C. S. Lewis

and the

Catholic Church

C. S. Lewis

and the

Catholic Church

JOSEPH PEARCE

SAINT BENEDICT+PRESS
Charlotte, North Carolina

This book was first published in the United States by Ignatius Press in 2003. This Saint Benedict Press edition has been re-typeset and revised. Revisions include occasional spelling, punctuation, and typography corrections. This edition also includes a new introduction by Fr. Dwight D. Longenecker, and a new appendix by the author.

Typeset by Lapiz.

Cover design by Caroline Kiser.

Cover images: *St. Peter's Basilica* ©iStockphoto.com/ToniFlap. *Portrait of C. S. Lewis* (1898–1963), United Kingdom, 1958. (Photo by Wolf Suschitzky/Pix Inc./Time & Life Pictures/Getty Images).

ISBN: 978-1-61890-230-6

Published in the United States by
Saint Benedict Press, LLC
PO Box 410487
Charlotte, NC 28241
www.SaintBenedictPress.com

Printed and bound in the United States of America.

for
WALTER HOOPER

CONTENTS

FOREWORD

THE QUESTION of C. S. Lewis's churchmanship is a question that won't go away. When he billed himself, in the 1940s, as a "mere" Christian, it seemed a stroke of genius. Yes. Why not have an apologia for the ancient Faith that avoids all partisan matters, and lays out for the unbeliever (and for the believer too, for that matter) the nature of Christian belief, and the reasoning underlying that corpus of belief? Certainly the success of Lewis's apologetic work would seem to testify to the wisdom of the approach that he chose. How many people (millions?) would give Lewis the credit for having assisted them along to true, regenerating Christian faith?

Is it pettifogging, then, to raise, forty years after Lewis's death, the question of his particular churchmanship? Can we not simply leave it where he wished to leave it? He never tried to hide his Anglicanism; but he never wanted to give his description of the Faith any remotest Anglican tint. Surely this is praiseworthy?

Indeed. But difficulties do arise. Lewis wished to leave on one side various "peripheral" topics. But what if those topics are not peripheral to the most immense, most ancient, body of Christians? The nature of the Eucharist (and of all of the Sacraments, actually); and the role of the Blessed Virgin in the drama of Redemption; and the sacerdotal, apostolic

priesthood; and the office of Peter; and the Communion of
the Saints; and the doctrine of Purgatory—these can be called
"peripheral" only by an avowed partisan, namely, a Protestant.
And Protestantism is a late-comer to the Christian scene. So.
There is an anomaly here: Lewis wishes us to accept his identity as a "mere" Christian; but we find that the truth of the
matter is that he was a mere Protestant. Quite ferociously so,
as it happens. His Ulster background colored his attitudes
more garishly than he, in his coldly rational moments, might
have wished to admit. (He is furious, for example, when a
Catholic publisher of one of his books seems to want to mar-
ket it to "Dublin riff-raff.")

But there are more anomalies. Although he loathed
the whole business of "High," "Broad," and "Low"
churchmanship in the Church of England, he could not
avoid it all. He had nothing but contempt for the Broad
churchmen who diluted the Faith until it was a mere sickly
gruel (see his Anglican bishop in *The Great Divorce)*. And
he detested the "smells and bells," lace-cotta, biretta sort of
thing that one finds at Anglo-Catholic shrines, and which
formed the métier of T. S. Eliot. He just wanted to be left
alone, to go to church and be done with it.

But it was not so simple. In spite of himself, Lewis moved
more and more toward what can only be called a "catholic"
Anglicanism. Again—he hated the epicene punctilio of the
Anglo-Catholic *party:* but his faith came to embrace all
sorts of doctrines and practices that his evangelical readers
(who are his most enthusiastic clientele) must sedulously
ignore. He spoke of "the Blessed Virgin," and made his
confession to his priest regularly, and believed in purgatory,

and even came to refer to the Eucharist as—heaven help us all—*the Mass!*

Lewis's anti-Romanism remained with him until his death, however. The point of a book like this is not to quibble. Joseph Pearce is one of Lewis's strong allies. But Lewis's public will find here, I think, an enormous amount of material that is both fascinating and—it must be admitted—germane.

Thomas Howard
Manchester, Massachusetts

INTRODUCTION

A SERIOUS CASE OF ANGLO-PHILIA

AS AN American college student in the late 1970s I was afflicted with a severe case of a dangerous disease called Anglo-philia—the love of all things English—and C. S. Lewis was largely to blame. I had been brought up in an Evangelical Fundamentalist family, and after high school I visited England while on a mission trip to Europe.

I was captivated by the robust life of London, the wry humor of the people, the quaint antiquity of English villages, the living links to the literary history, and the mellow beauty of the countryside. I arrived home and said to my parents, "I'm going to live over there one day!"

The Protestant religion in our home was a quiet, sincere, and deep faith. Our Christianity was the "old, old story" of a human race lost in sin and the saving love of God who sent his son for our redemption. We were fervent believers, but our faith was not fiery. After high school, however, I attended Bob Jones University (the fundamentalist college in South Carolina), and there the temperature of the religion was rather warmer.

Dr. Bob Jones preached against the Catholic Church which was "the great whore of Babylon." Liberals were the enemy, the seminarian "preacher boys" were ready to roll, and hell was real. This rip snortin' religion wasn't for me. I had already imbibed deeply of English culture and as a Speech and English major I went further up and further in. I was discovering a form of Christianity which was deeper, broader, and more ancient than anything I had met with before. The problem was that fundamentalists considered this "other Christianity" of the mainline Protestant denominations to be "liberal" and "worldly." We were taught how modernism had infected the Protestant churches and that they were not to be trusted. In the midst of these intellectually stormy waters, C. S. Lewis threw me a lifeline.

Lewis provided a bridge between the historic, Biblical Christianity I had been taught as a boy and the real roots of that faith in the European tradition. Lewis's writings were orthodox and acceptable but they were also intelligent, witty, and fresh. He upheld something he called "Mere Christianity" which was the basic, Biblical historic Christian faith. That was what I believed, and yet Lewis was clearly not a funda-mentalist, Southern Baptist. What religion was he? Like T. S. Eliot, George Herbert, John Donne, and others it turned out that Lewis was a member of the Church of England, and that he believed it was possible to be a "mere Christian" within the Anglican Church.

I was delighted to find that an Anglican church existed in Greenville, South Carolina, and that we were permitted to go there. So with some other students I started attending the lit-tle stone church in the bad part of town, and was imme-diately taken with the Book of Common Prayer, lighting candles, singing decent hymns, and kneeling to pray. This was C. S. Lewis's church! Someone gave me a picture book called *C. S. Lewis: Images of His World.* It was full of photographs of golden green Oxford quadrangles and people punting on the River Cam. There were pictures of Lewis and the Inklings smoking pipes and swilling beer in cosy English pubs. The book was all misty fields, quiet English rivers, the hobbiton-like hills of rural England, the heavenly glories of Cambridge chapels, and the homely glories of country churches.

I was hooked. It was in that little Anglican Church in the heart of the American South that I was baptized and confirmed into the Anglican Church and heard my own call to the ordained ministry.

THE APPEAL OF ANGLICANISM

The Anglicanism of C. S. Lewis is attractive to many American Evangelicals because it gives historical and philosophical roots to the subjective, free flowing, and wide ranging experience of modern American Protestantism. The classical Anglican position is that the Church of England (and by extension the other churches of the Anglican Communion) are the ancient Catholic Church properly reformed. Anglicans like to insist that their church is one of the three ancient apostolic churches along with the Roman Catholic and Eastern Orthodox, but that it has affirmed all that is good from the Protestant Reformation.

Anglicans claim that they have retained the ancient faith while excising the excesses and excrescences of Roman Catholicism. Anglicanism, they argue, is a Catholic form of Protestantism, and holds together the good parts of both in a *via media*—a middle way. One of the reasons C. S. Lewis was committed to Anglicanism was because he believed this *via media* was the best place to preach the simple Christian faith which he termed "mere Christianity."

This was Anglicanism's main appeal for me. I felt I could be Catholic without being *Roman* Catholic. I could share in the ancient tradition, culture, and spirituality of Catholicism, without all the foreign fuss, frippery and folderol. I could be Catholic without all the tiresome rules and regulations, or the unnecessary additional doctrines, decrees, and dogmas. Within Anglicanism I could be a "mere Christian" with C. S. Lewis.

However, as I became first an Anglican, then an Anglican priest I found it increasingly difficult to define what "mere Christianity" consisted of. There were too many other dilemmas to consider in the life of faith and the life of the church, and how was one to make a decision? C. S. Lewis proposed "mere Christianity" but in his sermon *Transposition,* Lewis warns against the "merely mentality." The person who determines everything by "merely" or "only" or "nothing but" sees all the facts but not the meaning. Any attempt to reduce something great to something small should be resisted.

Lewis argued valiantly that his "mere Christianity" was the "highest common factor" between Christians, but it's not that easy to define just what "mere Christianity" consists of. Is mere Christianity defined only by the historic creeds or are there certain moral teachings that are required? If so which ones are mandatory and which are not? Are certain disciplines and devotions necessary? If not, why not? What about sacraments? If so which ones and how many? Who decides? Is the definition of mere Christianity up to the individual? Up to the particular church and its leadership? If so, how do we decide which church is best?

CHURCH? WHAT CHURCH?

The biographers tell us that J. R. R. Tolkien tried to persuade Lewis to move on from Anglicanism to Catholicism. Lewis had other friends who were Catholic and one of them was convinced that Lewis never considered converting. Fr. Charles Smith says Lewis never became a Catholic "because there was too much of the Northern Ireland Protestant in him. There was always this anti-Romanism."

To understand this comment we must understand a bit about the history of Lewis's homeland. For about 500 years after the Norman invasion of Britain in 1066, Ireland was overshadowed by English rulers, but it wasn't until Henry VIII broke with the pope that an English king tried to dominate Ireland completely. Henry sought to impose his new Protestant religion not only on the people of England, but also on the Irish. He failed.

As they couldn't make the Irish Protestant, the English monarchs decided to import Protestants from Scotland and England. The English and Scots settlers in the royal plantations displaced the Irish from their land and established a Protestant stronghold in the Northeastern part of Ireland. The occupation of what is now called Northern Ireland engendered ethnic, political, and religious strife which continued for over 450 years. Lewis was born into the middle of it on the Protestant side of the line.

Despite his intelligence and open-mindedness, Lewis retained a bias against Catholics—equating them with the Irish who were the historic enemy.

While this is an aspect of Lewis's reluctance to become Catholic, I think the answer is more simply explained. As his world expanded, Lewis came to understand the roots of his own bigotry, and Joseph Pearce explains how he came to appreciate Catholic worship and spirituality. More importantly than any anti-Catholic bias he may have harbored, Lewis's continued loyalty to the Church of England had more to do with his Protestant understanding of the church.

How did Lewis conceive of the Body of Christ? Who exactly were members of Christ's Church and how did one become a member? Lewis ascribed to the historic creeds in which he professed belief in the "One, Holy, Catholic and Apostolic Church" but what did he mean by those words if he never took the step to become a full member of the only church that has a claim to be "One, Holy, Catholic and Apostolic"?

According to classic Protestant ecclesiology the Body of Christ—the Church—is invisible. By this a Protestant means that the church is made up of all true believers in every place and in every time down through the ages who have put their trust in Jesus Christ. Their number and identity is known by God alone and cannot be determined by baptismal registers, membership forms, church attendance, or denominational allegiance.

For the Protestant this invisible church is "One" because all true believers are united in their heartfelt faith and commitment to Jesus Christ. It is "Holy" because all true believers have been "washed in the blood of the Lamb" and share in the righteousness of Christ by faith. This invisible body of believers is "Catholic" because it is universal and spread by allegiance of faith across all continents and all times and places around the world. The invisible church of Jesus Christ is "Apostolic" inasmuch as it preaches and lives the simple gospel message first preached by the Apostles and recorded in the Bible. The classic Protestant belief is that all these true believers are united by faith in a core set of shared fundamental beliefs, and by obedience to a shared set of gospel values. These values and beliefs are so basic and obvious that they scarcely need stating. They are what Lewis dubbed, "mere Christianity."

THE HALL AND THE SIDE ROOMS

A firm conviction that the Church of Christ is invisible—
that it is composed of all true believers in all places and in all
times down the ages—must mean that particular denominations are, at best, a necessary evil. Whether one is Methodist
or Mennonite, Anglican or Assembly of God, Baptist, Bible
Believer, Presbyterian, or Pentecostal doesn't really matter.
What matters is that you truly have faith in Jesus Christ and
try to follow him.

This intentional indifference to denominational religion
lies at the root of C. S. Lewis's idea of "Mere Christianity." As
he explained in the preface of *Mere Christianity*:

> The reader should be warned that I offer no help to
> anyone who is hesitating between two Christian
> "denominations." You will not learn from me whether
> you ought to become an Anglican, a Methodist, a
> Presbyterian or a Roman Catholic. This omission is
> intentional. . . . There is no mystery about my own
> position. I am a very ordinary lay man of the Church
> of England, not especially "high" nor especially "low"
> nor especially anything else. . . . Ever since I became a
> Christian I have thought that the best, perhaps the only
> service I could do for my unbelieving neighbours was
> to explain and defend the belief that has been common
> to nearly all Christians at all times.

The idea of Lewis's apologetic is to define and defend
the core beliefs of the Christian faith in a simple way for the
man in the street. His attempt to do so reveals Lewis's innate
Protestant assumptions about the church. As a Christian he
is expected to "share the gospel" and "introduce his neighbor

to Jesus Christ" and he means to do so in the same straight-forward and winning style typical of the best of Evangelical Christians.

Lewis wants to win people to belief in Jesus Christ without the encumbrance of denominational debates about doctrine, and in his preface to *Mere Christianity* he goes to some length to give three reasons why he will not get involved in more complex theological debates. His protestations that he is not a theological expert and that such topics are over his head has always struck me as disingenuous. Lewis had no difficulties grappling with complex ideas when he wanted to. Indeed, he was very skilled not only in mastering difficult philosophical or theological ideas but also translating them into simple language.

His second and third reasons for not delving into denominational and doctrinal differences were more persuasive: he didn't think debates about doctrine helped win non believers, and he felt there was a more urgent need to defend and explain "mere Christianity" rather than focus on finer points of doctrine. "That part of the line" he wrote, "where I thought I could serve best was also the part that seemed to be thinnest. And to it I naturally went."

Lewis tried to limit the definition to assent to the Apostle's Creed. However, there are various interpretations of the Apostle's Creed. What an Anglican or a Methodist means by the phrase, "One, Holy, Catholic and Apostolic" is very different from what a Baptist or Catholic means. The same flexibility of interpretation applies to nearly every formula in the creed. You might affirm that "God the Father Almighty" is "maker of heaven and earth"? But what do you mean by "God the Father" and in what way is he "maker of heaven and earth"? Must you be a creationist? What about evolution? And what do you mean by "heaven" anyway?"

For there to be a definition of what mere Christianity is, there must be an agreed authority to make the definition and defend it. This question of authority is one that Lewis steadfastly refused to confront, and it is this fundamental question which is the elephant in the hall.

Lewis explains in the preface to *Mere Christianity* that to accept the Christian faith and commit to Christ is like entering a hall from which one enters various side rooms—the side rooms being the Christian community one decides to join.

> I hope no reader will suppose that "mere" Christianity is here put forward as an alternative to the creeds of the existing communions—as if a man could adopt it in preference to Congregationalism or Greek Orthodoxy or anything else. It is more like a hall out of which doors open into several rooms. If I can bring anyone into that hall I shall have done what I attempted. But it is in the rooms, not in the hall, that there are fires and chairs and meals. The hall is a place to wait in, a place from which to try the various doors, not a place to live in. . . . You must keep on praying for light; and . . . above all you must be asking which door is the true one; not which pleases you best by its paint and panelling. In plain language the question should never be, "Do I like that kind of service" but, "Are those doctrines true?"

Lewis is correct that one should not choose a Christian community according to personal taste or preference, but even the most ardent of Lewis's admirers must see the elephant in the hall—the unanswered question, the looming conundrum and the riddle refused.

If one must choose a room not by personal preference, but because the doctrines are true, then the rooms cannot not be of equal value. The doctrines in some rooms must be more reasonable, more true and more complete than in others. Otherwise why would there be different rooms? According to Lewis's own dictum one must search for the expression of Christianity which is most true, most holy, most historically reliable, most faithful to Scripture and fullest in its explanation and application of Christianity.

Is one to go on such a quest and make such a decision on one's own? How does one decide which side room is the fullest and most complete? Where can the searcher find not only more Christianity but most Christianity? If each new mere Christian makes his own decision how can he avoid making a choice which is merely subjective? At some point he will have to accept guidance. He will face the necessity to submit to a greater authority than himself, and this quest must lead the mere Christian to face the question of authority or "How do I decide which side room is the most true?"

C. S. LEWIS AND THE CATHOLIC CHURCH

If every mere Christian must eventually face this elephant in the hall, the puzzle remains, "Why did the incredibly brilliant C. S. Lewis so studiously avoid that same question?" Joseph Pearce takes us on the journey which explores this famous riddle. He does so with skill and meticulous research—leading us on a journey of exploration and allowing us to fit the pieces of the complex puzzle together.

This book explains the social, familial, intellectual, and theological influences on Lewis's life and traces both the very real Catholic elements in Lewis's brilliant thought as well as the lingering Protestant assumptions which kept him from seeing the need to "come home to Rome."

I am often asked whether C. S. Lewis would have become a Catholic if he had lived for another twenty years. If Lewis had seen the changes in the Catholic Church brought about by the Second Vatican Council, and if he witnessed the wholesale capitulation to modernism in his own Church of England would he have joined his friend J. R. R. Tolkien and entered into full communion with the Catholic Church?

Perhaps he would have, but one of the other aspects of the Protestant understanding of the church is that every church is imperfect and incomplete. Every church is flawed by human weakness. That is why so many "mere Christians" remain in churches that are wounded by sin and divided by heresy and schism. They accept the broken-ness, and with a resigned pragmatism, feel that they could not do much better elsewhere, and that the real demand is one of personal holiness rather than institutional conversion. Believing that any other church would be just as flawed, they stay where they are out of loyalty and pragmatism, and I sense that C. S. Lewis may have done the same.

Fr. Dwight D Longenecker
Greenville, South Carolina

INTRODUCTION TO
THE FIRST EDITION

IF ONE desires a thumbnail sketch of C. S. Lewis's attitude toward the centuries-old conflict between Protestants and Catholics, one might reflect on the pair of epigraphs by which he chose to introduce *The Screwtape Letters*.

> The best way to drive out the devil, if he will not yield to texts of Scripture, is to jeer and flout him, for he cannot bear scorn.
> —*Luther*

> The devil . . . the prowde spirit . . . cannot endure to be mocked.
> —*Thomas More*

Both quotations say basically the same thing; to paraphrase Saint Paul, "Laugh at the devil, and he will flee from you." Aside from this extraordinary advice, what is remarkable about Lewis's choice of epigraphs is the identity of the two authors. Not only is Luther a Protestant and More a Catholic, but these two men are also accounted champions of their respective parties, each having fought fearlessly for his own position. What is more, many of their fiercest confrontations were fought against one another, often in scathing letters and treatises. That Lewis, himself an Anglican, should choose these two voices for his epigraph creates an unmistakable impression. Here stand side by side two men, a Protestant and a Catholic, who opposed one another relentlessly during their earthly lives, seeming now to speak with one reassuring voice, "folded in a single party." The fact that both voices recommend laughter at the absurdity of evil is a testament to a conviction, seen elsewhere in Lewis's works, that the Christian perspective of comedy, in both the lighthearted and in the cosmic sense, will in the end win out over the tragic divisions that have historically beset the Body of Christ on earth.

This harmonious juxtaposition of Luther and More may say more about Lewis's approach to the Protestant/Catholic question than most of his explicit comments, which are indeed sparse. Not only does he seem here to desire reunion, but he also suggests that a kind of union already exists beneath the surface even of bitter disunion. Lewis was no stranger to such bitterness, having been raised in Protestant Belfast amid acrimonious conflicts between Protestants and Catholics. His reasons for avoiding open discussions of the question, as the present book makes clear, can be partly explained through an understanding of his formative years in Protestant Ulster.

Although Lewis did for the most part manage to avoid openly discussing the Protestant/Catholic question throughout most of his life, the question did not always avoid him. When his autobiographical allegory *The Pilgrim's Regress* was published in 1933, its richly traditional imagery and sacramental plot line caused many people in Oxford to speculate that Lewis had in fact already become a Catholic. In a sense, the question of his relation to Catholicism would haunt him for the rest of his days. By 1952, when *Mere Christianity* was first published as a book, Lewis had grown so sensitive to questions about his denominational stance that he wrote a

Preface in which he confesses up-front to being an Anglican, and then proceeds very carefully and at some length to defend his unbroken silence on these matters throughout the rest of the book.

His stated reasons for avoiding ecclesiastical controversies in *Mere Christianity* are simple. He says, first of all, that he is a mere layman, and that he is not qualified to navigate such deep waters. Second, he says that he has avoided discussing such disputes precisely because they have "no tendency at all to bring an outsider into the Christian fold. So long as we write and talk about them we are much more likely to deter him from entering any Christian communion than to draw him into our own."[1] His mission in this book, as he understood it, was to present Christianity as a unified front to an unbelieving world, speaking to non-Christians about the profound witness and power of the Christian faith across the centuries. This mission would, it seems, characterize much of his other work as well. As regards the question of reunifying the Christian Church, Lewis does go so far in this Preface as to say that "if I have not directly helped the cause of reunion, I have perhaps made it clear why we ought to be reunited."[2]

In some ways, Lewis's project has been doubly successful. Legions of nonbelievers have testified to being brought to faith in Christ by reading the works of C. S. Lewis. In addition, however, Lewis's works have resonated profoundly within the global Christian fold as well. Father Joseph Fessio, S.J., has commented on the striking phenomenon of Lewis's universal appeal to Christians worldwide, which was considerable in Lewis's own day, and which has only grown since his death in 1963. Father Fessio made these remarks during a theological conference in the mid-1990s, which Peter Kreeft recalled in

1998 as "the most memorable moment of the most memorable conference I ever attended." Attending the meeting, says Kreeft, were "dozens of high-octane Roman Catholics, Anglicans, Eastern Orthodox and Protestant Evangelicals," who, despite their noted theological differences, converged near the end of the conference in a crescendo of agreement. Kreeft continues:

> In the concluding session Father Fessio got up and proposed [tongue in cheek] that we issue a joint statement of theological agreement among all the historic, orthodox branches of Christendom saying that what united us was Scripture, the Apostles' Creed, the first six ecumenical councils and the collected works of C. S. Lewis. The proposal was universally cheered.[4]

As this spectacle of cheering across party lines might suggest, Protestants, Catholics, and Eastern Orthodox have managed to find areas of substantial agreement in Lewis's works, and a separate study could be made on this topic alone. Areas of broad agreement include such subjects as the centrality to salvation history of Christ's atoning death on the Cross, the historicity of the Resurrection, the authority of Sacred Scripture, the objective reality of moral law, the unchanging nature (and beauty) of human sexuality, and the value of the Christian family.

Moreover, Protestants and Catholics have tended to read Lewis in ways that show an ingenious versatility on Lewis's part. Each can find passages in Lewis that seem to resonate profoundly with his own tradition. Lewis has, for example, an uncanny knack for speaking dramatically of conversion, of making a decision to give one's life to Christ, which then leads to transformation in holiness. The poignant climax in his conversion story, told in his autobiography *Surprised by Joy*, has been celebrated by many Protestants who tend to understand salvation as a dramatic, and even singular, saving act of faith:

> You must picture me alone in that room in Magdalen, night after night, feeling, whenever my mind lifted even for a second from my work, the steady, unrelenting approach of Him whom I so earnestly desired not to meet. That which greatly feared had at last come upon me. In the Trinity Term of 1929 I gave in, and admitted that God was God, and knelt and prayed: perhaps, that night, the most dejected and reluctant convert in all of England.[4]

Those Christians who have come to faith by "praying to receive Christ as their personal Lord and Savior" often identify profoundly with Lewis's conversion narrative—even though, in the passage above, Lewis had been converted only to belief in God, and not yet to faith in Christ, which he narrates in a later chapter. In this sense, Lewis has appealed historically to "born-again Christians," and, subsequently, to many of their Evangelical cousins, even though modern Evangelicals have moved in recent years toward a more complex view of salvation, emphasizing not merely the initial act of faith, but subsequent conversion of character as well. This is a topic to which I shall return.

If Protestant circles have tended to see Lewis as a catalyst for dramatic conversion, so also have Catholic circles focused on the subject of Lewis and conversion, albeit in a slightly different light. In a development that has puzzled some of his Protestant champions to no end, Lewis has been credited (or blamed) in recent years with setting numerous people on the road to Rome. Such Catholic converts have included many of the serious scholars and disciples of Lewis, some of whom knew him before he died, and who considered him a friend and mentor. Many of these converts have gone on to become well-known Catholic writers, editors, and teachers in their own right, and their ranks include Walter Hooper, Sheldon Vanauken, Thomas Howard, Peter Kreeft, and others. The ubiquitous presence of C. S. Lewis's name among specifically American Catholic converts is also noted in Walker Percy's introduction to *The New Catholics: Contemporary Converts Tell Their Stories,* by Daniel O'Neill. At one point, Percy summarizes the litany of Catholic books and authors which have most often induced people to investigate the claims of the Catholic Church. In all of these accounts, he says, there was one unlikely name which kept reappearing:

> Books and reading figure here as largely as one might expect, and the writers one might expect, from Aquinas to Merton. But guess who turns up most often? C. S. Lewis! Who, if he didn't make it all the way, certainly handed along a goodly crew.[5]

Some Catholics may blush and accuse Percy of a whimsical triumphalism here, but his observation sheds light on a strange phenomenon. Given this late twentieth-century surge of converts into the Catholic Church, many of whom cite Lewis's theological writing as a common lodestar, one might reasonably ask two questions. First, what is it about Lewis's works that makes Catholicism seem so attractive to so many? Second, given this gravitational pull toward Catholicism in his work, why did Lewis himself never convert?

Joseph Pearce is just the writer to answer both these questions. In his detailed study on the topic of twentieth-century

English converts to Catholicism, *Literary Converts: Spiritual Inspiration in an Age of Unbelief,* Pearce chronicles and analyzes converts from among the most prominent English men and women of letters during the last century, including G. K. Chesterton, Ronald Knox, Evelyn Waugh, Edith Sitwell, and J. R. R. Tolkien. His approach finely integrates biography with spiritual and theological commentary showing how the lives of these literary Catholics were deeply intertwined over time, through the written and the spoken word. In Pearce's accounts, as in Percy's introduction, C. S. Lewis's name also figures prominently. Again, the question arises: why, given the network of Catholic converts in whose society he moved, did Lewis himself never convert? Hence the subject of the present book, *C. S. Lewis and the Catholic Church,* on which no one is more qualified to speak than Joseph Pearce.

In order to see more clearly the poignancy of the question which Pearce sets about answering, it will be worthwhile to look briefly at two traditionally Catholic theological subjects, as treated in the pages of Lewis. These two subjects are Purgatory and the Real Presence of Christ in the Eucharist, both of which Lewis seems to have understood remarkably well, and to have believed in strongly. As Lewis treats both these subjects, moreover, there emerges in his writing a decidedly Catholic understanding of grace, which is perhaps the most subtle and yet the most psychologically powerful dimension of his work.

Broadly speaking, the development mentioned earlier within some Evangelical communities, of thinking of salvation as a one-time event, and yet also as an ongoing, perilous and often painful process, also highlights a tension within Lewis's own best writings. On the one hand, Lewis emphasizes the dramatic nature of faith in Christ and the necessity for personal conversion. On the other hand, his writings also show a profound understanding of the gradual and often painful process of this transformation, as the whole person is remade into the image and likeness of Christ through the agency of the Holy Spirit. With incredible precision, Lewis delineates the psychological twists and turns by which grace works its changes, both in initial conversion, as well as in daily conversion, as the Christian virtues slowly emerge over time, often through suffering. This psychological complexity in Lewis's approach to grace has attracted both Protestants and Catholics alike, all of whom find new light shed on what it means to take up their crosses daily and follow Christ.

The soul's actual transformation by grace, which Catholics and Protestants both call "sanctification," is a subject to which both parties tend to assign a high degree of importance. As to the manner in which this transformation occurs, however, wide disagreements have historically arisen, not only between Protestants and Catholics, but also within the ranks of both parties. It is this difficult subject in particular on which Lewis writes with astounding clarity of interior vision. In *The Screwtape Letters,* for example, instead of speculating as to the theological mode of the soul's transformation, or lack thereof, Lewis gets down to the more practical and illuminating business of dramatizing the psychological movements of good and evil within the soul itself, portraying the overtures of grace made by the enemy (God), along with the Devil's ingenious and self-deceptive defenses against grace that whisper through the soul more often than most Christians would like to admit. By depicting these movements of grace within the human psyche, Lewis appeals both to Protestants and to Catholics in what amounts to a common language.

Lewis's gift for describing the transformative effects

of grace is also evident in his portrayal of what he calls the "Christ-life" in *Mere Christianity*. When he speaks of the universal mission of Christ in the Incarnation, he does so, as was his habit, by means of an analogy. He makes a distinction between *bios*, the Greek term for biological life, "the sort that comes through Nature," and *zoē*, another Greek term for "life," by which he means "the Spiritual life which is from God from all eternity, and which made the whole natural universe."[6] *Bios*, in other words, is natural life, and *zoē* is supernatural life. Christ, in short, came to infuse the fallen human race, whose *Nos* is running out, with a saving dose of His own *zoē*, or "Christ-life," which cannot die. To help readers understand Christ's promise of eternal life "to all who receive Him," Lewis develops the analogy by imagining a tin soldier being brought to life, bit by painful bit, in order to become a real boy.

It is precisely because Lewis saw the transformation and purification of the soul by grace in such clear and dramatic terms that he came ultimately to find the doctrine of Purgatory more and more essential, and even illuminating. He wrote of the concept at some length in his final book, *Letters to Malcolm: Chiefly on Prayer*, published posthumously in 1963:

> Our souls *demand* Purgatory, don't they? Would it not break the heart if God said to us, "It is true, my son, that your breath smells and your rags drip with mud and slime, but we are charitable here and no one will upbraid you with these things, nor draw away from you. Enter into the joy"? Should we not reply, "With submission, sir, and if there is no objection, I'd *rather* be cleaned first." "It may hurt, you know"—"Even so, sir."

Lewis's treatment here, as elsewhere, of the soul's purification has tended to raise eyebrows across the Protestant spectrum, from low Baptist to high Anglican. Belief in Purgatory is of course expressly forbidden in article 22 of the Thirty-Nine Articles in the Anglican Book of Common Prayer. That Lewis should believe in such a Catholic doctrine even in the face of explicit opposition from his own denomination has understandably caused the average reader to ask, "Why then wasn't C. S. Lewis a Catholic?"

In addition to believing in the cleansing and ultimately purgative effects of grace on the soul, both in this life and the next, Lewis tended to think of the operation of grace as working in cooperation with the body and the will of man rather than viewing it in exclusively spiritual terms, as the Holy Spirit, for example, mysteriously dwells in the "temple" of each Christian body. It is true that some Christians have understood grace in this way by reading 1 Corinthians 3:16, where Saint Paul reminds us: "Do you not know that you are God's temple and that God's spirit dwells in you?" Lewis, however, tended to understand grace as also a mysterious force that works not merely inside the body but by means of the body, as the life of a flower works its way by means of the stem to generate its blossom. For many Protestants, Holy Communion and baptism merely symbolize the spiritual action of grace, which the believer has attained through faith alone. They believe these physical actions neither participate in nor facilitate that grace. Catholics, however, have tended to understand grace both in spiritual and in bodily terms, seeing such sacramental actions as Holy Communion and baptism not as mere symbols but as effective and generally necessary means of infusing grace into the soul. The Catholic tradition has thereby defended the dogma that grace is mediated through physical elements in the same way that Christ's human body mediated His divine presence to those whom He physically touched.

In one well-known passage of *Mere Christianity,* Lewis is adamant about the physical nature of the sacraments in their ability to convey the *zoē,* or Christ-life, both to the Christian individual, and throughout the Body of Christ at large. "This new life is spread," he says, "not only by purely mental acts like belief, but by bodily acts like baptism and Holy Communion."[8] These Christian sacraments, he says, are evidence of God's love for matter in general, and for the body in particular. He drives his point home by saying that "there is no good trying to be more spiritual than God. God never meant man to be a purely spiritual creature. That is why He uses material things like bread and wine to put the new life into us. We may think this rather crude and unspiritual. God does not: He invented eating. He likes matter. He invented it."[9]

Lewis's view of grace as the supernatural life of God, infused into the Christian soul through the physical action of sacraments, demonstrates a remarkably Catholic perspective, which again was bound to raise questions as to his denominational affiliation. A definition of grace strikingly similar to Lewis's appears in the *Modern Catholic Dictionary,* where Father John A. Hardon, S.J., refers to "Sanctifying Grace" as "the supernatural state of being infused by God." He continues, seeming even to echo Lewis, by calling it "a vital principle of the supernatural life. . . . It is called sanctifying grace because it makes holy those who possess the gift by giving them a participation in the divine life. It is *zoē* (life), which Christ taught that he has in common with the Father and which those who are in a state of grace share."[10] In the course of the Christian journey, moreover, the Eucharist, the Bread of Life, has always been seen by Catholics as the "source and summit" of this divine life, which nourishes and restores grace in the soul.

Given what appears to be a markedly Catholic understanding of grace in Lewis, specifically in his thinking on Purgatory and on the Eucharist, it is not hard to understand why so many Catholic converts have referred to Lewis as a "Signpost to Catholicism," giving him primary credit for setting them on the road to Rome. The question then remains: If he was so theologically and spiritually sympathetic with Catholicism as to induce other people to convert, why did C. S. Lewis never become a Roman Catholic? Thomas Howard recently gave a succinct and twofold answer to this question in his aptly titled essay "Why Did C. S. Lewis Never Become a Roman Catholic?" The first reason, Howard says, is simple. "He didn't want to. Period."[11] The second, he says, is like unto the first. "Lewis thought Rome was wrong."[12] Specifically, the two areas where Lewis found the most difficulty seem to have been the authority of the pope and Marian devotion. Why did these doctrines serve as barriers to Lewis, whereas Purgatory and the Real Presence of Christ in the Eucharist apparently did not? The shape of the puzzle becomes more and more curious.

Rather than attempting to solve the puzzle once and for all, Joseph Pearce has done both Catholics and Protestants a tremendous service by putting all the pieces on the table and letting the reader assemble them for himself, with only occasional hints from the author as to where a certain piece might fit. Some of the pieces are biographical, some pieces are historical, some pieces are literary, and some pieces are theological. Of special interest is Pearce's treatment of Lewis's abiding friendship with J. R. R. Tolkien, who constituted a deeply Catholic presence throughout Lewis's life. Also discussed are

Lewis's literary and theological relations with Catholic prede-
cessors such as Newman and Chesterton, both of whom profoundly affected Lewis's understanding and practice of the
Christian faith. The result here is a book which manages to
set forth the objective shape of Lewis's theological and spiritual works in their relation to the Catholic Church, while at
the same time making no claim to remain entirely dispassionate. The subject is, after all, a passionate one.

In one sense, Pearce's book makes it safe for Protestants
and Catholics to come together and discuss the theological
conundrums that arise in Lewis's works, owing both to the
clarity and pertinence of the information he presents, and
to the good humor and congeniality he brings to the discussion. In so doing, Pearce adds his voice to a lively conversation
begun in 1981 by Christopher Derrick's book *C. S. Lewis and
the Church of Rome,* which examines many of the same issues
raised by Pearce. Derrick, a lifelong friend of Lewis's and a
Catholic himself, writes from an unambiguously Catholic perspective, and frequently subjects Lewis's writing to the same
kind of logical analysis which Lewis himself seems to have
greatly prized. As such, Derrick's book meets Lewis in many
ways on his own high intellectual ground, and occasionally in
Lewis's own combative style. Pearce's book, by contrast, may
give a broader readership new insights into the question of
Lewis's relationship with the Catholic Church, in ways that
will inspire reflection and fruitful dialogue of its own kind.

If Pearce's book makes it safe for Catholics and Protestants
to read and discuss Lewis together, it also makes Lewis more
dangerous than ever to read while sitting at home alone. The
threat of personal conversion lurks on every page. In his early
book, *The Allegory of Love,* Lewis highlighted the perilous ways
in which both Catholics and Protestants tend to go wrong:

> When Catholicism goes bad it becomes the world-
> old, world-wide *religio* of amulets and holy places and
> priestcraft; Protestantism, in its corresponding decay,
> becomes a vague mist of ethical platitudes.[13]

Lewis remained perpetually vigilant against these corruptions, both in himself and in his readers. His passion for traditional Christian practices was always animated by practical Christian charity. For that reason, no Catholic or Protestant who is guilty of either of the above-mentioned errors is ever quite safe reading C. S. Lewis. In approaching Lewis, Protestants who claim to hold to a merely "spiritual" version of Christianity, whether liberal and "vaguely ethical," or conservative and "spirit-filled," will be in perpetual danger of having their neat and tidy dualism between spirit and flesh challenged by Lewis's sacramentalism, his liturgical sense and his potent grasp of the often nitty-gritty process of sanctification. More traditional forms of sacramental Christianity may begin to seem alluring to such readers, and who can see where such allurements will lead? On the other hand, cradle Catholics who have drifted into hollow ritualism, whether overzealously superstitious or underzealously mechanical, will be in continual danger of discovering the true meaning and spirit that animates both liturgy and sacraments, and will run the risk of plunging headlong into genuine Catholic spirituality. Insofar as Joseph Pearce's book draws us closer to the real C. S. Lewis, he makes these dangers of illumination for both parties ever more present, and the peril of growth in holiness ever more real.

R. A. Benthall
Ave Maria College
Ypsilanti, Michigan

ACKNOWLEDGMENTS

SUCH IS the popularity of C. S. Lewis that any author embarking on a study of his life and work can find a rich source in the many experts who are willing to offer their assistance at considerable cost to themselves in terms of time and commitment—and at no cost to the author except his heartfelt gratitude for their labors on his behalf. It is, therefore, with heartfelt gratitude that I pour forth these acknowledgements.

Not for the first time, I find myself indebted to the gracious assistance of Walter Hooper. Having offered his help during my research on earlier books, such as *Literary Converts* and *Tolkien: A Celebration,* he was, as the world's foremost expert on Lewis, more valued than ever during my work on this particular volume. It would hardly be an exaggeration to say that he was the inspiration for the writing of this study in the first place, and I am as indebted to him for his encouragement as for his expertise.

I am grateful to Brad Birzer and Philip Nielsen for the sharing with me of their painstaking research at Wheaton College, and to the former in particular for his willingness to offer assistance and advice whenever either was sought. Father Peter Milward, S.J., was kind enough to permit me to quote at length from his book *A Challenge to C. S. Lewis,* the extract from which, thus quoted, has enriched my volume with the force of his argument.

I have been blessed throughout my work on this volume with the assistance of my colleagues at Ave Maria College. Most particularly, Christopher and Sarah Beiting, William Riordan, and Al Benthall have been tireless in their offering of advice, expertise and honest toil on my behalf. I am especially indebted to the last of these, whose careful appraisal of the manuscript helped me iron out the creases during the final revision. He has also been good enough to grace this volume with an introduction.

I am indebted indirectly to Father Jerome Bertram of the Oxford Oratory for his expertise on the concept of the Refrigerium. His research into this subject was not carried out with the present book in mind but, nonetheless, was extremely useful in helping to unravel the inspirational background to Lewis's delightful book *The Great Divorce*. Others who helped this volume indirectly include Barbara Reynolds, Christopher Derrick and Owen Barfield, whose interviews with me during my research for previous books have been resurrected for use in the present work. I must also confess a debt to Dwight Longenecker for being the originator, as far as I know, of the play on words between "mere Christianity" and "more Christianity" which I have used on several occasions.

My wife, Susannah, has been unceasingly supportive, not merely in the specific assistance she offered during the writing of this work, particularly in her reading of each chapter as it was written, but also in the more general sense of being a constant companion and inspiration. Our son, Leo Patrick, born on Saint Patrick's Day 2002, was in gestation during the period that this work was in its embryonic stages. Paradoxically, he has acted as a great source of inspiration, even on those occasions when he has been a great source of distraction!

The penultimate acknowledgement must be reserved for Father Joseph Fessio, S.J., Mark Brumley, Tony Ryan, and the other dauntless workers at Ignatius Press. Particular thanks are due to Father Fessio for his faith in, and support for, my work.

The ultimate acknowledgement belongs to C. S. Lewis himself, without whom this work would, of course, be impossible. I am as indebted to him as are many millions of others throughout the world, and I hope that this volume will serve as a tribute to his timeless gifts.

In addition to offering a resounding reiteration of my acknowledgements to all those who helped me research and write the first edition of this book, I would like to offer additional acknowledgement to those who have made possible this new, expanded edition.

First and foremost, I'd like to thank the folks at Saint Benedict Press for their enthusiastic support, especially Robert and Conor Gallagher, Rick Rotondi, and Christian Tappe. It was Rick Rotondi's idea that we should enhance the new edition with an appendix on those Catholic converts who were helped on their path to Rome by the works of Lewis. This addition has really enhanced the scope and sweep of the book and has added a degree of gravitas to its content. As one whose own conversion was influenced significantly by the reading of Lewis's work (see my book, *Race with the Devil: A Journey from Racial Hatred to Rational Love*), I leapt at the idea of assembling the *illustrissimi* of Lewisian converts into one place. I was helped significantly in this rewarding task by John Beaumont, author of *Roads to Rome* (St. Augustine's Press), who is the world's premier expert on Catholic converts.

The final acknowledgement must be given to those well-known Catholics who responded to my request that they send me their own accounts of Lewis's role in their conversions. I was humbled by the precious gift of time that these very busy men and women bestowed upon me. It is, therefore, with the deepest gratitude that I acknowledge the generosity of Mark Brumley, Ronda Chervin, Michael Coren, Thomas Howard, Peter Kreeft, Al Kresta, Jef and Lorraine Murray, Kevin O'Brien, Carl Olson, and Thomas Storck. I hope that this volume, which is in part the fruit of their labors, will serve as adequate recompense for their sacrifice of time.

PREFACE

A CONFESSION

MY PREFATORY comments on the following work will have to be something of a confession. It was always my hope that I could write a book on the subject of C. S. Lewis and the Catholic Church that could be read with equal enjoyment, or at least with equal fruitfulness, by Protestants and Catholics alike. Having now written the book, I remain hopeful that this can still be the case. The task, however, has not been easy. With the writing of most works of nonfiction a diligent and honest author need only concern himself with his adherence to objective truth. If he is diligent in his research and honest in the way the research finds its way onto the written page he will have done his job. With this particular book, however, this dimension only constitutes a part—and, in fact, the easiest part—of the job.

Apart from the need to adhere to objectivity, there is the need to discuss the contentious and controversial issues that a book such as this inevitably raises in a language that will engage, but not enrage, the reader. This is much more difficult to achieve satisfactorily.

It is not possible for the author to remain neutral on these issues; neither is it likely that many, if any, of his readers will be neutral on these issues. Some will argue, no doubt, that Lewis was anti-Catholic; others that, on the contrary, he was a closet Catholic; still others will argue that the Catholic Church is irrelevant to an understanding of Lewis and his work; others will counter that the influence of Catholicism is central to Lewis's life and work. To some, Lewis was too Catholic, to others he was not Catholic enough.

Logically speaking, the contending parties who might take opposing views on the whole contentious subject of C. S. Lewis and the Catholic Church fall into four distinct categories. First, there are those who despise both Lewis *and* the Catholic Church. Those falling into this category are hardly likely to take the time and trouble to read any book on the subject and consequently do not concern us. Second, there are those who admire Lewis but dislike the Catholic Church. Members of this group will, I hope, learn much from the following pages. Third are those who admire the Catholic Church but dislike Lewis. These might have something to learn from the present work, but it was most emphatically not written with this group in mind. Finally there are those who admire both Lewis *and* the Catholic Church. As with the second group, this group will, I hope, have much to learn from this book.

The book was written with the second and fourth groups in mind. I have written for those who share my love for Lewis, regardless of whether they share my love for the Catholic Church. This brings me to another matter for confession. I confess, here and now, that I am a Catholic, having been received into the Church on Saint Joseph's Day, 1989. My conversion was influenced largely by Chesterton and Belloc, though Lewis's role was not insignificant. To a degree, therefore, my work is not merely a labor of love, but also an act of thanksgiving.

I realize that some Protestants might be somewhat suspicious of reading a book on this subject written by a Catholic. They will argue, not unjustly, that the author will be biased. Perhaps so. To reiterate, it is impossible for any author to write on this subject from a neutral perspective. If he is Catholic he will see things from a Catholic perspective; if Protestant, he will see them from a Protestant perspective. Nonetheless, both sides will agree, as lovers of Lewis we must, that we do not live in a relativist universe. The truth is out there. Our duty is not to cherish our own position, but to discover the true one.

What, exactly, was Lewis's relationship with the Catholic Church? This is the question that I have asked, and it is the question that I have done my best to answer. I have tried to be objective; I have tried to be balanced; I have tried to be fair. I have tried, but I'm not sure that I have always succeeded. This brings me to a further confession. I confess an element of culpability in the manner in which I have pursued the answer to the question. On occasion, when I have felt that Lewis has himself been culpable, I have highlighted his culpability in a somewhat rhetorical fashion. It has not been my conscious intention merely to score points for the Catholic Church—indeed it *has* been my conscious intention to avoid doing so—but I am aware that it might seem that this is something to which I have sometimes stooped. If this causes offense, I regret utterly that it has done so.

Why, therefore, it might be asked, have I failed to remove these potentially offensive passages? My answer is one that I am confident would have won Lewis's approval, which is why I have no feelings of guilt for having left them in. There is, as Chesterton said and as Lewis demonstrated, a world of difference between an argument and a quarrel. "I am glad to think," wrote Chesterton of his relationship with his brother, "that through all those years we never stopped arguing; and we never once quarrelled."[1]

I have endeavored to treat the contentiousness and controversy that must inevitably surround this subject as an edifying and efficacious argument. It is never (Heaven forbid!) a quarrel. If the question is to be asked and answered, we must accept the necessity of an argument. Silence is not an option. It would in fact be a sin of omission. Argument, properly understood and subject always to charity, is merely a dialogue in which both parties intend to arrive at the truth, or at least end up closer to it. The argument must never deteriorate into a quarrel, something which must be considered scandalous among Christians of whatever persuasion, but if we do not argue these issues how can we ever agree—even if ultimately we only agree to differ?

The central question that this book asks and attempts to answer is one which no Christian has the right to shun. Christ has asked that we all be one. Our differences, as Lewis never failed to remind us, are a failure to do God's will. *Vive la différence* is not an option. Unity is an imperative. Lewis sought this unity in his advocacy of "mere Christianity." This volume, in its own humble way, has the same intention. Lewis would, I hope, be pleased that it has been written. My readers, I hope, will enjoy the argument!

ESCAPE FROM PURITANIA

I dreamed of a boy who was born in the land of
Puritania and his name was John.
                                    —*The Pilgrim's Regress*[1]

T HE OPENING sentence of *The Pilgrim's Regress*, C. S.
Lewis's first attempt at autobiography, serves as an appropriate place at which to commence our quest to understand
Lewis's complicated and often problematic relationship with
the Catholic Church. The boy of whom Lewis was dreaming was in fact himself. In the preface to the third edition of
The Pilgrim's Regress, Lewis described John's "Regress" as "my
journey,"[2] indicating unequivocally that he was the Pilgrim at
the center of the autobiographical allegory. It is also significant that Lewis chose the medium of allegory as the means
by which to write his autobiography, since the juxtaposition
of *allegory* and *autobiography* signifies that there is an underlying *meaning* to *life*. Our goal, therefore, will be to follow
Lewis in the manner by which he meant to lead us. We shall
endeavor to understand the meaning of his life by trying to
understand his life as a pilgrimage in search of the meaning
of life itself. This was his intention in writing *The Pilgrim's
Regress* and also his intention in writing his other autobiographical works, *Surprised by Joy* and *A Grief Observed*. We

shall take him as he meant to be taken and shall follow in his footsteps, and mind-steps, as he traveled in search of the Truth.

Lewis's journey begins in Puritania, a place that has two levels of meaning. On the allegorical or metaphysical level—the level of Truth—it represents Puritanism; on the physical level—or the level of Fact—it represents Lewis's childhood in the Puritanical atmosphere of Protestant Belfast.

It would be a grave mistake to ignore the importance of Lewis's place of birth on the subsequent shaping of his mind, heart and life. It would also he a mistake to ignore the extent to which the poisonous twins of pride and prejudice exert a vice-like grip on those brought up in the sectarian shadow of Ulster in general, and Belfast in particular. For those who have never been to Belfast, and who have never savored the bitterness that descends like an omnipresent fog over its war-weary and war-worried inhabitants, no words will convey the power that all-pervasive prejudice wields on both sides of the religious divide.[3] Yet, having commenced with an insistence that it would be a serious error to ignore the importance of Lewis's Ulster Protestant roots, it is necessary to insist, with equal vehemence, that it is possible to err in the direction of overemphasizing its importance. There is a real danger of stressing the power of Puritania to such an extent that it becomes a substitute for any serious consideration of Lewis's religious position. There is a danger of believing that Puritania predestined Lewis to become the sort of Christian that his admirers and detractors have come to love or loathe. Lewis, whose works are awash with the importance and the potency of free will, would have been horrified at such a deterministic interpretation of his life and beliefs. As such, we will be doing him a grave injustice should we fall into the trap of translating

Puritania's importance into a presumed omnipotence. It is important but it is not *that* important.

In essence, although Puritania remained a powerful presence in Lewis's life, it was by no means an all-powerful presence. It would be truer to say that Puritania cast a shadow across the length of his life. Sometimes it was a shadow from which he sought to escape in order to discover the brightness beyond its domain; at other times it was a welcome shade, or shield, in which, and behind which, he hid from the heat of controversial debate.

There is, however, little doubt that the first twenty years of C. S. Lewis's life were dominated by the influence of Puritania and by his desire to escape from it. His grandfather, the Reverend Thomas Hamilton, was a clergyman of the Church of Ireland whose view of the Catholic minority in Belfast was colored by the theology of bigotry. Catholics were, in his estimation, the devil's own children,[4] and he "never tired of deprecating the Catholic Church from his pulpit."[5] Lewis insisted, however, that his father, as distinct from his maternal grandfather, was "far from being specially Puritanical" but, on the contrary, "was, by nineteenth-century and Church of Ireland standards, rather 'high.'"[6] For those unversed in the ecclesial position of the Church of Ireland, Lewis's words will be misleading. Although the Church of Ireland is part of the Anglican church it is far "lower," that is, far more Protestant, than the Church of England. The key to understanding Lewis's words is found in the sub-clause, "by nineteenth-century and Church of Ireland standards." The truth is that what might be considered "rather 'high'" by the standards of the Church of Ireland in the nineteenth-century would be considered very "low" by the standards of the Church of England at the time. Certainly there was no question of Lewis's father adopting the "high church" position of the Oxford Movement and its followers. On the contrary, he would have disapproved strongly of the "popery" of Pusey and Keble and would have been outraged by the "poping" of Newman. Lewis's words must, therefore, be taken in context. His "rather 'high'" father was, in fact, rather "low" in the wider spectrum of Anglican churchmanship. He was also, apparently, rather tepid in the practice of his faith and failed to convey any degree of faith or fervor to his son. "I was taught the usual things and made to say my prayers and in due time taken to church," Lewis wrote. "I naturally accepted what I was told but I cannot remember feeling much interest in it."[7] Recalling his childhood, Lewis remarked that "aesthetic experiences were rare" and that "religious experiences did not occur at all."[8] Such was the apparent indifference of his parents with regard to his religious instruction that Lewis recalled that he received his first inkling of spiritual truth from his Presbyterian governess, Annie Harper, who, during "a longish lecture," conveyed "the first thing I can remember that brought the other world to my mind with any sense of reality."[9] In summary, Lewis's religious upbringing seems to have been characterized by an inherited anti-Catholicism, whether implicit or explicit, combined with a tepid low-church Anglicanism spiced with Presbyterianism.

Consciously or subconsciously, Lewis reacted against the more Puritanical strictures of Ulster Protestantism, particularly in the way in which it manifested itself in the family life of his friend Arthur Greeves, The Greeves family had been Quakers for several generations but when Arthur was about twelve years old his father, Joseph, became a member of the Plymouth Brethren, perhaps the most puri-tyrannical of the Puritan sects. Insisting that his wife and children follow his lead, he had the entire family baptized in the bathtub. Lewis remembered that Joseph Greeves "was timid, prim, sour, at once oppressed and oppressive. He was a harsh husband and a despotic father. . . . My own father described his funeral as 'the most cheerful funeral he ever attended.' "[10] Years later, Lewis reiterated in a letter to Arthur Greeves his hostile reaction to Puritanism:

> I begin to see how much Puritanism counts in your make up—that both the revulsion from it and the attraction back to it are strong elements. . . . I feel that I can say with absolute certainty . . . that if you ever feel that the *whole spirit and system* in which you were brought up was, after all, right and good, then you may be quite sure that that feeling is a mistake. . . . My reasons for this are 1. That the system denied pleasures *to others* as well as to the votaries themselves: whatever the merits of self-denial, this is unpardonable interference. 2. It inconsistently kept *some* worldly pleasures, and always selected the worst ones—gluttony, avarice, etc. 3. It was ignorant. . . . Your relations have been found very ill grounded in the Bible itself and as ignorant as savages of the historical and theological reading needed to make the Bible more than a superstition. 4. "By their fruits ye shall know them." Have they the *marks* of peace, love, wisdom and humility on their faces or in their conversation? Really, you need not *bather* about that kind of Puritanism.[11]

It is interesting to note Lewis's criticism in this letter of what might be termed *bibliola* try—the superstitious and idolatrous worship of the Bible which results from its being read without due deference and reference to theological tradition.

Such was the sectarian apartheid, de facto, if not necessarily de jure, that existed in Ireland during the first years of the twentieth century that it is likely that Lewis had scarcely even met a Catholic prior to his arrival in England. This being so, it might be helpful to compare his cultural and psychological roots with those of another Protestant Irishman, George Bernard Shaw.

"All the influences surrounding Bernard Shaw in boyhood were not only Puritan," wrote G. K. Chesterton, "but such that no non-Puritan force could possibly pierce or counteract. He belonged to that Irish group which, according to Catholicism, has hardened its heart, which, according to Protestantism, has hardened its head, but which, as I fancy, has chiefly hardened its hide, lost its sensibility to the contact of the things around it. In reading about his youth, one forgets that it was passed in the island which is still one flame before the altar of St. Peter and St. Patrick."[12] Chesterton's assessment serves as a timely reminder that pride and prejudice are always obstacles to sense and sensibility: "It could never cross the mind of a man of the Garrison that before becoming an atheist he might stroll into one of the churches of his own country, and learn something of the philosophy that had satisfied Dante and Bossuet, Pascal and Descartes."[13]

Elsewhere in his study of Shaw, Chesterton discussed the fortress mentality of Protestant Unionists:

> Bernard Shaw is not merely an Irishman; he is not even a typical one. He is a certain separated and peculiar kind of Irishman, which is not easy to describe. Some Nationalist Irishmen have referred to him contemptuously as a "West Briton." But this is really unfair. . . . It would be much nearer the truth to put

the thing in the bold and bald terms of the old Irish song, and to call him "The anti-Irish Irishman." . . . This fairly educated and fairly wealthy Protestant wedge which is driven into the country . . . is a thing not easy superficially to summarise in any terms. It cannot be described merely as a minority; for a minority means the part of a nation which is conquered. But this thing means something that conquers and is not entirely part of the nation. . . . There is only one word for the minority in Ireland, and that is the word that public phraseology has found; I mean the word "Garrison." The Irish are essentially right when they talk as Wall Protestant Unionists lived inside "The Castle." They have all the values and limitations of a literal garrison in a fort.[14]

Chesterton's views are reflected by Michael Holroyd, Shaw's biographer: "No Shaw could form a social acquaintance with a Roman Catholic or tradesman. They lifted up their powerful Wellingtonian noses and spoke of themselves, however querulously, in a collective spirit (as people mentioning the Bourbons or Habsburgs) using the third person: 'the Shaws.'"[15]

There is, of course, a danger in taking the parallels between Shaw and Lewis too far. Shaw was born and raised in Dublin, an overwhelmingly Catholic city in which Protestants were the privileged minority; Lewis was born and raised in Belfast, a predominantly Protestant city in which the Catholics were a much-maligned—and, in consequence, an increasingly malignant—minority. Nonetheless, Protestant Unionists in both cities shared the same supercilious sense of superiority with respect to their Catholic neighbors.

The deeply-ingrained and all-pervasive prejudice of Lewis's childhood was recalled, with whimsical humor, by his brother, Warnie. "We went to church regularly in our youth, but even then one sensed the fact that church going was not so much a religious as a political right, the weekly assertion of the fact that you were not a Roman Catholic Nationalist. Our butcher and our grocer attended one suspected primarily to draw customers' attention to the fact that at their shops could be bought decent Protestant food untainted by the damnable heresies of Rome."[16] Warnie also recalled how he and his brother would play a game called "Catholics versus Protestants," much as children in England might play "Cowboys versus Indians" or "British versus Germans." In these sectarian games Lewis would always insist on taking the Protestant side.[17]

Further evidence of the anti-Catholicism that Lewis inherited as a child is provided in a letter he wrote to his father at the beginning of October 1908. Written shortly after his arrival at Wynyard School in Watford, the nine-year-old Lewis informed his father that he was shocked by the "highness" of the ritual in the local Anglican church. "I do not like church here at all because it is so frightfully high church that it might as well be Roman Catholic."[18] These sentiments, obviously expressed with the implicit assumption that his father would approve of his plaintive contempt for the "frightfully high" services, must throw into question Lewis's claim, many years later, that his father was "rather 'high'" in his churchmanship. In November 1909, more than a year after his initial complaint to his father, he recorded the following anti-papist appraisal in his diary: "We were obliged to go to St. John's, a church which wanted to be Roman Catholic, but was afraid to say so. A kind of church abhorred by respectful Irish Protestants. . . . In this abominable place of Romish hypocrites and English liars, the people cross themselves, bow to the Lord's Table (which they have the vanity to call an altar), and pray to the Virgin."[19]

Now, however, comes the first hint of the conundrum of apparent contradictions that appear to have accompanied Lewis, throughout his life, in his love-loathe relationship with Catholicism. Compare the virulence of the words written in his diary with Lewis's recollection of the effect that he later claimed that the Anglo-Catholicism at St. John's had on his youthful development.

> But I have not yet mentioned the most important thing that befell me at [Wynyard]. There first I became an effective believer. As far as I know, the instrument was the church to which we were taken twice every Sunday. This was high "Anglo-Catholic." On the conscious level I reacted strongly against its peculiarities—was I not an Ulster Protestant, and were not these unfamiliar rituals an essential part of the hated English atmosphere? Unconsciously, I suspect, the candles and incense, the vestments and the hymns sung on our knees, may have had a considerable, and opposite, effect on me. But I do not think they were the important thing. What really mattered was that I here heard the doctrines of Christianity (as distinct from general "uplift") taught by men who obviously believed them. As I had no skepticism, the effect was to bring to life what I would already have said that I believed.[20]

What is one to make of the palpable tension caused by the effect of Anglo-Catholicism on the young Lewis? Perhaps one has little option but to repeat the words, quoted earlier, which

Lewis wrote to Arthur Greeves: "I begin to see how much Puritanism counts in your make up—that both the revulsion from it and the attraction back to it are strong elements. . . ." These words might make some sense of the contradictory conundrum. The revulsion from Puritanism might have fed the attraction to Anglo-Catholicism, whereas the ingrained revulsion from Catholicism would have attracted Lewis back to his Puritan roots. The result, at any rate, was a confusion of mutually confounding faiths.

Ultimately, perhaps, the appeal of Anglo-Catholicism might have resided in nothing more, or less, than a deep-seated desire to escape from Puritania, once and for all. This was achieved, apparently at least, some time between 1911 and 1913, not by the embrace of Anglo-Catholicism but by the rejection of all forms of Christianity. "And so, little by little, with fluctuations which I cannot now trace, I became an apostate, dropping my faith with no sense of loss but with the greatest relief."[21] He had escaped from the clutches of Puritania or at least he fooled himself with the illusion that he had done so. Little did he realize that Puritania could not be shaken off so easily. It, or at least its shadow, would continue to haunt Lewis, like a ghost of his past, on every step of his quest for the truth.

2

A SOUND ATHEIST

A young man who wishes to remain a sound Atheist
cannot be too careful of his reading.

—Surprised by Joy[1]

O N December 6, 1914, Lewis, by now a confirmed atheist,
was confirmed into the Anglican church at Saint Mark's
in Belfast. He would later describe this act of hypocrisy and
blasphemy, although driven by a genuine if cowardly desire to
avoid offending his father, as "one of the worst acts of my life."

> I allowed myself to be prepared for confirmation, and
> confirmed, and to make my first Communion, in total
> disbelief; acting a part, eating and drinking my own
> condemnation. As Johnson points out, where courage
> is not, no other virtue can survive except by accident.
> Cowardice drove me into hypocrisy and hypocrisy into
> blasphemy. It is true that I did not and could not then
> know the real nature of the thing I was doing: but I
> knew very well that I was acting a lie with the greatest
> possible solemnity.[2]

By 1916, Lewis was writing to Arthur Greeves that he
believed in no religion, adding that there was "absolutely no
proof for any of them, and from a philosophical standpoint

Christianity is not even the best." All religions were merely mythologies of man's own invention, "Christ as much as Loki." Christianity was only "one mythology among many, but the one that we happen to have been brought up in." Lewis buttressed his atheism with the sort of scientism and chronological snobbery that he would later condemn in the most forthright terms. His views were simply a reflection of "the recognized scientific account of the growth of religions." Superstition had always "held the common people, but in every age the educated and thinking ones have stood outside it." As a self-styled "educated and thinking one," the precocious seventeen-year-old expressed mild disappointment that his friend had not followed his example by becoming "emancipated from the old beliefs."[3] While conceding that "Jesus did actually exist," the figure of "Christ" was merely "the mythological being into whom he was afterwards converted by popular imagination" and around whom there arose "legends about his magic performances and resurrection" and "all the other tomfoolery about virgin birth, magic healing, apparitions and so forth. . . ."[4]

Evidently, if his letters to Arthur Greeves are to be believed, his rejection of Christianity was perceived as a liberation. "[S]trange as it may appear I am quite content to live without believing in a bogey who is prepared to torture me forever and ever if I should fail in coming up to an almost impossible ideal. . . . In fact I should think it horrible to feel that if life got too bad, I daren't escape for fear of a spirit more cruel and barbarous than any man. . . . The only reason I was sad was because I was disappointed in my hope that you were gradually escaping from beliefs which, in my case, always considerably lessened my happiness. . . ."[5]

Paradoxically, or perhaps perversely, Lewis's "liberation"

failed to prove very liberating. He confessed to discovering within himself "a vein of asceticism, almost of puritan practice without the puritan dogma. I believe in no God, least of all in one that would punish me for the 'lusts of the flesh': but I do believe that I have in me a spirit, a chip, shall we say, of universal spirit; and that, since all good & joyful things are spiritual & non-material, I must be careful not to let matter (= nature = Satan, remember) get too great a hold on me, & dull the one spark I have."[6] It seems that Lewis, having escaped from Puritania, had wandered into a jungle of half-digested heresy, a spiritual wasteland of garbled Gnosticism and pseudo-Manichaeism. His theological reductionism had led to a logical *reductio ad absurdum*. Believing in "no God" he apparently believed wholeheartedly in Satan. Refusing to believe in any god that would punish him for the "lusts of the flesh," he refused to succumb to these very same lusts because they were Satanic. The best, or at least the most amusing, riposte to Lewis's peculiarly incredible creed is to be found in G. K. Chesterton's satirical gibe at puritanical "heathenism" in his poem "The Song of the Strange Ascetic."

> If I had been a Heathen,
>   I'd have praised the purple vine,
> My slaves should dig the vineyards,
>   And I would drink the wine.
> But Higgins is a Heathen,
>   And his slaves grow lean and grey,
> That he may drink some tepid milk
>   Exactly twice a day
>
> If I had been a Heathen,
>   I'd have crowned Neaera's curls,

> And filled my life with love affairs,
> My house with dancing girls;
> But Higgins is a Heathen,
> And to lecture rooms is forced,
> Where his aunts, who are not married,
> Demand to be divorced.

Certainly Chesterton's depiction of "Higgins the Heathen" could serve equally as a lampoon of Lewis and all those strange ascetics who "sin without delight,"

> Of them that do not have the faith,
> And will not have the fun.[7]

By September 1918, Lewis's puritanical atheism had developed, or dissolved, into what might almost be termed a quasi-Satanic agnosticism. He now believed "that nature is wholly diabolical & malevolent and that God, if he exists, is outside of and in opposition to the cosmic arrangements."[8] Early in the following year, Warnie wrote to his father, denigrating his brother's "atheism," but dismissing it as a juvenile aberration that would pass with time. "Even at 23 one realizes that the opinions and convictions of 20 are transient things. Jack's Atheism is I am sure purely academic, but even so, no useful purpose is served by endeavouring to advertise oneself as an Atheist."[9] His father agreed: "He is young and he will learn in time that a man has not absolutely solved the riddle of the heavens above and the earth beneath and the waters under the earth at twenty." In the same letter, alluding to the fact that his son was now at University College, Oxford, Albert Lewis expressed the hope that "Oxford does not spoil him."[10]

Oxford would, in fact, have much to do with the maturing of Lewis. The ecclesially "high" atmosphere that surrounded its dreaming spires, and the eclectic mix of ideas that collided catalytically within its walls, would lead the young undergraduate further than ever from the provincial confines of Puritania. Oxford, after all, had been the bastion of Royalism during the English civil war, whereas its arch-rival, Cambridge, had been a stronghold of Cromwell's Puritan forces. Aware of these historical connections, Lewis, soon after he had learned that he had been elected to a scholarship at University College Oxford, would write of Macaulay that he was "too much of a whig and puritan for my taste: the old cavaliers were at any rate gentlemen."[11] These views would hardly have been endorsed by any of Lewis's Ulster relatives. Quite the contrary. When he ventured to voice some mild criticism of Cromwell he was reminded by his Aunt Kittie that "Cromwell's mother was some connection of ours."[12] Such was the entrenched cultural and religious position of the families of the Protestant Ascendancy in Ireland that the quarrels and wars arising from the English Reformation were not merely matters of familiar history, they were matters of family honor.

There was, however, far more of the "whig and puritan" in Lewis than perhaps he cared to admit. In the very same week in which he had written in praise of the "old cavaliers," he wrote to Arthur Greeves observing with opprobrium that Obadiah Walker had been at University College while observing with approbation that so had Shelley.[13] The denigration of the one and the praising of the other were significant. They constituted, on Lewis's part, an affirmation of his newfound skepticism and a reiteration of his timeworn anti-Catholicism. Obadiah Walker had been Master of University College between 1676 and 1688 but, upon the advent of the "Glorious" Revolution and the destruction of the Catholic monarchy, was imprisoned in the Tower of London because of his Roman Catholic beliefs. Shelley, on the other hand, had been expelled from University College in 1811 for circulating a pamphlet entitled *The Necessity of Atheism*. In his championing of Shelley he was nailing his colors to the atheist mast, while, in treating Walker with derision, he was still clinging to the anti-popery of his youth. Hence the colors that Lewis nailed to the atheist mast were emphatically Orange; that is to say, with self-contradictory irony, that they were emphatically "whig and puritan"![14] He might be an atheist, but he wanted it to be known that he was at least a loyal Protestant atheist.

Nonetheless, the catholic (and Catholic) flavor of Oxford began to exert an increasing influence on Lewis's tastes, removing the appetite for the provincialism of Puritanism. The Orange began to fade in the warm light of intellectual day. Thus, soon after arriving in Oxford, he could write to Arthur Greeves that "partly from interest in Yeats and Celtic mythology, partly from a natural repulsion to noisy drum-beating, bullying Orange-men and partly from association with Butler, I begin to have a very warm feeling for Ireland in general. I mean the real Ireland of Patsy Macan etc., not so much our protestant north. Indeed, if I ever get interested in politics, I shall probably be a nationalist (another subject for us to quarrel on, you see)."[15] The man named Butler, referred to in this letter, was Theobald Richard Fitzwalter Butler, whom Lewis had met during his first term at University College. Although Butler was "an Irishman & a nationalist" and "a violent Home Ruler," Lewis wrote that he liked him "exceedingly" and, through him, had been introduced to the work of Joseph Mary Plunkett, "one of the lately executed Sinn Fein poets."[16] Clearly Butler, who was four years Lewis's senior, had exerted a profound influence, balancing in Lewis's political and national consciousness the Orange of Ulster loyalism with the Green of Irish nationalism. His horizons were broadening.

Lewis's horizons were broadened still further by his association with John Robert Edwards, described by Lewis as "the other most interesting person" at the College. "[W]hat interests me about him is that he was an atheist till lately, and is now engaged in becoming a Catholic, or is very near it."[17] Edwards was "an ardent Newmanite" and he and Lewis discussed "religion, Buddhism, poetry and everything else."[18]

In spite of being introduced to real Catholics and would-be Catholics for the first time (as distinct from the bogey-Catholics of the embittered and bigoted imagination of Protestant Belfast), Lewis was far from wishing to become a Catholic himself. Instead, the impressions of Catholicism that he received from his friends were thrown into the catalytic cauldron, steeping along with all the other influences that fought for dominance in Lewis's hungry mind. One result of this strange brew of conflicting influences was a rather confused approach to the issues of the day, particularly with regard to the turbulent political developments in Ireland. Thus, for instance, he wrote to his father in July 1916, shortly after the ranks of the Ulster Volunteer Force had been decimated during the Battle of the Somme, that the "Ulster Division what there are of them now—must have silenced the yapping politicians for ever."[19] Compare this unequivocal support for the militant Unionism of the UVF with the sympathetic attitude to Irish nationalism that characterized his letters following his arrival at Oxford and his acquaintance with Sinn Fein sympathizers, such as Butler. Adding to the conundrum and the confusion with regard to the true nature of Lewis's position was an enigmatic reference in a letter to Arthur Greeves "as to the subject about Catholics and Protestants," evidently in response to some comments on the subject by Greeves. Lewis refused to be drawn into the discussion, stating simply that "I fear me that my views would only annoy you."[20]

Lewis's brief sojourn in Oxford came to an abrupt end in November 1917 when, having enlisted with the Somerset Light Infantry, he embarked for France. He arrived at the frontline trenches on his nineteenth birthday. At the beginning of February 1918, he fell ill with what the doctors called PUO (pyrexia, unknown origin), but which was known to the troops simply as "trench fever." He was sent to convalesce at a British Red Cross field hospital at Le Treport, and it was here that, for the first time, he came across the writing of G. K. Chesterton.

> I had never heard of him and had no idea of what he stood for; nor can I quite understand why he made such an immediate conquest of me. It might have been expected that my pessimism, my atheism, and my hatred of sentiment would have made him to me the least congenial of all authors. It would almost seem that Providence, or some "second cause" of a very obscure kind, quite over-rules our previous tastes when It decides to bring two minds together. Liking an author may be as involuntary and improbable as falling in love. I was by now a sufficiently experienced reader to distinguish liking from agreement. I did not need to accept what Chesterton said in order to enjoy it. His humour was of the kind which I like best—not "jokes" imbedded in the page like currants in a cake, still less (what I cannot endure), a general tone of flippancy and jocularity, but the humour which is not in any way separable from the argument but is rather (as Aristotle would say)

the "bloom" on dialectic itself. The sword glitters not because the swordsman set out to make it glitter but because he is fighting for his life and therefore moving it very quickly. For the critics who think Chesterton frivolous or "paradoxical" I have to work hard to feel even pity; sympathy is out of the question. Moreover, strange as it may seem, I liked him for his goodness. I can attribute this taste to myself freely (even at that age) because it was a liking for goodness which had nothing to do with any attempt to be good myself. . . . It was a matter of taste: I felt the "charm" of goodness as a man feels the charm of a woman he has no intention of marrying.[21]

Goodness, however, can be contagious. Lewis would find over the following years that his reading of Chesterton would lead him progressively closer to the God that Chesterton worshipped, a love for Chestertonian prose leading irresistibly to a love for Chestertonian praise. "In reading Chesterton, as in reading MacDonald, I did not know what I was letting myself in for. A young man who wishes to remain a sound Atheist cannot be too careful of his reading. There are traps everywhere. . . . God is, if I may say it, very unscrupulous."[22]

Lewis had discovered George MacDonald, the other key literary figure responsible for his eventual conversion to Christianity, almost two years earlier. "I have had a great literary experience this week," he wrote excitedly to Arthur Greeves on March 7, 1916. "I have discovered yet another author to add to our circle—our very own set: never since I first read 'The well at the world's end' have I enjoyed a book so much—and indeed I think my new 'find' is quite as good as Malory or Morris himself. The book, to get to the point, is George MacDonald's 'Faerie Romance,' *Phantastes.* . . . At any rate, whatever the book you are reading now, you simply MUST get this at once. . . ."[23]

"I have never concealed the fact that I regard him as my master," Lewis would write of MacDonald thirty years later; "indeed, I fancy I have never written a book in which I did not quote from him."[24] Describing the immediate impact of his reading of *Phantastes,* Lewis implied that it had baptized his imagination and had saved him from a possible slide from Romance to Decadence.

> I knew that I had crossed a great frontier. I had already been waist deep in Romanticism; and likely enough, at any moment, to flounder into its darker and more evil forms, slithering down the steep descent that leads from the love of strangeness to that of eccentricity and thence to that of perversity. Now *Phantastes* was romantic enough in all conscience; but there was a difference. Nothing was at that time further from my thoughts than Christianity and I therefore had no notion what this difference really was. I was only aware that if this new world was strange, it was also homely and humble; that if this was a dream, it was a dream in which one at least felt strangely vigilant; that the whole book had about it a sort of cool, morning innocence. . . . What it actually did to me was to convert, even to baptize . . . my imagination. It did nothing to my intellect nor (at that time) to my conscience. Their turn came far later with the help of many other books and men.[25]

MacDonald, like Chesterton, conveyed to the seemingly "sound atheist" the contagious "charm" of goodness, planting hidden seeds, or hinted suggestions, of unlooked for, and unnoticed, virtue that would come to fruition years later.

In his purgatorial romance, *The Great Divorce*, published in 1945, Lewis paid MacDonald the ultimate literary tribute of placing him in the role of Dante's Virgil, almost perhaps his Beatrice. MacDonald appears in Lewis's dream of purgatory as his "Teacher" and guide, helping him make sense of the mystical visions presented to him. "I tried, trembling, to tell this man all that his writings had done for me. I tried to tell how a certain frosty afternoon at Leatherhead Station when I first bought a copy of *Phantastes*. had been to me what the first sight of Beatrice had been to Dante: *Here begins the New Life*. I started to confess how long that Life had delayed in the region of imagination merely: how slowly and reluctantly I had come to admit that his Christendom had more than an accidental connexion with it, how hard I had tried not to see that the true name of the quality which first met me in his books is Holiness."[26]

The extent of Dante's direct impact on Lewis at this time is unclear. Although the Italian master's influence would grow in profundity throughout the following decade, there are relatively few mentions of him in Lewis's correspondence during the years of his youthful literary formation. In February 1917, he informed his father that he was learning Italian and that he had read the first two hundred lines of the *Inferno* in its original language.[27] He also expressed approval that Dante was among the favored poets of his Irish nationalist friend Theobald Butler.[28] There is, however, no exposition of Lewis's critical response to the *Divine Comedy*. Perhaps, therefore, it is fair to assume that he had not yet acquired a taste for what Dorothy L. Sayers referred to as Dante's "passionate intellect," much less a taste for the passionate faith that inspired his infernal, purgatorial, and beatific vision.

Lewis's introduction to the Catholic vision of Purgatory, a vision that would prove inspirational and instrumental in his writing of *The Great Divorce,* appears to have come from his reading of John Henry Newman. Lewis had read Newman's poems as early as 1914, while he was still at Malvern College, declaring to his father that they were "very, very delicate and pretty . . . almost too delicate for my taste: it is a kind of beauty that I can't very much appreciate." Significantly, however, he adds forcefully that "I must except from this criticism the 'Dream of Gerontius' which is very strongly written."[29] The forceful presence of Newman's purgatorial "Dream" remained with Lewis throughout his life. Half a century later, he would write in his last published book that the "right view" of Purgatory "returns magnificently in Newman's *Dream.* There, if I remember rightly, the saved soul, at the very foot of the throne, begs to be taken away and cleansed. It cannot bear for a moment longer 'With its darkness to affront that light.' "[30]

The works of MacDonald, a non-conformist minister, and those of Newman and Chesterton, both Catholics, formed a powerful Christian cocktail in Lewis's imagination, christening the romanticism at a subconscious level. Consciously, he still considered himself an atheist, battling against the faith that informed their works. He continued, obstinately, in his attempt not to see that the true name of the quality which he had first met in their books was Holiness.

Perhaps, however, there is evidence that Lewis's first introduction to Chesterton had softened his attitude towards the Catholic faith. Walking in the countryside around the field hospital at Le Treport within days of his first having read Chesterton, Lewis was impressed by the physical marks of Catholicism punctuating the landscape. "The roofs are all of old tiles and there are lots of old stone crucifixes, with their little offerings of grass & beads & things on them. Catholic Christianity is certainly more picturesque than Puritanism."[31] Even more surprising were his remarks in a letter to Arthur Greeves, written from Le Treport and also within days of his first reading Chesterton, about the anti-Catholicism in the work of George Borrow. "I am most violently out of sympathy with the author at times—when he is loudly patriotic . . . or when he indulges in vulgar invective against the parent church. Of course *that* is probably agreeable enough to you— eh?, old puritan."[32] This passage is particularly intriguing, not so much for the implicit anti-puritanism as for the revealing reference to Catholicism as "the parent church."

Returning to Oxford after the war, Lewis found his own immature atheism being tossed once more into the eclectic cauldron of competing ideas. His history tutor, George Hope Stevenson, was a devout Anglo-Catholic, whereas his tutor in philosophy, Edgar Frederick Carritt, rejected Christianity and placed all his faith in the cause of left-wing socialism. In such company Lewis was caught between the proverbial devil and the deep blue sea, or, more literally, between the Christian God and the deep red abyss. Although, like Carritt, he had rejected Christianity, he also felt an avowed aversion to bolshevism and the dialectical materialism it espoused. If Christianity remained unattractive, the socialist alternative was anathema. Finding himself in the no man's land between both parties, he could have been forgiven for echoing Shakespeare's Mercutio in the plaintive plea that a plague be placed on both their houses.

Lewis was, however, becoming more sympathetic to Catholicism, or, at least, he was becoming more sensitive to prejudiced puritanical attacks upon the Catholic Church.

In fairness, if not in faith, he felt duty-bound to defend the Church against her enemies. Returning to the work of George Borrow, Lewis wrote that "I still dislike the anti-Catholic propaganda," adding that he thought he had "found an explanation which might account for Borrow's rampant protestantism—it lies in the extreme Northernness or Saxonism of his nature. He thrilled, as we once did, to everything Norse.... I am glad to see that he knew the Kalevala. Hence, of course, a thoroughly Southern, Latin & Mediterranean thing like the Church was antipathetic. . . ."[33]

In spite of his sympathy with the Church, or rather his attempts at empathy towards her, he had no intention of abandoning his skeptical approach towards religion. Religious faith, he wrote in a letter to a friend in 1921, was "unsuitable for us who are alive now: we know too much and see life too widely and it is culpable not to make use of our widened landscape." Theirs was not the "comfortable little universe with heaven above and hell beneath, an absolute up and down and a bare six thousand years of recorded history." In effect, Lewis seemed to be saying that the sum of human experience was too little for the young generation and that previous generations had precious little to teach them. "I feel that we ought to use our own data even if they lead only to destruction."[34]

One senses in this further example of chronological snobbery the influence of H. G. Wells, a writer whom Lewis had read and enjoyed since childhood. In 1920, Wells had published the first volume of *The Outline of History*, a project which purported to be an objective account of the history of the world but which, in fact, was a retelling of history according to Wells's own philosophy of materialistic determinism. Although the smugly atheistic Lewis could not have known it at the time, the controversy surrounding this particular book would prove to be a further significant milestone on his eventual conversion to Christianity.

In essence, Wells's *History* began with the presumption that human society was "progressing" towards perfection and that, in consequence, the past was always inferior to the present. This was chronological snobbery enshrined as scholarship, art masquerading as science. Wells believed that human "progress" was blind, beneficial, and utterly unstoppable and inexorable. He perceived history as the product of invisible and immutable evolutionary forces that were coming to fruition in the twentieth century. The history of man had begun in the caves and was reaching a climax in the modern age with the triumph of science over religion. This, in turn, heralded a new dawn, a brave new world where happiness would be ushered in by technology. Wells's *Outline of History* was also tacitly anti-Christian, devoting far less space to the historical impact of Christ than to the Persians' campaign against the Greeks.

Wells's book had an enormous impact. It was heralded as a thoroughly modern view of history, a view of history unshackled by the prejudices and superstitions of the past. It was history as if God did not matter. In 1923, Joy Davidman (who was destined many years later to become Lewis's wife) had read *The Outline of History* as an impressionable eight-year-old and had immediately declared herself an atheist.

The most vociferous critic of Wells's "history" was Hilaire Belloc, whose many articles attacking Wells's "provincialism" and "ignorance" were collected and published in 1926 as *A Companion to Mr. Wells's "Outline of History."* Wells responded with *Mr. Belloc Objects,* to which Belloc, determined to have the last word, replied with *Mr. Belloc Still Objects*. At the end of the six-year controversy, Belloc claimed to have written more than 100,000 words in refutation of the central arguments of Wells's book. It was not, however, Belloc's response to Wells's *History* that would prove influential in edging Lewis closer to Christ but the book that Belloc's friend, G. K. Chesterton, wrote in response to the controversy.

In the midst of the acrimony and controversy generated by the six-year struggle between Wells and Belloc, Chesterton wrote *The Everlasting Man*. Intended as an answer to Wells, but wholly different in tone from Belloc's bellicosity, the book represented Chesterton's own attempt at an "outline of history." It was, in many respects, an antidote to Wells's book. Whereas Wells had made Christ peripheral, Chesterton had made Him central: "I have . . . divided this book into two parts: the former being a sketch of the main adventure of the human race in so far as it remained heathen; and the second a summary of the real difference that was made by it becoming Christian."[35]

The opening chapter of *The Everlasting Man* begins with a discussion of evolution and the limits of its application to any understanding of human history.

> Most modern histories of mankind begin with the word evolution, and with a rather wordy exposition of evolution. . . . There is something slow and soothing and gradual about the word and even about the idea. As a matter of fact, it is not, touching these primary things, a very practical word or a very profitable idea. Nobody can imagine how nothing could turn into something. . . . It is really far more logical to start by saying "In the beginning God created heaven and earth" even if you

only mean "In the beginning some unthinkable power
began some unthinkable process." . . .

But this notion of something smooth and slow,
like the ascent of a slope, is a great part of the illusion. It is an illogicality as well as an illusion; for
slowness has really nothing to do with the question. An event is not any more intrinsically intelligible or unintelligible because of the pace at which it
moves. . . . Yet there runs through all the rationalis-
tic treatment of history this curious and confused idea
that difficulty is avoided, or even mystery eliminated,
by dwelling on mere delay or on something dilatory in
the process of things.[36]

The effect on Lewis of reading *The Everlasting Man*
was staggering. Ever since discovering Chesterton, Lewis
had continued to read his works, and those of George
MacDonald, enjoying the charm of their goodness but refusing to be charmed by their Christianity. "George MacDonald
had done more to me than any other writer; of course it was
a pity he had that bee in his bonnet about Christianity. He
was good in *spite of* it. Chesterton had more sense than all the
moderns put together; bating, of course, his Christianity."[37]
This had been his view for seven years, ever since first reading
Chesterton in the field hospital at Le Treport. In the interim,
he had continued to read his works voraciously, allowing
Chesterton's religious orthodoxy to drip-feed itself into his
heart without ever, consciously, admitting it into his head.
"Then I read Chesterton's *Everlasting Man* and for the first
time saw the whole Christian outline of history set out in a
form that seemed to me to make sense."[38]

Lewis's atheism had been shaken to its foundations by

Chesterton's book. It would be a further six years before, under the influence of another Catholic, he would finally accept the Christian faith as his own. There was, however, no going back to the naivete of his youthful atheism. Life after *The Everlasting Man* would never be the same.

3

"NEVER TRUST A PAPIST . . ."

At my first coming into the world I had been (implicitly) warned never to trust a Papist, and at my first coming into the English Faculty (explicitly) never to trust a
philologist. Tolkien was both.

—Surprised by Joy [1]

O N January 18, 1927, Lewis recorded in his diary that he
was struggling to disentangle the conflicting philosophies battling for supremacy in his mind and heart.

Was thinking about imagination and intellect and the
unholy muddle I am in about them at present: undi-
gested scraps of anthroposophy and psychoanalysis
jostling with orthodox idealism over a background of
good old Kirkian rationalism. Lord what a mess! And
all the time (with me) there's the danger of falling back
into most childish superstitions, or of running into
dogmatic materialism to escape them. [2]

On the following day, Lewis appears to have sought a resolu-
tion of the "unholy muddle" in the perennial freshness of the
Romantic poets. He resolved to study "the whole doctrine of
Imagination in Coleridge" as soon as he had time—"and the
thought of Wordsworth was somehow very reassuring. That's

the real imagination, no bogies, no Karmas, no gurus, no damned psychism there." He had been "astray among second rate ideas too long. . . ."[3]

In seeking the Romantic antidote to the poison of parapsychology or psychoanalysis, Lewis was once more treading on dangerous ground. As with his reading of Chesterton, the sound Atheist-turned-Theist could not be "too careful of his reading." The Romanticism of Coleridge and Wordsworth, heralded by their collaboration on the *Lyrical Ballads* of 1798, had been a reaction against the supercilious "rationalism" of the so-called "Enlightenment." The Romantic revolution that they instigated was the reaction of the heart to the idolatry of the head. There was, however, a danger inherent in such a revolution; the danger that the reaction could become an over-reaction. The Romantics were always prone to the temptation to transplant the idolatry of the head with the idolatry of the heart, heart-worship supplanting head-worship, a temptation to which the darker romantic poets—Byron, Shelley, and Keats—succumbed. The self-indulgent melancholia of the dark romantics led logically and inexorably to the self-indulgent experimentation of the Decadents; Byron, Shelley, and Keats serving as the forerunners of Baudelaire, Verlaine, and Wilde. It is significant, therefore, that Lewis sought the sobriety of the light romantics, Wordsworth and Coleridge, and not the drunkenness of the dark romantics or Decadents.

Unlike many of those who followed in their wake, Wordsworth and Coleridge perceived the danger of divorcing the heart from the head. They understood the folly of asserting faith without reason as an antidote to the previous century's reason without faith, the folly of replacing one self-evident absurdity with another. Both men sought, and believed they had found, a synthesis between the promptings of the heart and the predicates of the head, a marriage of faith and philosophy. In both cases, their quest for the meaning of life led them from agnostic or atheistic proto-communism, in the form of a fervor for the anti-clericalism of the French Revolution, to an acceptance of Anglican Christianity. In Coleridge's case, his Anglicanism was so permeated with a real understanding of orthodox theology that he served to plant the seeds of traditionalism and Anglo-Catholicism that would blossom in the years after his death in the flourishing of the Gothic Revival and the Oxford Movement. His robust philosophical defense of religious orthodoxy places him, in relation to the Catholic literary revival of the nineteenth century, in a parallel position to that of Chesterton in the twentieth century. At the beginning of both centuries, Coleridge and Chesterton were catalysts for much that followed.

Certainly it is more than a little intriguing that Lewis should discover a solution to his "unholy muddle" in the works and philosophy of Samuel Taylor Coleridge, a poet and philosopher whose Romanticism would lead others to the very gates of Rome.

Lewis was also influenced during this crucial period of "unmuddling" by the work of Coventry Patmore, a Catholic convert poet whose Romanticism had taken him beyond the very gates of Rome into the full satisfying embrace of the Church. In June 1930, Lewis had read Patmore's *Angel in the House* and was greatly impressed by the "half philosophic, half religious odes on the author's theory of marriage as a mystical image of & approach to divine love." Although parts of the poem "would be very easy to parody," it was "surprising how one feels less and less inclined to sneer," especially as the poem was "really often sublime."[4] "Amazing poet! How all of a piece it is—how the riveted metre both expresses and illustrates his almost fanatical love of incarnation."[5]

Two weeks later, a more "amazing poet" was having an even greater effect. In early July, Lewis and his friend Owen Barfield had finished reading Dante's *Paradiso*. "I think it reaches heights of poetry which you get nowhere else: an ether almost too fine to breathe," he wrote excitedly to Arthur Greeves. "It is a pity that I can give you no notion what it is like. Can you imagine Shelley at his most ecstatic combined with Milton at his most solemn & rigid? It sounds impossible I know, but that is what Dante has done."[6] The divine poet's beatific vision in *Paradiso* had "really opened a new world to me":

> I had never seen at all what Dante was like before . . . the impression is one so unlike anything else that I can hardly describe it . . . —a sort of mixture of intense, even crabbed, complexity in language and thought with (what seems impossible) *at the very same time* a feeling of spacious gliding movement, like a slow dance, or like flying. It is like the stars endless mathematical subtility of orb, cycle, epicycle and elliptic, unthinkable & unpicturable, & yet at the same time the freedom and liquidity of empty space and the triumphant certainty of movement. I should describe it as feeling more *important* than any poetry I have ever read. . . . It is seldom homely: perhaps not *holy* in our sense—it is too Catholic for that: and of course its blend of complexity and beauty is very like Catholic theology—wheel within wheel, but wheels of glory, and the One radiated through the Many.[7]

In the midst of the "unholy muddle" and the productive process of "unmuddling," Lewis was forging a friendship with a young professor of Anglo-Saxon, J. R. R. Tolkien. Friendship with Tolkien, Lewis would write in *Surprised by Joy*, would mark "the breakdown of two old prejudices": "At my first coming into the world I had been (implicitly) warned never to trust a Papist, and at my first coming into the English Faculty (explicitly) never to trust a philologist. Tolkien was both."[8]

Tolkien had first come to Lewis's attention on May 11, 1926, during a discussion of faculty business at an "English Tea" at Merton College. "I had a talk with him afterwards," Lewis recorded in his diary "He is a smooth, pale, fluent little chap. . . . No harm in him: only needs a smack or so."[9] From these indifferent and inauspicious beginnings, a friendship soon developed which would become increasingly important to both men.

Shortly before this first meeting, Tolkien had formed the Coalbiters, a club among the dons dedicated to the reading of the Icelandic sagas and myths. Its name derived from the Icelandic *Kolbítar*, a lighthearted term for those who lounge so close to the fire in winter that they bite the coal. Membership of this informal club had been restricted initially to those with a reasonable knowledge of Icelandic but the restrictions were waived to enable enthusiastic beginners such as Lewis to attend. By January 1927, Lewis was a regular frequenter of meetings of the Coalbiters, finding the company of like-minded scholars invigorating.

Through his friendship with Tolkien, and his being a member of the Coalbiters, Lewis found his love for the "northernness" that had so inspired the imagination of his youth rekindled. It was not long before Tolkien, six years Lewis's senior, had become not merely a friend but also a mentor. On December 3, 1929, Lewis wrote to Arthur Greeves that he had been up until 2:30 in the morning "talking to the Anglo-Saxon professor Tolkien . . . discoursing of the gods and giants of Asgard for three hours," adding that "the fire was bright and the talk was good."[10]

A few days after this late-night conversation, Tolkien decided to show Lewis his Beren and Luthien poem. On December 7, Lewis wrote to Tolkien, expressing his enthusiasm:

> I can quite honestly say that it is ages since I have had an evening of such delight: and the personal interest of reading a friend's work had very little to do with it—I should have enjoyed it just as well if I'd picked it up in a bookshop, by an unknown author. The two things that come out clearly are the sense of reality in the background and the mythical value: the essence of a myth being that it should have no taint of allegory to the maker and yet should *suggest* incipient allegories to the reader.[11]

If Lewis had discovered in Tolkien a much-valued mentor, Tolkien had found in Lewis an appreciative and sympathetic audience for his, as yet unpublished, work. "The unpayable debt that I owe to him," Tolkien wrote of Lewis years later, "was not 'influence' as it is ordinarily understood, but sheer encouragement. He was for long my only audience. Only from him did I ever get the idea that my 'stuff' could be more than a private hobby."[12] This view of Lewis's importance as an "encourager" was reiterated by Tolkien in a letter to Professor Clyde Kilby on December 18, 1965. "I have never had much confidence in my own work," Tolkien wrote, "and even now when I am assured (still much to my grateful surprise) that it has value for other people, I feel diffident, reluctant as it were to expose my world of imagination to possibly contemptuous eyes and ears. But for the encouragement of C. S. L. I do not think that I should ever have completed or offered for publication *The Lord of the Rings*."[13]

Tolkien's "unpayable debt" to Lewis would actually be paid in full through the profound debt that Lewis owed to Tolkien. Specifically, Lewis was indebted to Tolkien for his final conversion to Christianity. According to Walter Hooper, Lewis's friend and biographer, "a realisation of the truth in mythologies triggered Lewis's conversion" to Christianity:

> This came about after a long discussion in 1931 with Tolkien and Hugo Dyson which continued until four o'clock in the morning. At the end of this marathon discussion Lewis believed that myths were real and that facts took the shine off truth, emptying truth of its glory. Thereafter he became an excellent Christian apologist.[14]

This meeting, which was to have such a revolutionary impact on Lewis's life, took place on September 19, 1931, after Lewis had invited Tolkien and Dyson to dine at his rooms in Magdalen College. After dinner the three men went for a walk beside the river and discussed the nature and purpose of myth. Lewis explained that he felt the power of myths, but that they were ultimately untrue. As he expressed it to Tolkien, myths were "lies, even though lies breathed through silver."

"*No*," Tolkien replied emphatically. "*They are not.*"

Tolkien resumed, arguing that myths, far from being lies, were the best way of conveying truths which would otherwise be inexpressible. "We have come from God [continued Tolkien], and inevitably the myths woven by us, though they contain error, will also reflect a splintered fragment of the true light, the eternal truth that is with God." Since we are made in the image of God, and since God is the Creator, part of the *imageness* of God in us is the gift of creativity. The creation—or, more correctly, the sub-creation—of stories or myths is merely a reflection of the image of the Creator in us. As such, although "myths may be misguided, . . . they steer however shakily towards the true harbor," whereas materialistic "progress" leads only to the abyss and to the power of evil.

"In expounding this belief in the inherent *truth* of mythology," wrote Tolkien's biographer, Humphrey Carpenter, "Tolkien had laid bare the centre of his philosophy as a writer, the creed that is at the heart of *The Silmarillion*."[15] He had also laid bare the fatuity of the "unholy muddle" in which Lewis still found himself. Listening almost spellbound as Tolkien expounded his philosophy of myth, Lewis felt the foundations of his own theistic philosophy crumble into dust before the force of his friend's arguments.

Buttressed by the support of Dyson, who substantially shared his beliefs, Tolkien developed his argument to explain that the story of Christ was the True Myth, a myth that works in the same way as the others, but a myth that really happened—a myth that existed in the realm of fact as well as in the realm of truth.[16] In the same way that men unraveled the truth through the weaving of story, God revealed the Truth through the weaving of history.

Tolkien's line of reasoning struck a particular note of poignancy with Lewis because he had examined the historicity of the Gospels and had come to the almost reluctant conclusion that he was "*nearly* certain that it really happened."[17] Indeed the discussion with Tolkien and Dyson had been foreshadowed by a previous conversation five years earlier. Shortly after he had read Chesterton's *The Everlasting Man,* the book that had shaken his agnosticism to its foundations, "something far more alarming" happened to him.

Early in 1926 the hardest boiled of all the atheists I ever knew sat in my room on the other side of the fire and remarked that the evidence for the historicity of the Gospels was really surprisingly good. "Rum thing," he went on. "All that stuff of Frazer's about the Dying God. Rum thing. It almost looks as if it had really happened once."

"To understand the shattering impact" of the atheist's admission, Lewis wrote, "you would need to know the man (who has certainly never since shown any interest in Christianity)." He was "the cynic of cynics, the toughest of toughs."[18]

Now, five years later, it seemed that Tolkien was making sense of it all. He had shown that pagan myths were, in fact, God expressing Himself through the minds of poets, using the images of their "mythopoeia" to reveal fragments of His eternal truth. Yet, most astonishing of all, Tolkien maintained that Christianity was exactly the same except for the enormous difference that the poet who invented it was God Himself, and the images He used were real men and actual history. The death and resurrection of Christ was the old "dying god" myth except that Christ was the *real* Dying God, with a precise and verifiable location in history and definite historical consequences. The old myth had become a fact while still retaining the character of a myth.

Tolkien's arguments had an indelible effect on Lewis. The edifice of his unbelief crumbled and the foundations of his Christianity were laid. Twelve days later, Lewis wrote to Arthur Greeves that he had "Just passed on from believing in God to definitely believing in Christ in Christianity," adding that his "long night talk with Dyson and Tolien had a good deal to do with it."[19]

The full extent of Tolkien's influence can be gauged from Lewis's letter to Greeves on October 18:

> Now the story of Christ is simply a true myth: a myth working on us in the same way as the others, but with this important difference that *it really happened:* and one must be content to accept it in the same way, remembering that it is God's myth where the others are men's myths: i.e. the Pagan stories are God expressing Himself through the minds of poets, using such images as He found there, while Christianity is God expressing Himself through what we call "real things." Therefore, it is *true,* not in the sense of being a "description" of God (that no finite mind could take in) but in the sense of being the way in which God chooses to (or can) appear to our faculties. The "doctrines" we get out of the true myth are of course *less* true: they are translations into our *concepts* and *ideas* of that which God has already expressed in a language more adequate, namely the actual incarnation, crucifixion, and resurrection.[20]

Tolkien was also affected deeply by the long discussion with Lewis, feeling sufficiently inspired by their encounter to write the poem "Mythopoeia," his finest achievement in verse. The poem takes the form of the reply of "Philomythus," that is, the lover of myth, to "Misomythus," the hater of myth, and is dedicated "To one who said that myths were lies and therefore worthless, even 'though breathed through silver.'" The allusion to Lewis as "Misomythus" is a trifle unfair. He was never a hater of myths. On the contrary, he shared with Tolkien a passionate love for mythology, a love that stretched back far beyond their "long night talk" to the days of his childhood. Now, thanks to Tolkien's exposition of his philosophy of myth, the two men shared more than a *love* for mythology; they also shared the *belief* that mythology was a conveyer of truth.

Having found agreement in a shared philosophy, the friendship between Tolkien and Lewis flourished as never before. In October 1933, Tolkien recorded the following entry in his diary: "Friendship with Lewis compensates for much, and besides giving constant pleasure and comfort has done me much good from the contact with a man at once honest, brave, intellectual—a scholar, a poet, and a philosopher—and a lover, at least after a long pilgrimage, of Our Lord."[21]

For Lewis the friendship was even more important. Had he never met Tolkien, it is possible that his "long pilgrimage" would never have reached its conclusion. As with the influence of Chesterton five years earlier, Lewis was discovering that the old prejudiced notion that he should "never trust a Papist" was a cankerous and cantankerous lie. Had he never trusted a Papist, it is at least possible that he might never have met Christ. Certainly the path he had taken to "mere Christianity" was very largely the Roman road along which guides such as Chesterton and Tolkien, and Patmore and Dante and Newman, had led him.

MEETING MOTHER KIRK

On the floor of *Peccatum Adae* stood Mother Kirk crowned and sceptered in the midst of the bright moonlit circle left by the silent people. All their faces were turned towards her, and she was looking eastward to where John slowly descended the cliff. . . .

"I have come to give myself up," he said.

"It is well," said Mother Kirk. "You have come a long way round to reach this place, whither I would have carried you in a few moments. But it is very well."

"What must I do?" said John,

"You must take off your rags," said she, "as your friend has done already, and then you must dive into this water."

"Alas," said he, "I have never learned to dive."

"There is nothing to learn," said she. "The art of diving is not to do anything new but simply to cease doing something. You have only to let yourself go."

—*The Pilgrim's Regress*[1]

IN THE same week Lewis and Owen Barfield finished reading Dante's *Paradiso*, the poem that had taken Lewis to "heights of poetry which you get nowhere else," he experienced another major milestone on his path to conversion which would plunge him into depths of profundity which he had never previously experienced. Having reached the heights with Dante, the depths were plumbed, literally and figuratively, while bathing with Barfield in the river Thame. It was here that Lewis learned to dive, an event that he described as "a great change in my life" which had "important (religious) connections."[2] The act of diving, and, more specifically, the act of learning to do so for the first time, was, for Lewis, an incarnate metaphor for the leap of faith required for religious conversion. The inability to dive was linked to the desire for self-preservation, itself a metaphor for the sin of pride, whereas the first successful dive required an abandonment of self-centered fear, a metaphor for the virtue of humility. Its significance was highlighted to dramatic effect in *The Pilgrim's Regress,* the autobiographical allegory published in 1933 in which Lewis charted his "long pilgrimage" to Christianity through the process of unlearning or "unmuddling" the inherited and accumulated prejudices of his life. At the culmination of his pilgrimage, the figure of Mother Kirk (that is, Mother Church) tells him that he must dive into the living waters if he is to achieve his heart's desire. She is unimpressed by John's (that is, Lewis's) protestations that he has never learned to dive. "There is nothing to learn. . . . The art of diving is not to do anything new but simply to cease doing something. You have only to let yourself go." It was not a question of learning, but of unlearning. One did not learn humility; one gained humility by abandoning pride. Unlearning pride was the key to humility and, under grace, the prerequisite for conversion.

The "great change" in Lewis wrought by his having learned to dive can be discerned from the nature of his letters in the weeks following this pivotal event in his life. Thereafter,

Lewis values humility above all else and denigrates the place of worldly ambition, insisting that the desire to gain approval as a writer was not the side of his character that was "really worth much":

> And depend upon it, unless God has abandoned us, he will find means to cauterize that side somehow or other. . . . And honestly, the being cured, with all the pain, has pleasure too: one creeps home, tired and bruised, into a state of mind that is really restful, when all one's ambitions have been given up. Then one can really for the first time say "Thy Kingdom come." . . .[3]

In this frame of mind, or heart, Lewis began to dabble in theology, reading the work of Baron von Hugel, the Catholic theologian and biblical scholar, and Thomas Traherne, the seventeenth-century mystical poet. One detects the influence of both these writers, and perhaps particularly von Hugel's *The Mystical Element in Religion,* in Lewis's exposition of a mystical aestheticism. "Beauty descends from God into nature: but there it would perish and does except when a Man appreciates it with worship and thus as it were *sends it back* to God: so that through his consciousness what descended ascends again and the perfect circle is made."[4]

Having learned the paradoxical truth of myth with Tolkien and Dyson, and having learned to dive, physically, with Barfield, and metaphysically, with Humility, Lewis had finally "passed on from believing in God to definitely believing in Christ—in Christianity."[5] "Thereafter," as Walter Hooper states, "he became an excellent Christian apologist."

Lewis's vocation as a Christian apologist commenced with his writing of *The Pilgrim's Regress* during August 1932. This book, Lewis's first and one of his finest, presents tantalizing insights into the "unmuddling" process that led to his conversion. Writing with disarming clarity and candour, Lewis, through the character of "John," his allegorical self-portrait, takes the reader on an intellectual journey in which we discover how the author finally succeeded in making holy sense of his "unholy muddle." As "John" progresses on his "Regress" from misconception and prejudice to the conception of Christian reality, the reader begins to understand Lewis's own religious position in the months immediately after his conversion.

The initial idea of something similar to *The Pilgrim's Regress* appears to have arisen in Lewis's mind prior to his reaching the stage of "definitely believing in Christ." As early as 1930, when he had returned to a belief in God but was still to reconcile himself with the Christian conception of Him, Lewis attempted a prose description of "the process by which I came back, like so many of my generation, from materialism to a belief in God."[6] Alluding to the recent high-profile conversions of writers such as T. S. Eliot to Anglo-Catholicism, in 1928, and Evelyn Waugh to Roman Catholicism, in 1930, Lewis betrayed an element of irritation at the fact that the religious revival of that time was tending towards "classicism in art, royalism in politics, and Catholicism in religion." Clearly uncomfortable at this papist tendency, Lewis countered with the statement that there could be "a *via media* between syllogisms and psychoses," and that "Thomas Aquinas and D. H. Lawrence do not divide the universe between them."[7]

The reference to "classicism in art, royalism in politics, and Catholicism in religion" was a direct quotation of Eliot. They were the words Eliot had chosen to announce his conversion to Anglo-Catholicism and were themselves a reiteration of the position of Eliot's mentor, Charles Maurras, whose views had been described in the March 1913 edition of the *Nouvelle revue francaise* as the embodiment of a traditionalist trinity: "classique, catholique, monarchique." Lewis disliked Eliot's poetry intensely and clearly disliked the "catholic" form that his conversion had taken with equal intensity

He was, however, far more favorably disposed towards Evelyn Waugh. He had written a highly favorable review of Waugh's biography of Dante Gabriel Rossetti in 1928 and would no doubt have been aware of Waugh's much publicised reception into the Catholic Church in September 1930. Commenting on Waugh's conversion, a writer in the *Bystander* noted that the "brilliant young author" was "the latest man of letters to be received into the Catholic Church. Other well-known literary people who have gone over to Rome include Sheila Kaye-Smith, Compton Mackenzie, Alfred Noyes, Father Ronald Knox and G. K. Chesterton."[8] The list was far from exhaustive. By the 1930s the tide of Roman converts had become a torrent, and throughout that decade there were some twelve thousand converts a year in England alone. This, then, was the background to Lewis's concern that the universe was being divided into the two extremes of Catholic "syllogisms," as represented by Saint Thomas Aquinas, and materialistic and sensual "psychoses," as epitomized by D. H. Lawrence. His task, he felt, was to discover a via *media* between these two extremes. His own position was so much in a state of flux in 1930, however, that the task had to be abandoned. It was not until two years later, after his transition from Theism to Christianity had been completed, that he was able to return to the task he had set himself.

During the spring of 1932, Lewis began another abortive effort at writing an autobiographical account of his conversion, this time in verse. Only thirty-four lines have survived of what Lewis's biographers Roger Lancelyn Green and Walter

Hooper have labeled his "Chestertonian 'voyage'": "As Lewis had read most of Chesterton's theological books by this time it does not seem fanciful to suppose that Lewis's idea of a spiritual "voyage" was based on an idea suggested by Chesterton in his book on *Orthodoxy*."[9]

By the time Lewis returned to the charting of his spiritual conversion in August 1932, he had abandoned any thought of rendering it in verse. He chose instead the medium of strict, or formal, allegory. The title he selected, *The Pilgrim's Regress,* is, of course, strongly suggestive of Bunyan's allegory Apart from the similarity of title, however, and the choice of formal allegory as the medium, there is little similarity between Bunyan's *Progress* and Lewis's *Regress.* The former's Puritanism was anathema to the latter's aesthetic sensibilities. As such, the influence of Bunyan on Lewis, beyond the superficial similarities of form, should not be overstated. Bunyan's influence on *The Pilgrim's Regress* is similar to the influence of H. G. Wells on Lewis's Space Trilogy. The fact that Lewis had been influenced by Wells in his choice of science fiction as the medium for the Trilogy does not indicate that Wells had any influence on the theological dimension of the novels. On the contrary, the novels were written as an answer to Wells's scientism and as an antidote to its poison. Similarly, *The Pilgrim's Regress* was an answer to Bunyan's Puritanism in the sense that Lewis's Pilgrim escapes the joylessness of Puritania and discovers Joy beyond its borders. In fact, considering Lewis's implicitly anti-Catholic comments during his first effort at spiritual autobiography in 1930, we shall discover that the deeper influences on the writing of *The Pilgrim's Regress* were surprisingly "Catholic."

Lewis's view as to what constituted the "extremes" and what constituted the *via media* had changed considerably from that which characterized his Theistic stance two years earlier. In *The Pilgrim's Regress* it seemed as though Catholicism, far from being one of the extremes, had become, in some vague and ill-defined expression of "orthodoxy," the *via media* itself. The "syllogisms" were now represented as being the idols of the head, whereas the "psychoses" were the idols of the heart. Among the "syllogisms" to the "north" of the *via media*, depicted in the allegory as physical places symbolizing the idea they represent, were Puritania, representing the spirit of Puritanism; Zeitgeistheim, representing the spirit of the age or the slavery of fashion; and Superbia, representing the sin of Pride. To the "south" of the *via media*, among the "psychoses," are Orgiastica, representing Lust enshrined; Quietismus, representing the quietism of the Quakers and others, within which are to be found Luxinterna and Hunch, representing the dangers of following the promptings of blind faith without the light of reason; Occultica, representing the Occult; Aesthetica, representing the worship of Beauty or Art for its own sake; and Sodom, representing, well, Sodom!

The influence of Coleridge and Wordsworth is clearly present in the placing of the *via media* of orthodoxy between the extremes of heresy or idolatry. In true Coleridgean fashion, Lewis now believed that the true path between the "syllogisms" of the head and the "psychoses" of the heart was through the establishment of the correct relationship between faith and reason. The *via media*, or the path of truth, represented the *marriage* of faith and reason whereas the heresies to "north" and "south" of the true path were ideas that had *divorced* themselves from this marriage. To the "north" is the reason-without-faith of the eighteenth-century "Enlightenment" against which Wordsworth and Coleridge had reacted; to the "south" is the faith-without-reason and the self-indulgence of the Dark Romantics and Decadents, representing the over-reaction to eighteenth-century rationalism that Wordsworth and Coleridge had also rejected.

Even more powerful than the presence of Wordsworth and Coleridge on the structure of *The Pilgrim's Regress,* and therefore by inference on the state of Lewis's mind shortly after his conversion, is the presence of Dante. Lewis's placing of the sins of the head to the "north" and those of the heart to the "south" represents a near reflection of the division and categorizing of the seven deadly sins in the *Divine Comedy.* In the *Inferno,* Dante places those guilty of sins of incontinence or the appetite (such as the lustful, the gluttonous, the hoarders and the spendthrifts) in Upper Hell; he places those guilty of sins of fraud or malice in Lower Hell. Broadly speaking, and allowing for the inadequacy of our "word hoard" as a tool for grasping these metaphysical nuances, the former follow the follies of the heart, the latter the follies of the head. Similarly, in the *Purgatorio,* Dante places those guilty of Excessive Love of Secondary Goods, such as the Avaricious, the Gluttonous and the Lustful in Upper Purgatory; he places those guilty of Love Perverted, that is, the love of neighbors' harm, such as the Proud, the Envious and the Wrathful, in Lower Purgatory. Again, and broadly speaking, the former were followers of the follies of the heart, the latter of the follies of the head. Since Dante himself was merely following the categorization of these sins by his mentor, Saint Thomas Aquinas, in the latter's *Summa Theologiae,* it can be seen that Saint Thomas Aquinas emerges as the preeminent and towering influence on the structure of Lewis's allegorical "Regress." Thus we can see that Aquinas was no longer on one of the "extremes" but was now exerting a strong pull on the very center of Lewis's *via media.* Whether Lewis was consciously aware of Aquinas's centrality is perhaps open to question. It is at least possible that Dante had succeeded in "smuggling" the theology of his Master into the thoughts of Lewis without Lewis's fully realizing the fact. If this is so, there is, of course, a delicious irony, or what Dante might have called a Divine Comedy or Symmetry, in the fact that Lewis had succumbed to the very "theological smuggling" that would become one of the purposes of his own works of fiction. Perhaps indirectly, Lewis had clearly come a long way in the two years since his idea of writing the story of his conversion had been initially conceived.

Apart from the obvious influence of Coleridge and Wordsworth, and the towering influence of Dante and, through him, Aquinas, other influences also abound throughout the pages of *The Pilgrim's Regress.* It is difficult to view the work as a whole, panoramically, without being reminded insistently, of Aristotle's *Ethics,* and clues to some of the other influences are provided by Lewis himself in the epigraphs he employs at the commencement of each book of the *Regress.* These include quotations from Plato, Boethius, Spenser, Milton, Pascal, Virgil, Bunyan, and George MacDonald.

Significantly, an epigram by the Anglican theologian Richard Hooker is included at the commencement of Book One, indicating that Lewis was already acquainted with the work of the theologian who would become, and would remain, possibly the most important to him throughout his life. Although Hooker is a theologian of the Church of England, his position within the context of Anglican churchmanship is singularly "Catholic." It was Hooker, perhaps more than any other Anglican theologian, who argued against the Puritan position of his day, and the Protestant Fundamentalist and "Evangelical" position of today, that Scripture is the sole guide of human conduct. Against this creed of *sola scriptura,* or what might be termed bibliolatry, Hooker maintained in his *magnum opus, Laws of Ecclesiastical Polity,* that the sacraments were central to Christian worship and that sacred tradition, sanctioned by the authority of the Church, was an integral part of the deposit of faith. Certainly there is no escaping the fact, though Lewis sometimes endeavored to do so, that in selecting Hooker as the theologian to whom he owed the greatest debt, Lewis was hanging his coat of allegiance within the Church of England firmly on the "high" Hook of Anglo-Catholicism.

The anti-Puritan stance of *The Pilgrim's Regress* is apparent from the outset, indeed from the very first sentence of the book: "I dreamed of a boy who was born in the land of Puritania and his name was John."[10] Even the title of the opening chapter, "The Rules," signifies Lewis's equating Puritanism with Pharisaism, those who know the letter of the Law but are blind to its spirit. God is known as "the Landlord." He is, however, seen very much as an absentee Landlord, more conspicuous by His absence than His presence. He is loved in theory only, but feared in practice, and, one suspects, loathed in secret. The rules are rigid but are bent through the tacit acceptance of hypocrisy. Religious practice is performed by the donning of masks, illustrating its artificiality, and by the wearing of "ugly and uncomfortable clothes," illustrating its joylessness.[11] All in all, the Puritan "Landlord" emerges as an Orwellian "Big Brother," a theoretically benign tyrant.

It is little surprise that John seeks to escape. He leaves Puritania and, before he has traveled very far, meets Mr. Enlightenment, the spirit of atheistic rationalism, who informs him with the utmost solemnity that the Landlord does not exist.[12] He wanders onwards, entering "darkest Zeitgeistheim," a land ruled by "the Spirit of the Age."

Here he meets Sigismund Enlightenment, a personification of Freudianism, who is Mr. Enlightenment's son. Sigismund speaks of his father with contempt as "a vain and ignorant old man, almost a Puritanian."[13]

John is imprisoned by the Spirit of the Age but is freed by Reason, a beautiful woman on a black stallion: ". . . she was so tall that she seemed to him a Titaness, a sun-bright virgin clad in complete steel, with a sword naked in her hand."[14] The potent imagery of Reason as Ever Virgin, purity personified, needs no further explanation. She destroys the Spirit of the Age and leads John to freedom. Explaining the errors of the age, Reason explains that those enslaved to the Spirit of the Age "have ceased to listen to the only people who can tell them anything about it."

"Who are they?" asks John.

"They are younger sisters of mine, and their names are Philosophy and Theology."[15]

After Reason has led him back to the main road, the *via media,* John meets with Vertue and they proceed along the road together. Soon, however, "the road ran up without warning to the edge of a great gorge or chasm and ended in the air, as if it had been broken off?[16] Vertue and John begin to argue about which is the best way down when they are interrupted by "a third voice": "You have neither of you any chance at all unless I carry you down." The voice is that of an old woman, Mother Kirk, that is, Mother Church. "Some of the country people say she is second-sighted," Vertue whispers to John, "and some that she is crazy."

"I shouldn't trust her," John whispers in return. "She looks to me much more like a witch." Considering how old and frail she looks, John asks the old woman how she intends to carry them down, adding that, if anything, they were more likely to be able to carry *her* down. Mother Kirk replies that she could do it "by the power that the Landlord has given me."

"So you believe in the Landlord, too?" said John.

"How can I not, dear," said she, "when I am his own daughter-in-law?"[17]

Having declared herself, implicitly, the Bride of Christ, Mother Kirk explains that the great chasm in the road was caused by a catastrophe, that is, the Fall: "And at the moment he put out his hand and plucked the fruit there was an earthquake, and the country cracked open all the way across from North to South: and ever since, instead of the farm, there has been that gorge, which the country people call the Grand Canyon. But in my language its name is *Peccatum Adae*."[18]

It is intriguing, perhaps indeed a little odd, that Lewis should make a point of ending Mother Kirk's monologue with the assertion that the language of Mother Church is Latin. The Anglican Church, which Lewis had joined following his conversion, had long since succumbed to the vernacular, whereas the liturgy of the Catholic Church at the time Lewis was writing was exclusively conducted in Latin, her official language.

It is also more than a little intriguing that Lewis includes a satire, through the introduction of the characters "Mr. Broad" and "Neo-Angular," of the divisions in the Church of England between low-church Broad Churchmen and high-church Anglo-Catholics. It is also strange that John only meets these characters *after* he has left Mother Kirk to follow his own path. Writing to an Irish acquaintance, Canon Claude Chavasse, in February 1934, about the purpose of the satirical approach he had adopted towards the factions within the Church of England, Lewis wrote that the Broad Church suffered from a "confusion between mere natural goodness and Grace which is non-Christian" and was "what I most hate and fear in the world." If, however, he hated and feared the non-Christian confusion within the Broad Church, he was less than enamored with the High Church as well. "What I am attacking in Neo-Angular is a set of people who seem to me . . . to be trying to make of Christianity itself one more high-brow, Chelsea, bourgeois-baiting fad" and "T. S. Eliot is the single man who sums up the thing I am fighting against."[19]

Writing to his friend Sister Penelope, after she had also inquired as to the meaning of the satire on Anglican churchmanship in *The Pilgrim's Regress*, Lewis wrote: "To me the real distinction is not high and low, but between religion with a real supernaturalism and Salvationism on the one hand and all watered-down modernist versions on the other."[20] Clearly, if forced to choose between the devil of Broad Church modernism and the deep-blue "C" of conservative-Chelsea-"Catholic" High Church, and "high-brow," Anglicanism *à la* Eliot, Lewis would, reluctantly, choose the latter. He was not, however, at home with either.

Lewis's reluctant preference for the high church over the low becomes apparent at the end of *The Pilgrim's Regress* when John finally gives himself up to the embrace of Mother Kirk, and is preparing to dive into the pool of baptism. As he endeavors to find the courage to die to himself so that he can dive into life, the wraiths of the skeptics that he had met on his journey attempt to dissuade him from taking the final decisive step of conversion. Old Mr. Enlightenment and his son, Sigismund, appear before him, the latter dismissing his desire for conversion as a case of "religious melancholia": "Stop while there is time," he warns. "If you dive, you dive into insanity."[21] Several others also appear, the last of whom is Broad, the personification of Broad Church Anglicanism, who seeks to dissuade John from joining Mother Kirk: "My dear boy, you are losing your head. These sudden conversions and violent struggles don't achieve anything. We have had to discard so much that our ancestors thought necessary. It is all far easier, far more gracious and beautiful than they supposed."[22] Ultimately, however, it is not the presence of Mr. Broad among the skeptics that is significant but the absence of Neo-Angular. In the end, grudgingly, Lewis admits that Eliot and the Anglo-Catholics are at least seeking Mother Kirk, even if they have not found her.

After John finally dives into the waters of baptism he hears "another voice . . . from behind him," the Word of God Himself, who explains the riddle of existence in terms remarkably similar to those employed by Tolkien during the "long night talk" of the previous year:

> Child, if you will, it *is* mythology. It is but truth, not fact: an image, not the very real. But then it is My mythology . . . this is My inventing, this is the veil under which I have chosen to appear even from the first until now. For this end I made your senses and for this end your imagination, that you might see My face and live. What would you have? Have you not heard among the Pagans the story of Semele? Or was there any age in any land when men did not know that corn and wine were the blood and body of a dying and yet living God?[23]

Thus, in a final coup de grace, Lewis has the Word of God Himself explaining the profound importance of the Blessed Sacrament of His Body and Blood. Significantly, however, he does so in the language of Tolkien's philosophy of myth. Perhaps, therefore, as an illuminating parallel to Lewis's treatment of the subject, it might be helpful and appropriate to quote Tolkien's own words on the importance of the Blessed Sacrament, written in a letter to one of his sons.

> Out of the darkness of my life, so much frustrated, I put before you the one great thing to love on earth: the Blessed Sacrament. . . . There you will find romance, glory, honour, fidelity, and the true way of all your loves on earth, and more than that: Death: by the divine paradox, that which ends life, and demands the surrender of all, and yet by the taste (or foretaste) of which alone can what you seek in your earthly relationships (love, faithfulness, joy) be maintained, or take on that complexion of reality, of eternal endurance, which every man's heart desires.[24]

Following the publication of *The Pilgrim's Regress,* several reviewers assumed that Lewis must be another of the growing list of converts to Roman Catholicism. The *Downside Review,* published by the Benedictines, hailed Lewis for his "notable contribution to Catholic literature." A review in *Blackfriars,* a Dominican publication, was equally effusive, describing Lewis's "revival of the allegorical method" as "very successful." *Catholic World,* published by the Paulist Fathers in New York, praised *The Pilgrim's Regress* as a "brilliantly written volume" and "a caustic, devastating critique of modern philosophy, religion, politics, and art." W. Norman Pittenger, an Anglican priest teaching at the General Theological Seminary in New York, writing in *The Living Church,* assumed, on the evidence of the book alone, that the pilgrim "lands up in the end in a resting place which we fancy is none other than the Church of Rome. Anglicans may wish that he had come their way, but Mr. Lewis, who is a Roman Catholic, does not see it so. . . . We are sure that the book will find many delighted readers, even if they do not all arrive in the happy haven of Roman Catholicism."[25]

It was hardly surprising that many people perceived that Lewis had become a Catholic. All the evidence of his encounter with Mother Kirk in *The Pilgrim's Regress* would seem to suggest that he could be nothing else. Catholics might indeed have wished that he had come their way, but Mr. Lewis, who was an Anglican, did not see it so.

INKLINGS AND REACTIONS

C. S. L.'s reactions were odd. Nothing is a greater tribute to Red propaganda than the fact that he (who knows
they are in all other subjects liars and traducers) believes
all that is said against Franco, and nothing that is said
for him. . . . But hatred of our church is after all the real
only final foundation of the C of E—so deep laid that it
remains even when all the superstructure seems removed
(C. S. L. for instance reveres the Blessed Sacrament, and
admires nuns!). Yet if a Lutheran is put in jail he is up in
arms; but if Catholic priests are slaughtered—he disbelieves
it (and I daresay really thinks they asked for it).

—*J. R. R. Tolkien*[1]

"**M**OST CRITICS supposed Lewis to be more Catholic
than he believed himself to be," wrote Lewis's biographers Green and Hooper, commenting on the reaction to
the publication of *The Pilgrim's Regress*.[2] Apart from the presumption of the reviewers that the book's author must be a
Catholic, rumours began to circulate around the hallowed
halls of Oxford that Lewis had converted to Catholicism.
Paul Elmer More, the American literary critic and philosopher, visited Oxford in July 1933, shortly after having read
The Pilgrim's Regress. Puzzled by the nature of Lewis's allegory,

he asked his friend John Frederick Wolfenden, a tutor in philosophy at Magdalen College, whether Lewis had succumbed to the hire of Rome. "I asked him about Lewis, what the story of his experience was and whether he had become a Roman Catholic, and what was meant by 'Mother Kirk' to which his Pilgrim returns. Wolfenden said he didn't know much about it all, but was sure Lewis had not become an R.C."[3]

Christopher Derrick, in *C. S. Lewis and the Church of Rome,* remarked that it was indeed "understandable" that the figure of Mother Kirk should lead many to the assumption that Lewis must be a Catholic.

> Very little is proved, of course, by the fact that Mother Kirk's language appears to be Latin. But it is surely significant that she claims obedience as by right, that the pilgrim's best course is to find her "at the very beginning" and "from infancy;" that God ("the Landlord") keeps leading men back to her; that "if all goes well" the Pagan finds her; that the pilgrim is, in the last resort, directed to her by the fact of death, and "must" go to her if he hopes to find Christ; and that although shabby and witch-like at her first appearance, she is "crowned and sceptred" and with all faces turned towards her when the pilgrim's moment of decision finally comes.
>
> All this points towards a very high and even specifically Roman Catholic notion of what "the Church" is. Even Mother Kirk's name carries a suggestion of that kind, since "our holy Mother the Church" is an expression which comes naturally and traditionally to Roman Catholic but seldom to Anglican lips. Nor is she to be simply equated with Christ, who makes one personal appearance in the story, briefly but crucially,

and is clearly distinct from her; she is in fact his Bride, as the Church, when not called his body, is traditionally said to be.[4]

Perhaps the most surprising aspect of *The Pilgrim's Regress* is not the impression gained by most of its readers that it was Catholic, but the author's surprise that his readers should think it so. In *The Allegory of Love*, Lewis alluded to "a man in our own time who wrote what he intended to be a general apologetic allegory for 'all who profess and call themselves Christians,' and was surprised to find it both praised and blamed as a defence of Rome."[5] Clearly this "man" was a literary fiction and Lewis was referring to his own experience with *The Pilgrim's Regress*. His efforts to distance himself from the alleged Catholicism of *The Pilgrim's Regress* were made explicit in the preface to the third edition, published in 1943. "The name *Mother Kirk*," he insisted, "was chosen because 'Christianity' is not a very convincing name. Its defect was that it not unnaturally led the reader to attribute to me a much more definite *Ecclesiastical* position than I could really boast of. The book is concerned solely with Christianity as against unbelief. 'Denominational' questions do not come in."[6] Lewis's insistence on the ambivalence of the meaning of Mother Kirk is not "very convincing" and, as Christopher Derrick observed, "his argument here was distinctly weak."[7] Throughout *The Pilgrim's Regress,* Derrick observed, Lewis "had displayed great ingenuity in devising allegorical personal names and place names to signify every possible kind of philosophical or religious position; and had he so chosen, he could easily have devised such a name for 'mere Christianity,' seen as somehow distinct from Christ himself but without any ecclesiastical implication. 'Evangelia,' 'Faith,' and 'Christina' are among the obvious possibilities. His choice of 'Mother Kirk' as a name for this character was not made *flute de mieux,* as he tried to suggest."[8] Derrick concludes, convincingly in my judgment, that the "real explanation" as to the choice of "Mother Kirk" in particular, and the all-pervasive tone of Catholicism in general, throughout the pages of *The Pilgrim's Regress,* lies in the fact that it was written in one uninterrupted stream of consciousness in the space of less than a fortnight. "Such high-speed writing must necessarily help the less conscious part of an author's mind to betray itself more frankly than leisure and deliberation would permit; and it seems likely that in 1932, Lewis's natural or instinctive understanding of 'the Church' was far more Catholic than his conscious mind knew or desired it to be."[9] Thus his recent reading of Dante, Coleridge, and Chesterton, and his recent discussions with Tolkien and Dyson, had come together in the conceptual cauldron from which *The Pilgrim's Regress* emerged as a composite expression of cathartic (and Catholic) desire. "But," Derrick adds significantly, Lewis's "conscious mind appears to have regained control."

The problem, however, was that Lewis's conscious mind was under the powerful influence of subconscious prejudice.

The extent to which the looming and prejudiced presence of Puritania was preventing Lewis's escape from its shadow could be seen in Lewis's relationship with Sheed and Ward, the Catholic publishing company that published the second edition of *The Pilgrim's Regress.* "I didn't much like having a book of mine, and specially a religious book, brought out by a papist publisher, but as they seemed to think they could sell it, and Dent's clearly couldn't, I gave in."[10] Frank Sheed wrote the copy for the dust jacket of the Sheed and Ward edition, praising the work as full of wit and declaring that Lewis was certainly funnier than Bunyan. Sheed's faux pas, as far as Lewis was concerned, was to link Puritania with Ulster: "This story begins in Puritania (Mr. Lewis was brought up in Ulster). . . ." Since the story *did* begin in Puritania, since it was largely autobiographical, and since Lewis was born in Ulster, one might think that the statement was innocuous enough. It had, however, inflamed Lewis's prejudiced sensibilities. "If you ever come across anyone who might be interested," Lewis wrote to Arthur Greeves, "explain as loudly as you can that I was not consulted and that the blurb is a damnable lie told to try and make Dublin riff-raff buy the book."[11] Lewis's enraged reaction is almost shocking in its shrillness. Where, exactly, was the "damnable lie"? Why the presumption that the "papist" population of Dublin were "riff-raff"?

In the light of such an odd over-reaction, Tolkien's judgment as to Lewis's prejudiced response to all things "papist" is certainly noteworthy, though ultimately a trifle unjust:

> It was not for some time that I realized that there was more in the title *Pilgrim's Regress* than I had understood (or the author either, maybe). Lewis would regress. He would not enter Christianity by a new door, but by the old one; at least in the sense that in taking it up again he would also take up, or reawaken, the prejudices so sedulously planted in boyhood. He would become again a Northern Ireland Protestant.[12]

The injustice of Tolkien's statement relates to the assertion that Lewis would revert to being a stereotypical Ulster Protestant, that is to say, a virulently anti-Catholic and Puritanical "Christian." Lewis would, in fact, become nothing of the sort. As we shall see, his conception of "mere Christianity" was far more "Catholic," in its sacramentalism and its defense of

ecclesiastical tradition and authority than would be tolerable
to the typical Presbyterian or low-church Calvinist. In reality, Lewis's increasingly awkward positioning of himself on
a self-styled "center ground" of "mere Christianity" between
the Protestant and Anglo-Catholic wings of the Church
of England would be the result of a personal compromise
between the de facto "Catholicism" of his central beliefs and
the Protestant "prejudices so sedulously planted in boyhood."

Throughout the 1930s and 1940s, Lewis and Tolkien
fought their religious battles, with each other and with others,
within the ring of fellowship known as the Inklings, a group
of generally like-minded souls who met regularly, in Lewis's
rooms at Magdalen College and at the Eagle and Child, a pub
in central Oxford.

"The Inklings," wrote Warnie Lewis in his unpublished
biography of his brother,

> calls for a word of explanation. Properly speaking it was
> neither a club nor a literary society, but partook of the
> nature of both. There were no rules, officers, agenda, or
> formal elections, unless one accepts as a rule the fact that
> we met in Jack's rooms every Thursday evening after
> dinner. . . . From time to time we added to our original
> number, but without formalities. . . . [I]t was rarely that
> a name was put forward that was not generally accept-
> able, for all of us . . . knew the sort of man we wanted—
> and did not want. At the top of the latter class Jack put
> the type which dogmatises without evidence then when
> challenged, falls back on the cliche of bluster.[13]

The lack of formality makes it difficult to pinpoint the
date at which the Inklings began to meet. It is likely that the
group began to form itself in the early 1930s, at about the

time the Coalbiters ceased to meet. The latter came to a natural end after its reason for existence, the reading of all the principal Icelandic sagas culminating in the Elder Edda, had been achieved. The Inklings therefore fulfilled a need by filling the vacuum left by the dissolution of the earlier group. "There's no sound I like better than adult male laughter," Lewis wrote,[14] illustrating the need that he felt for the relaxed and relaxing fellowship of like-minded friends. Writing of friendship in *The Four Loves,* Lewis offers a clue as to why the Inklings became such a central part of his life from the time of its inception until his death a third of a century later. "In this kind, of love," he wrote, *"Do you love me?* means *Do you see the same truth?"* Or at least, "Do you *care about* the same truth?" The man who agrees with us that some question, little regarded by others, is of great importance, can be our Friend. He need not agree with us about the answer."[15]

From the beginning, the Inklings was never merely a substitute for the Coalbiters. Whereas the earlier group had been formed by Tolkien with a specific purpose, the Inklings centered on Lewis and had no specific agenda beyond a vague shared interest in literature among its members and a vague notion of a kinship of spirit existing between them. Lewis was the nucleus, without whom any gathering would have been inconceivable, but Tolkien was also almost always present. Barfield was considered a key member of the group even though his job as a London solicitor kept him from attending regularly. Other core members included Warnie Lewis; R. E. Havard, Catholic convert and Oxford doctor; Charles Williams, eclectically eccentric scholar and author of "theological thrillers"; and Hugo Dyson, lecturer in English at Reading University, who along with Tolkien had been instrumental in Lewis's conversion.

Typically, the Inklings met twice a week. On a weekday morning they would meet in a pub, normally on a Tuesday at the Eagle and Child, known familiarly and affectionately by members as the "Bird and Baby." On Thursday nights they would congregate in the spacious surroundings of Lewis's large sitting room in Magdalen College where one of the members would produce a manuscript—a poem, a story, or a chapter from a work in progress—and begin to read it aloud. This would be followed by criticism by the other members. "Out would come a manuscript and we would settle down to sit in judgement upon it," recalled Warnie Lewis. "Real, unbiased judgement too, for about the Inklings there was nothing of a mutual admiration society; with us, praise for good work was unstinted but censure for bad, or even not so good, was often brutally frank. To read to the Inklings was a formidable ordeal, and I can still remember the fear and trembling with which I offered the first chapter of my first book—and remember too my delight at its reception."[16] At the early meetings of the Inklings, Tolkien read the manuscript of *The Hobbit* and would later read the manuscript of *The Lord of the Rings,* chapter by chapter, as it was being written. Similarly, Lewis read the manuscripts of his own works, such as *The Screwtape Letters, The Problem of Pain* and *Out of the Silent Planet.*

When Lewis dedicated *The Problem of Pain,* published in October 1940, to "The Inklings," his former pupil and lifelong friend, Dom Bede Griffiths, wrote to ask him who exactly they were. Lewis replied that "Williams, Dyson of Reading, & my brother (Anglicans) and Tolkien and my doctor, Havard (your Church) are the "Inklings" to whom my *Problem of Pain* was dedicated."[17] Although Griffiths' religious vocation with the Benedictines prevented his own involvement with the Inklings, he was an important figure in Lewis's life. He was, in fact, another important piece in the jigsaw puzzle of influences that came together to forge Lewis's conversion to Christianity.

It was a discussion between Barfield, Lewis, and Griffiths which was to prove instrumental in edging Lewis closer to conversion. Barfield and Griffiths were lunching in Lewis's room when Lewis happened to refer to philosophy as "a subject." "It wasn't a *subject* to Plato," Barfield retorted, "it was a way." "The quiet but fervent agreement of Griffiths, and the quick glance of understanding between these two, revealed to me my own frivolity. Enough had been thought, and said, and felt, and imagined. It was about time that something should be done."[18]

Even though they unwittingly played such a crucial role in the coup de grace of Lewis's conversion, neither Barfield nor Griffiths was a Christian at the time of this providential conversation. By a strange coincidence, however, both Lewis and Griffiths converted to Christianity and received their respective First Communions within a day of each other at Christmas 1931, Griffiths as a Catholic on Christmas Eve and Lewis as an Anglican on Christmas Day.

Prior to his conversion to Catholicism, Griffiths had passed through a short Anglican phase and was preparing himself for ministry in the Church of England when a reading of Newman's *Essay on the Development of Christian Doctrine* changed his concept of Christianity and the Church.

> I believed that the Church which Christ had founded
> was a historical reality, that it had a continuous history
> from the time of the Apostles to the present day. I had
> thought that this continuity might be found in the

Church of England, but now the overwhelming weight
of evidence for the continuity of the Roman Church
was presented to my mind.[19]

A few months after his reception Griffiths decided to try
his vocation as a monk at Prinknash, the Benedictine Priory at
Winchcombe, and on December 20, 1932, he was clothed as
a novice. He made his solemn vows on December 21, 1936.

From the time of his conversion Griffiths began trying
to discuss with Lewis the merits of their respective positions.
Lewis, however, was reticent, refusing to discuss the doctrinal differences between Catholicism and Anglicanism. "The
result," wrote Griffiths, "was that we agreed not to discuss our
differences any more . . . there was always a certain reserve
therefore afterward in our friendship."[20]

Though reserved, their friendship remained, as did their
respective friendships with Owen Barfield, the only one of
the original trio who was still resisting conversion. Sixty years
later, Barfield remembered their friendship with nostalgic
affection.

Lewis, Griffiths and I went for long walks together.
We talked a good deal about theology. . . . I was with
Griffiths and I told him I was an agnostic and we got
talking about being damned and some remark he made
elicited the reply from me that "in that case I suppose
that I am damned." And I'll never forget the calm, collected way he turned round and said "but of course you
are." This amused Lewis very much of course when I
told him afterwards.[21]

Although Griffiths was not able to attend meetings of the
Inklings, there was a surprisingly large number of Catholics

among its members. Apart from Tolkien and Havard, other Catholic members included James Dundas-Grant, George Sayer, Father Gervase Mathew, O.P., and Tolkien's son Christopher. The significant Catholic presence was a source of some tension, particularly on the part of Hugo Dyson. Although a "high" Anglican, Dyson resented the large number of "papists" in their midst, a fact to which Warnie alluded in his diary entry on August 15, 1946. After Tolkien had invited J. A. W. Bennett, a Catholic at Queen's College, to a meeting of the Inklings, Warnie wrote:

> A small Inklings, only Ronald [Tolkien], Humphrey [Havard], ourselves [the Lewis brothers], and [Bennett] . . . brought in by Ronald from Queens. . . . I hear with dismay that Ronald has since talked of "bringing him in occasionally;" with dismay for two reasons, firstly that he is a dull dog, and secondly that he is an R.C. [Roman Catholic]. I don't mind his being one in the least, but Hugo, who has puzzlingly strong views on the matter has several times lately threatened that if any more Papists join the Inklings he will resign.[22]

Bennett became an occasional member of the Inklings nonetheless, and, although Dyson did not resign, it is clear that he was becoming increasingly disgruntled by the Catholic presence. The tension between Dyson and Tolkien found expression in Dyson's intense dislike of *The Lord of the Rings.* At a meeting on April 24, 1947, Tolkien and his son Christopher, along with Dr. Havard, Father Mathew, and the Lewis brothers, were just settling down to read the latest chapter when Dyson arrived. Warnie wrote that Dyson "came in just as we were starting . . . and as he now exercises a veto on it—most unfairly I think—we had to stop."[23]

The most intriguing example of the tensions that existed between the Catholic and non-Catholic elements within the Inklings arose three years earlier, in October 1944, after the unexpected arrival of the controversial Catholic poet Roy Campbell at the Eagle and Child during one of the regular gatherings of Lewis, Tolkien, and the others. The encounter with Campbell is particularly significant as a means of obtaining valuable insights into the complexities of Lewis's relationship with the Catholic Church.

When Tolkien arrived at the Eagle and Child in the company of Charles Williams on that particular Tuesday morning, he was surprised to discover the Lewis brothers "already ensconced." The conversation was "pretty lively" and Tolkien noticed "a strange tall gaunt man half in khaki half in mufti with a large wide-awake hat, bright eyes and a hooked nose sitting in the corner. The others had their back to him, but I could see in his eye that he was taking an interest in the conversation quite unlike the ordinary pained astonishment of the British (and American) public at the presence of the Lewises (and myself) in a pub."[24] The stranger reminded Tolkien of Strider in *The Lord of the Rings,* the mysterious Ranger who eavesdropped on the conversation of the hobbits at the Prancing Pony at Bree.

> All of a sudden he butted in, in a strange unplaceable accent, taking up some point about Wordsworth. In a few seconds he was revealed as Roy Campbell . . . Tableau! Especially as C. S. L. had not long ago lampooned him in the *Oxford Magazine.* . . . There is a good deal of Ulster still left in C. S. L. if hidden from himself. After that things became fast and furious and I was late for lunch. It was (perhaps) gratifying to find

that this powerful poet and soldier desired in Oxford
chiefly to see Lewis (and myself).[25]

The "lampoon" to which Tolkien referred was Lewis's poetic
riposte to Campbell's long poem *Flowering Rifle*. Campbell's
poem, published five years earlier, was a robust and often
embarrassingly jingoistic eulogy to the victorious Nationalist
forces in the Spanish Civil War. In a poem entitled simply
"To the Author of *Flowering Rifle*," published in *The Cherwell*
magazine on May 6, 1939, Lewis had condemned Campbell's
lack of charity, reminding him that "the merciful are promised mercy still." Campbell was a "loud fool" who had learned
the art of lying from his enemies on the left,

> . . . since it was from them you learned
> How white to black by jargon can be turned. . .

Lewis admired Campbell's poetic powers, declaring that his
verse "outsoars with eagle pride" the "nerveless rhythms" of
the left-wing poets. Yet his "shrill covin-politics" and that of
his enemies were "two peas in a single pod":

> . . . who cares
> Which kind of shirt the murdering Party wears?

Although Lewis's critique of Campbell's harshness and
lack of charity in *Flowering Rifle* was justified, his simplis-
tic approach to the religious and philosophical dynamics of
the war in Spain exposed his own political naiveté. Campbell
was actually living in Spain when the war began, and he and
his family were lucky to escape with their lives. Many of his
friends were not so lucky. The priest who had received Roy
and his wife, Mary, into the Catholic Church in 1935 was
murdered in cold blood in the following year by communist

militiamen, as were the Carmelite monks whom Roy and Mary had befriended in Toledo.[26] In seeing the war in Spain as a fight to the death between traditional Christianity and secular atheism, Campbell was closer to reality than was Lewis with his simplified depiction of a battle between "left" and "right." The war was beyond politics. It was a struggle for the religious heart and soul of Europe.

Campbell had read Lewis's attack on him, but it seems, from Tolkien's rendition of events, that he had taken the criticism in good spirits and that it was Lewis who became aggressive during the "fast and furious" discussion in the Bird and Baby. In spite of their differences, Lewis invited Campbell to a gathering of the Inklings in Lewis's rooms in Magdalen College two days later. Again, it was Lewis who became aggressive. According to Tolkien, Lewis "had taken a fair deal of port and was a little belligerent."[27] He insisted on reading out his lampoon again, but Campbell laughed the provocation aside.

If Lewis was belligerent towards Campbell, Tolkien was transfixed by him, listening intently as the assembled Inklings "were mostly obliged to listen to the guest." Paradoxically, Tolkien felt that Campbell was "gentle, modest, and compassionate," even though he and the others spent most of the evening listening to Campbell's embellished and highly romanticised account of his own life. Tolkien's report of the biographical monologue is awash with the combined effects of Campbell's exaggeration and Tolkien's faulty memory.

> What he has done . . . beggars description. Here is a scion of an Ulster prot. family resident in S. Africa, most of whom fought in both wars, who became a Catholic after sheltering the Carmelite fathers in Barcelona in vain, they are caught & butchered, and R. C. nearly

lost his life. But he got the Carmelite archives from the burning library and took them through the Red country. He speaks Spanish fluently (he has been a professional bullfighter). As you know he then fought through the war on Franco's side, and among other things was in the van of the company that chased the Reds out of Malaga. . . . But he is a patriotic man, and has fought for the B. Army since. I wish I could remember half the picaresque stories, about poets and musicians, etc., from Peter Warlock to Aldous Huxley. . . . However, it is not possible to convey an impression of such a rare character, both a soldier and a poet, and a Christian convert. How unlike the Left—the "corduroy panzers" who lied to America (Auden among them who with his friends got R. C.'s works "banned" . . .).[28]

If Campbell made a favorable impression on Tolkien, who thought him "old-looking war-scarred" and "limping from recent wounds," Lewis's attitude remained as combative as ever, much to Tolkien's evident chagrin.

C. S. L.'s reactions were odd. Nothing is a greater tribute to Red propaganda than the fact that he (who knows that they are in all other subjects liars and traducers) believes all that is said against Franco, and nothing that is said for him. . . . But hatred of our church is after all the real only final foundation of the C. of E.—so deep laid that it remains even when all the superstructure seems removed (C. S. L. for instance reveres the Blessed Sacrament, and admires nuns!). Yet if a Lutheran is put in jail he is up in arms; but if Catholic priests are slaughtered—he disbelieves it (and I daresay really thinks they asked for it). But R. C. shook him a bit . . .[29]

Following the meeting, Lewis stated that he "loathed . . . Roy Campbell's particular blend of Catholicism and Fascism, and told him so."[30] His judgment was unfair. Campbell never considered himself a Fascist, and his support for Franco's Nationalists was based on the simple and laudatory desire to defend traditional Christian culture from the destructive atheism of the communists. During the Civil War the communist and anarchist Republicans carried out horrific atrocities against priests, monks, and nuns. Priests had their ears cut off, monks had their eardrums perforated by rosary beads being forced into them, and the elderly mother of two Jesuits had a rosary forced down her throat. Before the war was over twelve bishops, 4,184 priests, 2,635 monks and about 300 nuns were killed. Churches were systematically destroyed, and George Orwell recorded that in Barcelona "almost every church had been gutted and its images burned." In *Homage to Catalonia,* Orwell wrote,

> Some of the foreign anti-Fascist papers even descended to the pitiful lie of pretending that churches were only attacked when they were used as Fascist fortresses. Actually churches were pillaged everywhere and as a matter of course. . . . In six months in Spain I only saw two undamaged churches, and until about July 1937 no churches were allowed to reopen and hold services, except for one or two Protestant churches in Madrid.[31]

Having been received into the Catholic Church in the year before the outbreak of the war, it was scarcely surprising that Campbell considered it his duty to defend the culture and traditions he had recently discovered and embraced. Furthermore, having witnessed the cold-blooded murder of his friends, it is scarcely surprising that Campbell was somewhat vociferous in his attacks on communism. He was, however, as vociferous in his attacks on Nazism. Before the Spanish war started, he had made the acquaintance of two Norwegians, also living in Spain. One was a communist and the other a Nazi but, Campbell observed, "they were both staunchly united in their hate of Christ and Christianity."[32] "From the very beginning my wife and I understood the real issues in Spain," Campbell wrote in his autobiography, ". . . now was the time to decide whether . . . to remain half-apathetic to the great fight which was obviously approaching—or whether we should step into the front ranks of the Regular Army of Christ. Hitler himself had said, even by then, how much more easy the Protestants were to enslave and bamboozle than the Catholics."[33] One can imagine Tolkien nodding sagely in agreement with Campbell's words, perceiving them as an example of Campbell's Strideresque wisdom in comparison with Lewis's naïve credulity and residual anti-Catholic prejudice.

It was possibly Campbell to whom Lewis was alluding in his Preface to the 1943 edition of *The Pilgrim's Regress* when he wrote that "One can even meet adult males who are not ashamed to attribute their own philosophy to 'Reaction' and do not think the philosophy thereby discredited."[34] If it *was* Campbell Lewis had in mind when these words were written, and considering his polemical attack on Campbell in "To the Author of *Flowering Rifle*" it does not seem unlikely, he was again doing him an injustice. Campbell had famously remarked that a body without reactions is a corpse, and he made no secret of his belief that the reaction of the "conservative" people of Spain to the communist and anarchist insurrection was proof that Spanish culture was vibrant and alive. Such belief in "healthy reaction" is, however, hardly the mark of a mindless reactionary, and Lewis presumably would have agreed with Campbell that the "reaction" of the Allies to the militaristic aggression of the Nazis was not "thereby discredited" but, on the contrary, was highly creditable. There is, in any case, a real sense that Lewis was the proverbial pot calling the kettle black in his accusing others of reactionary tendencies. Apart from Tolkien's conviction that Lewis's judgment about Campbell in particular, and the Spanish Civil War in general, was the result of a knee-jerk reaction arising out of his anti-Catholicism, it is difficult to see Lewis's continued dismissal of the poetry of the "Neo-Angular" T. S. Eliot as anything other than a wilful and reactionary blindness. As late as September 1947, Lewis was declaring Eliot's poetry to be "bilge" and was continuing to insist that Eliot "had nothing to say worth saying in any case."[35] Regardless of whether one could understand (if not necessarily sympathize with) Lewis's belief that Eliot's earlier verse was "bilge" which "had nothing to say,"[36] it is difficult to conceive how he could fail to appreciate the sublime Christian poetry of later years. In the face of "Ash Wednesday," "The Rock," *Murder in the Cathedral,* and *Four Quartets,* all of which had been published by 1947, Lewis's recalcitrance beggars belief. How can one view his obstinate refusal to accept the obvious merits of Eliot's work as anything other than the result of a singular critical blindness or else the bitter fruit of pure reaction, whether against the poet as an individual or against the "Catholicism" of his creed?

Happily, the differences between Campbell and Lewis did not prevent the development of a genuine friendship. Campbell's respect for Lewis was illustrated by his request for Lewis's advice on which selections from Milton would be best suited for broadcasting on the BBC, where Campbell was working as a producer. Lewis, reciprocating the expression of respect, replied that Campbell was "quite as able as I to choose," though he proceeded to make suggestions nonetheless. "Oddly enough," Lewis wrote in the same letter, "we were all talking about you last night. Next term you must break away and spend a Thursday night with us in College. (I can do dinner, bed, and breakfast.)"[37]

On November 28, 1946, Campbell returned to Oxford to attend another meeting of the Inklings at Lewis's rooms in Magdalen College. Lewis's brother recorded in his diary that Campbell was the main attraction of the evening. "A pretty full meeting of the Inklings to meet Roy Campbell . . . whom I was glad to see again; he is fatter and tamer than he used to be I think."[38] Lewis had also become somewhat tamer— and certainly far less belligerent. He seems, in fact, to have forgiven Campbell for *Flowering Rifle* and to have embraced him both as a friend and as a fellow Inkling. They still crossed swords at these lively literary gatherings, but they were now arguing as friends, not quarrelling as enemies. The difference in their relationship can be perceived in the tone of another of Lewis's poems, "To Roy Campbell," in which he complained that Campbell was wrong to dismiss Romantic poets such as Coleridge or Wordsworth merely because they were praised by untrustworthy critics. These poets, wrote Lewis, were "far more ours than theirs," indicating that Campbell was now accepted by Lewis as "one of us" in the battle against common literary foes.

One wonders, as Tolkien watched Lewis's slow acceptance of Campbell into the inner sanctum of the Inklings, whether he ever mused further on the parallels between Campbell and Strider. The parallels are certainly striking. The hobbits had regarded the Ranger with deep suspicion when they first met him in the convivial yet threatening surroundings of the Prancing Pony at Bree; Lewis had regarded the arrival of the Stranger with the same suspicion when they met in the equally convivial, though hardly threatening, surroundings of the Bird and Baby in Oxford. In both cases, the suspicions gave way to a warm-hearted trust. Roy "Strider" Campbell had walked out of the Prancing Pony of Tolkien's imagination into the Bird and Baby of Lewis's world. He had stepped out of the Fellowship of the Ring into the ring of fellowship known as the Inklings.

6

SMUGGLING THEOLOGY

... any amount of theology can now be smuggled into
people's minds under cover of romance without their
knowing it.

—*Letters of* C. S. *Lewis*[1]

IN MAY 1944, Lewis received "an amusing letter" from the
Society for the Prevention of Progress, of Walnut Creek,
California, inviting him to become a member and requesting
that he "forward his credentials." Responding with humorous
satisfaction, and evident relish, at having received the invitation, Lewis replied as follows:

> Dear Sir,
>
> While feeling that I was BORN a member of your
> society, I am nevertheless honoured to receive the out-
> ward seal of membership. I shall hope by continued
> orthodoxy and the unremitting practice of Reaction,
> Obstruction, and Stagnation to give you no reason for
> repenting your favor.
>
> I humbly submit that in my Riddell Lectures enti-
> tled "The Abolition of Man" you will find another work
> not all unworthy of consideration for admission to
> the canon.
>
> Yours regressively,
> Beverages not Beveridges
> (My motto).[2]

The signature, or motto, which Lewis appended to his reply was instigated or inspired by one of the Society's rules to which his attention had been called: "*Membership and the privileges of the Society are denied to such individuals as Henry A. Wallace and this fellow Beveridge.*" Risibility aside, there was a seriousness behind the rationale for the Society and Lewis's sense of affinity with it. It was not merely an excuse for Reaction for its own sake, which, as we have seen, Lewis had criticized specifically and explicitly in the preface for the new edition of *The Pilgrim's Regress* a year earlier. Rather it was the "healthy reaction" of those who viewed the increasing encroachments of the welfare or "nanny" state with suspicion. At the time Lewis received his "invitation," Henry A. Wallace was vice president to Franklin D. Roosevelt, whose New Deal policy he supported, and William Beveridge was being hailed as the architect of Britain's welfare state, following the publication of the Beveridge Report in 1942. Both men had become *bêtes noires* to those who perceived that their policies represented a further shift of power towards Big Government and, as an inevitable result, the further interference by Big Government in the lives of individuals, families and local communities.

In essence, the Beveridge Report called for wider involvement by the apparatus of the state in the lives of the populace, principally through a scheme of "social insurance" covering the whole population. Such a vision, hailed in Britain as a blueprint for post-war recovery and renewal, was seen by its opponents, of whom Lewis was representative, as the harbinger of a drab egalitarian future run by bureaucrats in which the sense of duty and responsibility would have no place amid the selfish demands for "rights."

As the "amusing letter" from California indicated, Lewis was not alone in his skepticism towards this further intrusion of an over-powerful, bureaucratic, and social-engineering state into the lives and liberties of individuals. Roy Campbell shared Lewis's "healthy reaction," deriding the Beveridge Report in a terse poem entitled simply "The Beveridge Plan," which consisted of a solitary quatrain of vitriol in which its underlying principles are attacked as "Fascidemokshevism." In this one morosely constructed word, Campbell had demonstrated that, far from being a "fascist," he was, at heart, a libertarian who believed that modern states, whether they called themselves fascist, democratic, or Bolshevist, were exerting too much power over the lives of individuals and families. In fact, bearing in mind his somewhat paradoxical grouping together of fascism, democracy and bolshevism, Campbell would no doubt have been wryly amused, though perhaps not entirely surprised, to discover that Josef Goebbels, Hitler's propaganda minister, was interested enough in the Beveridge Report to make a close study of it. Against the complex mechanisms and powerful bureaucracies advocated by Beveridge—and, for that matter, Goebbels—Campbell counterposed small, self-supporting communities of freely cooperating families, much as he had seen and experienced during the years he had spent living among the rustics of Provence and Spain.

Lewis's antagonism towards the "brave new world" of liberal secularism, with its creeping centralization, multinational capitalism, international socialism, and supercilious scientism, had been informed, no doubt, by his reading of Chesterton, whose advocacy of the creed of "distributism" was itself rooted in the social teaching of the Catholic Church, particularly in the Papal Encyclicals *Rerum Novarum* (Leo XIII, 189 I) and *Quadragesimo Anna* (Pius XI, 1930). What Chesterton calls "distributism" the Catholic Church calls "subsidiarity." In either case, the rose of political and economic smallness, by any other name, would smell as sweet amid the thorns of giantism. Solzhenitsyn—advocating the same response to state-centered social engineering as Lewis, Chesterton, or Campbell—spoke of the need for "self-limitation;" E. F. Schumacher, responding to Beveridge's presumption that big is best, coined the anecdotal antidote that "small is beautiful." Perhaps most memorably of all, Tolkien counterposed the imperialistic scientism of Sauron and Saruman in *The Lord of the Rings* with the humility of the hobbits and their desire to be left in peace to till the soil of the Shire. Sauron and Saruman are driven by the will to power; Frodo and Sam by the desire for liberty and peace. In a letter to his son, Tolkien declared that "the most improper job of any man, even saints (who at any rate were at least unwilling to take it on), is bossing other men. Not one in a million is fit for it, and least of all those who seek the opportunity."[3]

The extent to which Lewis shared Tolkien's vision of the Shire, and advocated, at least implicitly, Chesterton's distributism and the Church's subsidiarity, can be gauged from sentiments expressed in a letter to Arthur Greeves in 1930. Writing about the efforts of Griffiths, prior to his conversion to Catholicism in the following year, to live self-sufficiently with two friends in a cottage in the Cotswolds, Lewis waxed lyrical in his positive response to their endeavor.

> Their aim is, as far as possible, to use nothing which is the product of the factory system or of modern industry in general; for they think these things so iniquitous that every one is more or less party to a crime in using them. . . . There is certainly something attractive about the idea of living as far as may be on the produce of the land about you: to see in every walk the pastures

where your mutton grazed when it was sheep, the garden where your vegetables grew, the mill where your flour was ground, and the workshop where your chairs were sawn—and to feel that bit of country actually and literally in your veins.

Tolkien once remarked to me that the feeling about home must have been quite different in the days when a family had fed on the produce of the same few miles of country for six generations, and that perhaps this was why they saw nymphs in the fountains and dryads in the wood—they were not mistaken for there was in a sense a real (not metaphorical) connection between them and the countryside. What had been earth and air & later corn, and later still bread, really was in them. We of course who live on a standardized international diet (you may have had Canadian flour, English meat, Scotch oatmeal, African oranges, & Australian wine to day) are really artificial beings and have no connection (save in sentiment) with any place on earth. We are synthetic men, uprooted. The strength of the hills is not ours.[4]

In his yearning for the reunion of person with place, or soul with soil, and his criticism of the artificiality of modernity and the "synthetic men" it produced, Lewis was sharing the "healthy reaction" of Campbell, Chesterton, Leo XIII, Pius XI, Tolkien, Griffiths, Schumacher, and Solzhenitsyn, all of whom were (or were in the process of becoming) Catholics, albeit that Solzhenitsyn is "Orthodox" and "Catholic" in the Russian and not the Roman sense. This, of course, is not to say that such a reaction is the sole preserve or prerogative of Catholics, but it does place Lewis's response within a specifically Catholic sphere of influence. He had been inspired by his reading of Chesterton, by his speaking with Tolkien, and by the practical example of Griffiths in his arrival at these conclusions. Chesterton (definitely) and Tolkien (probably) had been inspired by the social doctrine of the Catholic Church, and specifically by the teaching of Popes Leo XIII and Pius XI, in the development of their own reactions to modernity and the social and cultural mechanization and standardization (or what Chesterton called "standardization by a low standard") that was one of modernity's chief characteristics.

Chesterton's antimodernity found its way into his novels, most particularly in *The Napoleon of Notting Hill* and *The Ball and the Cross,* whereas Tolkien's found its way into *The Lord of the Rings* through what he termed the "applicability" of events in Middle Earth to those in the world in which we live. Lewis's antimodernity had already surfaced in the allegorically satirical treatment of "Zeitgeistheim" and several other modern "heresies" in *The Pilgrim's Regress.* In September 1938, *Out of the Silent Planet,* the first of his space novels, was published, in which the character of Weston was introduced as a personification of the modern materialism and its "progressive" philosophical phantoms to which Lewis had a strong aversion.

Writing to Sister Penelope, an Anglican nun and trusted friend, about his motivation for writing *Out of the Silent Planet,* Lewis emphasized the real "danger of 'Westonism'":

> What set me about writing the book was the discovery
> that a pupil of mine took all that dream of interplan-
> etary colonization quite seriously, and the realization
> that thousands of people in one way and another
> depend on some hope of perpetuating and improving

the human race for the whole meaning of the universe—that a "scientific" hope of defeating death is a
real rival to Christianity. . . .[6]

In the same letter Lewis explained that he intended to counter
this materialistic philosophy through the smuggling of theology into his own novels.

You will be both grieved and amused to hear that out
of about 60 reviews only 2 showed any knowledge that
my idea of the fall of the Bent One was anything but an
invention of my own. But I think that this great ignorance might be a help to the evangelisation of England;
any amount of theology can now be smuggled into
people's minds under cover of romance without their
knowing it.[7]

Several influences seem to have converged into the catalytic collision that led to Lewis trying his hand at what, in
the broadest sense, could be called science fiction. In 1935
he had read David Lindsay's *Voyage to Arcturus,* which Lewis's
biographer Walter Hooper has described as a "ghastly and
unhallowed story."[8] Although Lewis himself thought that the
novel "was on the borderline of the diabolical,"[9] he read it
with a morbid and bitterly fruitful curiosity. "From Lindsay I
first learned what other planets in fiction are really good for;
for *spiritual* adventures," he wrote to the poet Ruth Pitter in
January 1947. "Only they can satisfy the craving which sends
our imaginations off the earth. Or putting it another way,
in him I first saw the terrific results produced by the union
of the kinds of fiction hitherto kept apart: the Novalis, G.
Macdonald, James Stephens sort and the H. G. Wells, Jules
Verne's sort. My debt to him is very great."[10]

In replying to Roger Lancelyn Green's inquiry about the impetus behind *Out of the Silent Planet,* Lewis wrote in December 1938 that what had "immediately spurred" him to write was Olaf Stapledon's *Last and First Men* and an essay entitled "The Last Judgement" in J. B. S. Haldane's *Possible Worlds,* "both of which seem to take the idea of such travel seriously and to have the desperately immoral outlook which I try to pillory in Weston. I like the whole planetary idea as a *mythology* and simply wished to conquer for my own (Christian) point of view what has always been used by the opposite side."[11]

An older influence, stretching right back to his childhood and to which he referred in his autobiography, *Surprised by Joy,* was what he termed the "scientification" of H. G. Wells:

> The idea of other planets exercised upon me then a peculiar, heady attraction, which was quite different from any other of my literary interests. . . . This was something coarser and stronger. The interest, when the fit was upon me, was ravenous, like a lust. . . . I may perhaps add that my own planetary romances have been not so much the gratification of that fierce curiosity as its exorcism. The exorcism worked by reconciling it with, or subjecting it to, the other, the more elusive, and genuinely imaginative, impulse.[12]

Since Lewis is said to have used Tolkien as the model for the virtuous character of Ransom, who is the hero of the *Space Trilogy* and Weston's archenemy and ultimately his nemesis, it is tempting to see Weston as the embodiment of Wells, in a specific sense, and not merely in the general abstract sense in which Wells represents the scientism and "scientification" that Lewis sought to condemn. Certainly there seems little doubt that Ransom, a professor of philology, was modeled in part on Tolkien. "As a philologist I may have some part in him," Tolkien wrote to his son Christopher in 1944, "and recognize some of my opinions and ideas Lewisified in him."[13] As for the connection between Wells and Weston, Christopher Beiting, in his essay "Science and Temptation in C. S. Lewis's Space Trilogy," detects a definite correlation. "The novel [*Out of the Silent Planet*] very consciously echoes the works of H. G. Wells, particularly *The First Men in the Moon,* and in the person of Weston, the evil physicist, presents a critique of many of the ideas of Wells and the assumptions of science."[14]

A graphic example of Weston's Wellsian *weltanschauung* is exhibited towards the end of *Out of the Silent Planet.* Standing before Oyarsa, the archangelic figure who governs Malacandra (Mars), Weston treats the superior spiritual being with contempt, being unable in the theological blindness of his philosophical materialism to *see* spiritual realities, and conveys, with a self-assured superciliousness that is oblivious of its ignorance, the creed of chronological snobbery that animates the works of Wells and was the atheistic animus behind Wells's *Outline of History:*

> I bear on my shoulders the destiny of the human race. Your trial life with its stone-age weapons and beehive huts, its primitive coracles and elementary social structures, has nothing to compare with our civilization—with our science, medicine and law, our armies, our architecture, our commerce, and our transport system which is rapidly annihilating space and time. Our right to supersede you is the right of the higher over the lower.[15]

In seeing the first two novels of the Space Trilogy as a war between the perennial wisdom of Ransom/Tolkien and the supercilious chronological snobbery of Weston/Wells, one sees a re-presentation of the battle between Belloc and Wells over the latter's *Outline of History* from which emerged Chesterton's *The Everlasting Man,* the reading of which had enabled Lewis "for the first time" to see "the whole Christian outline of history set out in a form that seemed to me to make sense." Whether intended consciously or unconsciously—or indeed whether intended at all—there is certainly a startling "applicability" between the struggle of Ransom to overcome the "scientification" of Weston and the struggle of the young Lewis—ably assisted by Belloc, Chesterton, and Tolkien—to overcome the "scientification" of Wells and the philosophical materialism and "progressive" modernity that he represented.

In *Perelandra,* the second novel of the Space Trilogy, the struggle between Ransom and Weston becomes deeper and darker. Science is no longer merely a substitute for religion; it has actually *become* a religion, or at least it imagines in its pride that it has become so. "I plunged into Biology," Weston explains to Ransom after they are reunited on Perelandra (Venus), "and particularly into what may be called biological philosophy. . . . I became a convinced believer in emergent evolution. All is one. The stuff of mind, the unconsciously purposive dynamism, is present from the very beginning."[16] Later, Weston explains that all notions of God and the devil, or heaven and hell, are only "portraits of Spirit, of cosmic energy . . . for it is the Life-Force itself which has deposited them in our brains."[17] In this exposition of a concocted cocktail of science, philosophy, and theology, Weston's ideas emerge beyond those of Wells to merge into a composite amalgam of the ideas of the Marxist biologist J. B. S. Haldane and those of Bernard Shaw. Ultimately, Weston encapsulates the progressive optimism that characterizes the ill-defined ramblings of all those who place their faith in the ultimate beneficence of science.

Westonism is the allegorical epitome of scientism, the idolatry of science as a god to which every knee must bow. It is, however, more than that. It is diabolical. It is devil worship. In following gods and not God, the idolaters are actually, even if unwittingly, following the Anti-God. In turning one's back on God, one does not find heaven, nor earth, nor progress, nor science, nor the Life-Force; one finds what one has always found. The path of "Progress" without religion is the road to hell. Thus, Weston is not merely a man lost in error, he is a man demonically possessed:

> Then horrible things began happening. A spasm like that preceding a deadly vomit twisted Weston's face out of recognition. As it passed, for one second something like the old Weston reappeared—the old Weston, staring with eyes of horror and howling, "Ransom, Ransom! For Christ's sake don't let them . . ." and instantly his whole body spun round as if he had been hit by a revolver bullet and he fell to the earth, and was there rolling at Ransom's feet, slavering and chattering and tearing up the moss by handfuls.[18]

One wonders if Weston's being possessed sprang from a satanic "prayer" that he exclaimed at the end of the previous book, *Out of the Silent Planet*. Having been told by Oyarsa that the idolization of Life, to the exclusion of the acceptance of Death, was contrary to the will of Maleldil (God) and was, in fact, the will of the Bent One (Satan), Weston replies defiantly in pidgin Malacandrian: "You say your Maleldil let all go dead. Other one, Bent One, he fight, jump, live—not all talkee-talkee. Me no care Maleldil. Like Bent One better: me on his side."[19] Having expressed the desire to sell his soul to the Bent One, his desire is granted. He enters hell or, more precisely, hell enters him. "I am the Universe," he exclaims immediately before collapsing into the spasms of demonic possession. "I, Weston, am your God and your Devil! I call that Force into me completely. . . ." With ironic symmetry, the proclamation of me-myself-I as God does not result in the attainment of godhood but the very loss of selfhood. Henceforth Weston becomes the "Un-man," a shell within which Satan has smuggled himself into the unfallen world of Perelandra, a tool with which to bring about the Fall of a new world.

The remainder of *Perelandra* is essentially a retelling of the story of the Fall in Genesis, with the possessed Weston endeavoring to corrupt Perelandra's "Eve" while Ransom attempts to prevent him from succeeding. Explaining the difficulties of characterizing and describing the unfallen "Eve," Lewis wrote to Sister Penelope in November 1941, while he was in the midst of writing the early chapters of the book. "I've got Ransom to Venus and through his first conversation with the 'Eve' of that world; a difficult chapter . . . I may have embarked on the impossible. This woman has got to be in some ways like a Pagan goddess and in other ways like the Blessed Virgin."[20] His difficulty was similar to that experienced by Tolkien in his characterization of Galadriel in *The Lord of the Rings.* After Father Robert Murray, a Jesuit friend, had compared the image of Galadriel to that of the Virgin Mary, Tolkien replied that the priest had been "more perceptive . . . than anyone else. . . . I think I know exactly what you mean . . . by your references to Our Lady, upon which all my own small perception of beauty both in majesty and simplicity is founded."[21]

The shadow of Puritania clouded Lewis's ability to see the Blessed Virgin in quite the same way as that afforded to Tolkien. Mistaking Marianism for mariolatry, that is, veneration for worship, Lewis had excluded himself from the vision of the First Eve which the clear and immaculate prism of the New Eve could have provided. The majestic simplicity of the Immaculate was beyond his conception. Consequently, Lewis drew his inspiration for Tinidril, the "Eve" of Perelandra, from the "divine" poet who saw the Immaculate as did no other. It was to Dante that Lewis turned as he endeavored to breathe life into his "Eve."

In a letter to an American critic, Lewis wrote that "Tinidril at her second appearance owes something to Matilda at the end of *Purgatorio*."[22] Matilda, an attendant and friend of Beatrice, appears in the twenty-eighth canto of that work. She is discovered in the Earthly Paradise, which Dante places at the summit of Mount Purgatory, a place beyond the effects of Sin. As Dante enters the Sacred Wood within the Earthly Paradise, which is itself the unfallen "divinely symmetrical" counterpart to the Dark Wood of Sin from which Dante had originally set out on his path through the Inferno, he sees a Lady, singing and gathering flowers on the farther bank of a brook.

> With feet I stayed, and with mine eyes I passed
> > Beyond the rivulet, to look upon
> > The great variety of the fresh may.
> And there appeared to me (even as appears
> > Suddenly something that doth turn aside
> > Through very wonder every other thought)
> A lady all alone, who went along
> > Singing and culling floweret after floweret,
> > With which her pathway was all painted over.[23]

Compare the vision thus depicted by Dante in *Purgatorio* with Lewis's vision in *Perelandra:*

> And there he stopped in astonishment. The Lady's island was floating beside his, divided only by five feet or so of water. . . . There was no expanse of sea now visible—only a flat wooded landscape as far as the eye could reach in every direction. . . . And there walking before him, as if on the other side of the brook, was the Lady herself—walking with her head a little bowed and her hands occupied in plaiting together some blue flowers. She was singing to herself in a low voice. . . .[24]

There is certainly, as Lewis admits, a great similarity in Dante's depiction of his encounter with the Lady in the Sacred Wood and Lewis's depiction of Ransom's encounter with his "Lady" in *Perelandra.* Perhaps, however, the similarity goes deeper than the merely descriptive; perhaps, in fact, the similarity is *prescriptive,* in the sense that Lewis owed much of the inspiration for the whole of his novel to the allegorical nature of the Earthly Paradise in Dante's *Purgatorio.*

In the *Purgatorio* the Lady Matilda answers Dante's questions about the Earthly Paradise, explaining that it is the place where Man was once innocent and happy. "In the *allegory*" wrote Dorothy L. Sayers in her commentary to this particular Canto, "the Earthly Paradise is the state of *innocence.* It is from here that Man, if he had never fallen, would have set out on his journey to the Celestial Paradise which is his ultimate destination; but because of sin, his setting-out is from that other Forest which is the degraded and horrifying parody of this one. His whole journey through Hell and Purgatory is thus a *return* journey in search of his true starting-place the return to original innocence. Natural innocence is not an end in itself, but the necessary condition of beginning: it was never intended that unfallen Adam should remain static, but that he should progress from natural to supernatural perfection. . . Once we remember that Eden is, and was always meant to be, a starting-place and not a stopping-place, we shall have little difficulty in finding a consistent and intelligible significance for the allegory."[25]

In the same letter in which Lewis had confessed the similarity between the respective descriptions of Tinidril and Matilda, he intimated that Dante had exerted a more general influence over *Perelandra*. Having alluded to the obvious parallels between *Perelandra* and *Paradise Lost,* Lewis played down the importance of Milton and seemed to imply that these were largely superficial and were grounded merely in the fact that the two works shared the same *genetic* roots. "Milton I think you possibly over-rate: it is difficult to distinguish him from Dante and St. Augustine."[26]

As to the influence of Saint Augustine upon the writing of *Perelandra,* Lewis's biographers Green and Hooper are in no doubt as to its centrality:

> The whole of the ninth chapter is based on one of the great theological issues. In the fourth century St. Augustine gave classical formulation to the Church's belief that Adam's Fall brought more good than evil. His expression, *Felix peccatum Adae,* is rendered "O happy fault, O necessary sin of Adam" in the Easter liturgy of the Catholic Church. The Un-man tries to convince the Lady that only by disobeying Maleldil will she emerge from her present "smallness" into "Deep Life, with all its joy and splendour and hardness." Finally, Ransom turns on the Un-man and, addressing

him as the Devil, says: "Tell her all. What good came to you? Do *you* rejoice that Maleldil became a man?" The remembrance of what the Incarnation still means to him causes the Un-man to howl like a dog, and he abandons the temptation.[27]

The idea for the third novel of the Space Trilogy, *That Hideous Strength*, appears to have arisen in Lewis's mind out of the controversy over the founding of an atomic plant near Blewbury fifteen miles from Oxford, or, if not the idea for the book itself, at least the conception of the National Institute of Co-ordinated Experiments, the sinister and ironically acronymed N.I.C.E., which represents the spectre of scientism within the novel. The dropping of the atomic bomb on Hiroshima and Nagasaki within weeks of the novel's publication in 1945 must have added potency to this "atomic" connection.

As world war mutated into Cold War, the chill of the "brave new world" ushered in by science sent shivers through the postwar literati, leading many other writers to share Lewis's disdainful mistrust of scientism. In September 1945, Edith Sitwell read an eyewitness description of the immediate effect of the atomic bomb upon Hiroshima. "That witness," she wrote, "saw a totem pole of dust arise to the sun as a witness against the murder of mankind. . . ."[28] Sitwell responded by writing one of her finest poems, *The Shadow of Cain*, the first of her "three poems of the Atomic Age" in which she lamented that "the womb from which all life began" had been broken.

The horrors of Hiroshima also inspired Siegfried Sassoon. In 1945 he wrote "Litany of the Lost," a verse which echoed the concerns expressed by Lewis and Sitwell and employed similar resonant religious imagery as a counterpoise to postwar pessimism and alienation. The litany listed the effects of the sins of scientism, the "breaking of belief in human good," the "slavedom of mankind to the machine," and the "terror of atomic doom foreseen." The world, wrote Sassoon, was chained to "the wheel of progress uncontrolled" and was "leaderless and sceptic-souled." Armed only "with our marvelous monkey innovations," we were "unregenerate still in head and heart." The refrain at the end of each verse served hauntingly as a prayer: *Deliver us from ourselves.*

In November 1945, Sheed and Ward, the "papist" publishers who had brought out the second edition of Lewis's *The Pilgrim's Regress,* published *God and the Atom* by Ronald Knox, the opening chapter of which was headed "Trauma: Hiroshima." In the same year, Orwell published *Animal Farm,* the first of his duo of novels that would encapsulate the postwar angst of the entire Cold War generation. The other, *Nineteen Eighty-Four,* published four years later, would immortalize and epitomize the postwar pessimism with more potency than any other novel of its generation. At the time of his sudden and untimely death in 1950 Orwell had been planning to write a study of Evelyn Waugh, whose *Brideshead Revisited,* also published in 1945, was another example of antiprogressive "reaction." Orwell believed that Waugh's genius had exposed the Marxist fallacy that art can be "good" only if it is "progressive."

Intriguingly, all these writers were either converts to Catholicism or would become so within the next decade or so—with the notable exception of Orwell, whose sudden death leaves a beguiling question mark over his likely destination had the "thief in the night" not intervened. Lewis, of course, would not convert but would continue to consider himself an "orthodox" and "traditional" Christian, intent on "smuggling theology" into his novels. As such, *That Hideous Strength,* which deserves a place of prominence alongside *Nineteen Eighty-Four, Animal Farm,* and *Brideshead Revisited* in the plaintive literature of postwar reaction against the myth of "progress," offers some tantalizing clues as to Lewis's religious position at the end of the Second World War.

The reaction against modernity that had earned Lewis the invitation to become a member of the Society for the Prevention of Progress runs through the third novel of the Trilogy almost as a leitmotif. In explaining the purpose of the N.I.C.E., one of the characters, Lord Feverstone, explains that "Man has got to take charge of Man. That means, remember, that some men have got to take charge of the rest."[29] Here one hears echoes of Orwell's *Animal Farm,* with all its animals being equal but some being more equal than others. Since the N.I.C.E. spurns Christian concepts of morality there is no question of their being "holier-than-thou," they are simply wiser-than-thou. Since, like nanny, the N.I.C.E. knows best, the demoniac and dogmatic scientists plan all the "progressive" wonders of the eugenically correct state: sterilization of the unfit, liquidation of backward races, selective breeding, prenatal education, vivisection, biochemical conditioning of the brain, and ultimately the supplanting of the organic with the chemical, real life with its synthetic substitute. Here are all the ingredients of Lewis's loathing for state-centralized social engineering and the "synthetic men" it produces. Indeed, we are not surprised that he conjures up, or resurrects, the ancient figure of Merlin to provide an Arthurian antidote to the "progressive" poison. Lewis, as a member of the Society for the Prevention of Progress, would rather drink mead with Merlin than be made to take the medicine of modernity. Beverages not Beveridges!

Lewis's ascribing of demoniac powers to the men of science in *That Hideous Strength* bore more than a marked similarity to Tolkien's treatment of the same issues in *The Lord of the Rings.* In fact, Lewis's description of *That Hideous Strength* serves, unwittingly, as one of the finest succinct descriptions of Tolkien's epic: "I think *That Hideous Strength* is about a triple conflict: Grace against Nature and Nature against Anti-Nature (modern industrialism, scientism and totalitarian politics):[30] This triple conflict between the supernatural, natural, and unnatural was, arguably, the key to both books.

There were, however, other affinities between *That Hideous Strength* and the work of Tolkien, specifically in Lewis's "borrowing" from his friend's unpublished work, *The Silmarillion.* In chapter six of *That Hideous Strength,* one of the characters, Frost, refers to "something much more remote" than the fifth century. "Something that comes down from long before the Great Disaster, even from before primitive Druidism; something that takes us back to Numinor, to pre-glacial periods."[31] "With regard to 'Numinor,'" Tolkien wrote in reply to an inquiry from Lewis's biographer Roger Lancelyn Green,

> in the early days of our association Jack used to come to my house and I read aloud to him *The Silmarillion* so far as it had then gone, including a very long poem: Beren and Luthien. Numinor was his version of a name he had never seen written (Numenor) and no doubt was influenced by *numinous.* Other things in other works are also derived from me: for instance Tor and Tinidril are clearly Tor and his elf-wife Idril blended with Tinuviel (the second name of Luthien). The Eldils also owe something to the Eldar in my work.[32]

Clearly, Lewis was not only "smuggling theology" into his work; he was also "smuggling mythology." Perhaps, however, it would be uncharitable to suggest that Lewis had ever *intentionally* plagiarized the work of his friend. Since Tolkien had read much of his mythology to Lewis, it is hardly surprising that some of Tolkien's "elvish" magic should have found its way into Lewis's books.

The most intriguing aspect of *That Hideous Strength*, at least from the perspective of the present study, does not revolve around something that Lewis smuggled into the story, but around something that he seems to have smuggled out of it. This curious case of "smuggling" takes place during a dialogue between Ransom and Merlin, the latter having been called back from the tomb after fifteen centuries of sleep. Since these two men appear to have the whole "hideous strength" of hell ranged against them, Merlin, unsurprisingly, asks Ransom if they cannot seek any powerful allies in their struggle. "This Saxon king of yours who sits at Windsor, now—is there no help in him?" Thus begins a litany of futility in which Merlin runs through a list of possible allies, always to be told by Ransom that they can offer no help in the struggle against the "hideous strength." The priests and bishops cannot help because "Nile Faith itself is torn in pieces since your day and speaks with a divided voice." There are no Christian princes left who can come to their aid.

"Then we must go higher. We must go to him whose office it is to put clown tyrants and give life to dying kingdoms. We must call on the Emperor."

"There is no Emperor."

"No Emperor. . . ." Merlin's voice dies away into the desert of desolation. "He sat still for some minutes wrestling with a world which he had never envisaged."[33]

Christopher Derrick, in *C. S. Lewis and the Church of Rome,* refers to "a significantly illustrative falsity" in this dialogue, "a falsity of some relevance to the theme of this book."

> Merlin is casting about for allies, for people whom he could expect to be crucially useful in his fight for Christendom; and as his enquiry proceeds progressively, he casts his net wider and looks higher. Can we get help from the king and his nobles? If not, can we get help from the priests and bishops? If not, can we get help from the Emperor? If not, can we get help from . . . ? But the obvious final and climactic question is not asked. Instead we get a pause, a brief silence which I take to be the silence of embarrassment, on Lewis's part rather than Merlin's. . . .
>
> The effect given is that of a crescendo which has been artificially denied its natural climax. Almost any other novelist who found himself devising such a sequence, whatever his personal belief or disbelief, would have considered it artistically right to make Merlin ask Ransom about the Bishop of Rome, the Pope: "Surely we can turn *there* for help?" So far as Christendom was concerned, it was to that last question that the crescendo pointed, as Lewis must surely have seen. But there was something within him which caused him to replace it, almost as though self-consciously, by silence, and thereby to inflict a palpable stress or falsity upon an otherwise effective sequence.[34]

The obvious reason for this artistic sin of omission would appear to be Lewis's residual Ulster Protestantism. "No Pope

of Rome" meant "no Pope of Rome" even when artistic con-
siderations appeared to point insistently at his presence. This,
however, is to over-simplify the curious absence of the Pope.
"If Lewis had retained that full confidence of anti-Catholicism
which Belfast confers upon some of its citizens," Derrick
continues, "he could have found good scope for this in the
sequence quoted."

> He could easily have represented Merlin as being aware
> of the papacy . . . and as putting the obvious question
> to Ransom in all innocence: "Then if all else fails, can
> we not call upon the Pope?" And into Ransom's disil-
> lusioning reply, Lewis, had he so chosen, could have
> packed all the worst things that have ever been said
> about the Scarlet Woman, the Whore of Babylon,
> perhaps associating that evil power with the N.I.C.E.
> itself, the organization which he devised to represent
> the operation of Satan in this world. . . . But his novel
> gave him that opportunity of saying harsh things about
> the papacy, or, alternatively, of saying friendly things
> about it; and he preferred what I have called the silence
> of embarrassment."

The embarrassing silence was the deafening silence, the
scream in a vacuum, of a soul trapped in the no-man's-land
between affirmation and denial. The power of Puritania continued to overshadow him, no longer strong enough in its
influence to elicit the anti-Catholic curses of a Belfast bigot
but powerful enough to place its Protestant finger on his lips
to keep him from saying anything that could be considered
"papist." In the meantime the Real Presence of Catholicism,
smuggled into Lewis's books through the enduring influence
of the two most important Doctors of the Church, Saint

Augustine (directly) and Saint Thomas Aquinas (indirectly via Dante), thumbed its nose at the embarrassing absence of the author's admission of the fact that it was there. Smuggling, after all, is a matter of secrecy.

LEWIS IN PURGATORY

"But I don't understand. Is judgement not final? Is there really a way out of Hell into Heaven?"

"It depends on the way ye're using the words. If they leave that grey town behind it will not have been Hell. To any that leaves it, it is Purgatory. And perhaps ye had better not call this country Heaven. Not *Deep Heaven,* ye understand." (Here he smiled at me.) "Ye can call it the Valley of the Shadow of Life."

—*The Great Divorce* [1]

IN 1945, the same year in which the last novel of the Space Trilogy was published, Lewis's purgatorial "Dream," *The Great Divorce,* also was published. In this book, more than in any of his others, the figure of Dante emerges as the principal source of inspiration. "Although it cannot, of course, compare in scope and plenitude with Dante's great poem," write Green and Hooper, "the book can certainly be said to be Lewis's *Divine Comedy* and the parallels between the two works are numerous."[2]

The parallels are indeed numerous but the differences between Dante's "dream" and Lewis's are nonetheless significant. The principal difference is that Lewis derived inspiration from what Tolkien described as "the medieval fancy of the

Refrigerium, by which lost souls have an occasional holiday in Paradise."[3] Lewis had originally come across the notion of the Refrigerium in August and September 1931 during his reading of the works of the seventeenth-century Anglican divine Jeremy Taylor. In one of his "Sermons," Taylor had written of the "Refrigerium" as an example of "papist" superstition:

> The church of Rome amongst other strange opinions hath inserted this one into her public offices; that the perishing souls in hell may have sometimes remission and refreshment, like the fits of an intermitting fever: for so it is in the Roman missal printed at Paris, 1626, in the mass for the dead; *Ut quia de ejus vitae qualitate diffidimus, etsi plenam veniam anima ipsius obtinere non potest, saltem vel inter ipsa tormenta quae forsan patitur, refrigerium de abundantia miserationum tuarum sentiat.*[4]

The Latin may be translated thus: *And since we are unsure about the character of his life, even if his soul is unable to obtain . . . the abundance of thy great mercies, among whatever crushing sufferings he endures.*[5] The wording is such that, contrary to Taylor's assertion, it might be said to be related to the suffering souls in purgatory and have no relation to the souls of the damned.

In the same sermon, Taylor mentions another source of the Refrigerium—the fourth-century Latin poet and hymn-writer Prudentius Aurelius Clemens, who wrote: "Often below the Styx holidays from their punishments are kept, even by the guilty spirits. . . . Hell grows feeble with mitigated torments and the shadowy nation, free from fires, exults in the leisure of its prison; the rivers cease to burn with their usual sulphur."[6]

The concept of the Refrigerium fired Lewis's imagination to such an extent that his brother recorded in his diary on

April 16, 1933, that Lewis had "a new idea for a religious work, based on the opinion of some of the Fathers, that while punishment for the damned is eternal, it is intermittent: he proposes to do sort of an infernal day excursion to Paradise."[7]

The "new idea" was more than a decade in gestation, coming eventually to fruition during 1944 and being published in the following year.[8] In spite of the elapse of so much time, the notion of the Refrigerium remained central to the story, as was made explicit by the spirit of George MacDonald, who appears in Lewis's "dream" as his guide, much as Virgil and Beatrice had appeared to Dante.

> "Sir," said I, ". . . It is about these Ghosts. *Do* any of them stay? Can they stay? Is any real choice offered to them? How do they come to be here?"
>
> "Did ye never hear of the *Refrigerium?* A man with your advantages might have read of it in Prudentius, not to mention Jeremy Taylor."
>
> "The name is familiar, Sir, but I'm afraid I've forgotten what it means."
>
> "It means that the damned have holidays excursions, ye understand."[9]

At this juncture, a more precise examination of the notion of the Refrigerium is necessary. Is it, as Jeremy Taylor asserted, merely a further example of papist superstition, one of the many "strange opinions" held by the Church of Rome, from which Anglicans had rightly distanced themselves? Doesn't the wording of the Roman Missal, quoted above, prove that the Church subscribed to such a doctrine? Also, over and above the heterodox or orthodox status of the Refrigeriurn, why did it exert such a powerful influence upon Lewis's imaginative faculties? Finally, was Lewis's treatment of this "medieval fancy" in harmony with the Catholic Church's teaching on heaven, hell, and purgatory?

Lewis would probably have been aware of the old tradition of the Refrigerium from his reading of the ninth-century *Voyage of Saint Brendan,* in which the hero meets Judas during one of his occasional days off from Hell, granted "as an indulgence."[10] This, alongside the subsequent reading of Taylor and Prudentius, was likely to have been one of the imaginative seeds from which *The Great Divorce* would have sprung. Although *The Voyage of Saint Brendan* suggests that the idea of the Refrigerium had become something of a commonplace in late first-millennium tradition, Father Jerome Bertram of the Oxford Oratory[11] states that it was "usually considered to date from the apocryphal *Apocalypse of Paul*" in the late fourth century, "in which Christ grants a day and a night's refreshment for ever on Easter Day." Significantly, however, and in answer to the first and second of the questions posited above, "the Church never gave any official countenance to the idea."

As for Taylor's claim that official sanction for the idea of the Refrigerium can be found in an early seventeenth-century Parisian missal, Father Bertram stresses that this particular missal "has not been traced." Nonetheless, "a feature of early Gallican missals was a Mass for one whose soul was in doubt, *Missa pro cuius anima dubitatur,* for which various formulae are cited. . . . The common theme is a prayer, if possible for the salvation of the deceased, but failing that at least for some mitigation of Hell." This Mass found its way into Italian missals in the late fifteenth century, which would at least admit the possibility that the untraced Parisian missal could have included the text quoted by Taylor. This particular Mass was, however, eliminated in the 1570 reform of the Roman Missal.

Perhaps the most authoritative source for the possibility of the Refrigerium, in some form or other, is to be found in the works of Saint Augustine, specifically in his *Enchiridion ad Laurentium de fide, spe, et caritate liber unus,* written in A.D. 421. In this work, Augustine states the possibility that God's mercy might even extend, should He so choose, to the very damned in hell:

> In vain, therefore, do some men, indeed, very many, because of human sentiment, bewail the eternal punishment of the damned and their perpetual, unending torments, without really believing that it shall be so. . . . But let them suppose, if it pleases them, that the punishments of the damned are, at certain periods of time, somewhat mitigated. For even thus it can be understood that they remain in the wrath of God, that is, in damnation itself,—for it is this that is called the wrath of God, not some disturbance in the divine mind:— that in His wrath, that is, by their abiding in His wrath, He does not shut up His mercies; yet, He does not put an end to their eternal punishment, but only applies or interposes some relief to their torments.[12]

Having discussed the source of the Refrigerium in Christian tradition, and the less than official sanction afforded it by the Church, one would appear to be at liberty either to accept Saint Augustine's "supposal" that some form of mitigation of punishment for the damned is possible or to take Tolkien's apparently more skeptical, or at least more whimsical, view that it was a mere "medieval fancy." The question remains, however, as to the importance of the Refrigerium in Lewis's writing of *The Great Divorce* and whether his treatment of the subject is heterodox or orthodox in relation to the teaching of the Church. To put it bluntly, does Lewis take liberties that the Catholic would not be permitted to take without straying into heresy, or does he deal with the whole subject in a manner that would receive the sanction of the Church?

Lewis answers this question himself, or rather he does so through the words of the spirit of George MacDonald, his guide. After MacDonald mentions the Refrigerium and cites Prudentius and Taylor, he defines, on the very next page, the deeper reality of the situation of these souls "on excursion" in terms that are surely orthodox, though colored with the use of imaginative license.

> "But if they come here they can really stay?"
>
> "Aye. Y'ell have heard that the emperor Trajan did."
>
> "But I don't understand. Is judgement not final? Is there really a way out of Hell into Heaven?"
>
> "It depends on the way ye're using the words. If they leave that grey town behind it will not have been Hell. To any that leaves it, it is Purgatory. And perhaps ye had better not call this country Heaven. Not *Deep Heaven,* ye understand." (Here he smiled at me.) "Ye can call it the Valley of the Shadow of Life."[13]

In this succinctly sublime dialogue, Lewis has presented a theological vision of purgatory that is almost Dantean in its orthodoxy and profundity. The souls who might have appeared to have been in hell discover, once they repent, that they were actually in purgatory all the time. Only the stubbornly impenitent are truly and actually in hell. They cannot escape hell because they do not want to. The "Holiday from Hell" is itself hell to them (since they cannot bear to be in purgatory or heaven) and they return to hell of their own free will and by their own volition. Hell is their true home, though they despise it. It is where they belong.

A few pages later, the shade of MacDonald elucidates the same truth even more succinctly and sublimely.

> Never fear. There are only two kinds of people in the end: those who say to God, "Thy will be done," and those to whom God says, in the end, "*Thy* will be done." All that are in Hell, choose it. Without that self-choice there could be no Hell.[14]

This dialogue represents the cardinal point of the whole work, in both senses. It comes in the middle of the book, halfway through, and is the point at which, and on which, the whole story hinges. Curiously, however, the crucial dialogue contains one faux pas that highlights the anomalous nature of Lewis's own position. "But there is a real choice after death?" Lewis asks MacDonald. "My Roman Catholic friends would be surprised, for to them souls in purgatory are already saved. And my Protestant friends would like it no better, for they'd say that the tree lies as it falls."[15] One suspects, in fact, that Lewis's Roman Catholic friends might have been a little surprised at Lewis's presumption that they would be surprised. Although the souls in purgatory are indeed "saved"—as, in fact, they are saved in *The Great Divorce* according to MacDonald's own definition—they do not lose their free will or "real choice" after death. It would be *implausible* for those in purgatory or heaven to choose hell, because of the fullness of their knowledge of God's Presence and the horror that the reality of their own sin evokes, but that does not negate their free will. It might place a limit on free will but such limits are always in place, both before and after death. One might be technically "free" to call a circle a square but one possessed of his sanity is not going to do so! On the same principle, one who has obtained salvation, with all the added perception that it offers with regard to primal reality, is not going to choose damnation. Certainly, Lewis's Roman Catholic mentor, Dante, would have been surprised to learn that Lewis believed that his penitents in purgatory were not truly penitent, since the absence of free will, or "real choice," would have made their repentance impossible. (If Lewis, as a character in the book, is actually implying that those who have died have, effectively, a second chance at getting it right, he is heterodox from every angle, Protestant and Catholic, but one assumes that this is not his intention. Even if it is, his guide, who is the voice of orthodoxy; clearly does not intend him to believe this.)

In spite of Lewis's apparent lack of understanding of the Church's teaching, he seems to have stumbled, evidently partially unwittingly, on the Church's true position. In short, and to answer the fourth of the questions posited above, Lewis handles the whole question of heaven, hell and purgatory in a manner with which Catholics need not feel awkward.

Yet, if Lewis has mastered the true nature of purgatory within the scheme of salvation, what about the Refrigerium? Should Catholics feel comfortable with this problematic pseudo- or quasi-doctrine, this "medieval fancy," which appears to be at the very heart of *The Great Divorce?* The answer, of course, is "of course"! The idea of the Refrigerium was used by Lewis as a "supposar," a literary device which Green and Hooper describe as "the hallmark of his novels."[16] Thus, for instance, the "supposar" at the heart of the first two novels of the Space Trilogy rested on the doctrine of the Fall: Suppose there are rational creatures on other planets? Suppose they are unfallen? Clearly we do not have to believe that there is rational life on Mars and Venus in order to enjoy *Out of the*

Silent Planet and *Perelandra.* Clearly the theological wisdom, or truth, within the novels does not depend on the supposal being literally factual. Similarly, one does not have to subscribe to the notion of the Refrigerium to enjoy *The Great Divorce.* Neither does the existence or nonexistence of the Refrigerium have any bearing on the validity of the relationship between heaven, hell, and purgatory which is at the center of Lewis's "dream." Those wishing to imply that *The Great Divorce* depends for its ultimate validity, either as literature or as a conveyer of truth, upon the validity of the Refrigerium, are arguing, *ipso facto,* that Dante's *Inferno* is invalidated by his placing Satan at the center of the earth, or that his *Purgatorio* is invalid because he describes purgatory as a physical mountain, or that his *Paradiso* lacks validity because heaven is structured as a reflection of the astronomical heavens. Dante did not believe that these physical images, employed as literary devices, were factually accurate depictions of hell, purgatory, and heaven, any more than Lewis imagined that his speculative allegory about the nature of salvation and damnation in *The Great Divorce* depended on the actual truth or falsehood of his "supposal" of the Refrigerium.

Placing the Refrigerium to one side, we can concentrate on Lewis in purgatory and discover what he saw there. One notices instantly that the Saved, those who have attained heaven, are "the solid people," while the Damned are transparent, like ghosts. Those who live in virtue, that is, in the Presence of God, are more Real, since God is the Source of all Reality; whereas those who deny God by following the life of sin are incomplete, unsubstantial, spiritually malnourished.

We see, in the encounter of the Murderer who had attained heaven and the self-righteous ghost who languishes in self-imposed hell, the perennial difference between the

Publican and the Pharisee. The repentant sinner is embraced by God; the holier-than-thou stickler-for-the-rules refuses the embrace. "I'd rather be damned than go along with you," the self-righteous ghost tells the Murderer-turned-Saint. "I came here to get my rights, see? Not to go snivelling along on charity tied onto your apron-strings. If they're too fine to have me without you, I'll go home."[17] Turning its back on its chance of salvation, the ghost moves away, in triumphant misery, heading for home. The "home" that is hell.

The next encounter is between an orthodox Christian and a modernist theologian; the former saved, the latter damned. The modernist, obstinate in his error, complains that his Christian friend had become rather "narrow-minded" toward the end of his life. "Why, my dear boy, you were coming to believe in a literal Heaven and Hell!" The Christian asks the modernist where he thinks he has just come from. He says that he hadn't thought of giving the drab, gray place where he has been residing any name. "You have been in Hell," he is informed; "though if you don't go back you may call it Purgatory." Unimpressed, the modernist, apparently disbelieving that either place exists, boasts proudly of how, before he became an Anglican bishop, he had "fearlessly" rejected the Resurrection. "You have seen Hell: you are in sight of Heaven. Will you, even now, repent and believe?"

"I'm not sure that I've got the exact point you are trying to make," replies the modernist ghost. There being none so blind, etc., the modernist informs his Christian friend that he must return to whence he had come because he is due to give a paper to the Theological Society on how "Jesus . . . would have outgrown some of his earlier views . . . if he'd lived": "I'm going to ask my audience to consider what his mature views would have been. A profoundly interesting question. What a different Christianity we might have had if only the Founder had reached his full stature!"[18]

Some time later, Lewis meets the ghost of a prudish woman who attempts to hide in the bushes from the Solid One who has been sent to try to save her from hell—or, more correctly, is sent to help her save herself from hell. "How *can* I go out like this among a lot of people with real solid bodies? It's far worse than going out with nothing on would have been on earth. Have everyone staring *through* me." "Friend," replies the Spirit, "Could you, only for a moment, fix your mind on something not yourself?" Thus, in an example of the real depth-psychology that Lewis had already exhibited to great effect in *The Screwtape Letters,* he equates prudishness with pride. Even more profound, however, is the imagery that he employs to cure the ghost of her prudishness. The Solid One, unable to save her with words, places a horn to his lips and blows a summons to a herd of unicorns, "white as swans but for the red gleam in eyes and nostrils and the flashing indigo of their horns": "I can still remember the squelching noise of the soft wet turf under their hoofs, the breaking of the undergrowth, the snorting and whinneyings; how their hind legs went up and their horned heads down in mimic battle. Even then wondered for what real battle it might be the rehearsal. I heard the Ghost scream, and I think it made a bolt away from the bushes . . . perhaps towards the Spirit, but I don't know."[19] The strongly erotic imagery is juxtaposed with the snow-white purity that the unicorn has always represented in the tradition of Catholic typology. The erotic and the pure, not as opposites, but as bride and groom in a nuptial embrace breeding humility. Thus we see how Lewis equates prudishness with pride but also, through the intimation of the intimate, purity with passion. By implication, the

prudish and the prurient—and the puritanical and the por-
nographic—are exposed as reverse sides of the coin of disor-
dered sexual love.[20] Instead of the icy coldness of Puritanism,
Lewis seeks the warming passion of purity. Never had Lewis
escaped so successfully from Puritania.[21]

Significantly, Lewis seems to imply that the ghost of the
prudish woman was indeed saved from returning to "Hell,"
in which case, to echo the words of the shade of George
MacDonald, whom Lewis meets immediately after this epi-
sode, she could not in fact have been in hell at all, but only
in purgatory. "If they leave that grey town behind it will not
have been Hell. To any that leaves it, it is Purgatory."

"And perhaps ye had better not call this country Heaven,"
MacDonald continues. "Not *Deep Heaven,* ye understand. . . .
Ye can call it the Valley of the Shadow of Life."[22] In these
words, MacDonald is saying, in fact, that the place in which
Lewis's "dream" is occurring is itself purgatory. In Dante's
Purgatorio, purgatory is found beyond "Peter's Gate," that
is, beyond the "gates of heaven." It is, however, not "Deep
Heaven," which is to be found in Paradise, but "the Valley of
the Shadow of Life" or, to employ Dante's imagery as opposed
to Lewis's, "the Mountain of the Shadow of Life."

There is a further parallel with Dante's *Purgatorio* in Lewis's
The Great Divorce, and one that harmonizes intriguingly with
Lewis's inspiration from the *Purgatorio* in *Perelandra.* Whereas
in *Perelandra* Lewis confessed to having derived inspiration
from canto xxviii of the *Purgatorio* for Ransom's encounter
with Perelandra's "Eve," there is a clear parallel between the
Pageant of the saint, Sarah Smith, presented to Lewis in chapter 12 of *The Great Divorce* and the Pageant of the Sacrament
presented to Dante in cantos xxix and xxx of the *Purgatorio.*
There seems, indeed, to be no limit to the inspiration that

Lewis drew from the fathomless well of Dante's imagination.

Having wandered through purgatory breathing in deep draughts of its Catholic theological atmosphere, Lewis concludes *The Great Divorce* with an explicit attack on Calvinism. "For every attempt to see the shape of eternity except through the lens of Time destroys your knowledge of Freedom," explains the spirit of MacDonald. "Witness the doctrine of Predestination which shows (truly enough) that eternal reality is not waiting for a future in which to be real; but at the price of removing Freedom which is the deeper truth of the two."[23]

It is an irony and a paradox, though not altogether surprising, that Lewis delved deeper into the truths of Christianity in the imaginary "dream" of *The Great Divorce* than in much of his prose didacticism. As a truly gifted writer and storyteller he shone more light onto the "shadowlands" from the heights of his imagination—from Mars, Venus, Narnia, and "Purgatory"—than from his prosaic expositions of "mere Christianity." It is, however, to the "merely Christian" that we now turn our attention.

8

MERE CHRISTIANITY

> If any man is tempted to think . . . that "Christianity"
> is a word of so many meanings that it means nothing
> at all, he can learn beyond all doubt, by stepping out of
> his own century, that this is not so. Measured against
> the ages "mere Christianity" turns out to be no insipid
> interdenominational transparency, but something posi-
> tive, self-consistent, and inexhaustible.
>
> —*Introduction to* The Incarnation of the Word[1]

LEWIS FIRST employed the term "mere Christianity" in 1944, in an introduction to a book by his friend Sister Penelope. From the very first he insisted that it was "no insipid interdenominational transparency," a clear indication of his resolute opposition to all forms of "ecumenism" involving the diluting of the central tenets of Christendom. Thereafter, the banner of "mere Christianity" became the standard to which he called all Christians to rally in defense of their common faith.

As early as 1933, in a reply to Dom Bede Griffiths, who had sought to engage him in a debate on the differences between Catholicism and Anglicanism, Lewis had written: "When all is said . . . about the divisions of Christendom, there remains, by God's mercy, an enormous common ground."[2] "Mere Christianity" was, therefore, the "enormous common ground" that was shared by Christians of all denominations. The challenge that Lewis set himself was to map out this ground so that Christians could see and understand what they held in common. This apparently laudatory aim was, however, always fraught with difficulties.

Perhaps the best way to begin a discussion of Lewis's efforts to define "mere Christianity" is to quote, and then analyze, the passage which first brought the name and notion of "mere Christianity" to Lewis's mind. It seems that Lewis first came across the term "mere Christian" in the works of the seventeenth-century Christian writer Richard Baxter. In his *Church-history of the Government of Bishops,* published in 1680, Baxter had written:

> You know not of what Party I am of, nor what to call me; I am sorrier for you in this than for my self; if you know not, I will tell you, I am a CHRISTIAN, a MERE CHRISTIAN, of no other religion; and the Church that I am of is the Christian Church, and hath been visible where ever the Christian Religion and Church hath been visible: But must you know of what Sect or Party I am of? I am against all Sects and dividing Parties: But if any will call *Mere Christian* by the name of a Party, because they take up with *mere Christianity, Creed,* and *Scripture,* and will not be of any dividing or contentious Sect, I am of that Party which is so against Parties: If the name CHRISTIAN be not enough, call me a CATHOLIC CHRISTIAN; not as that word signifieth an hereticating majority of Bishops, but as it signifieth one that hath no Religion, but that which by Christ and the Apostles was left to the Catholic Church, or the body of Jesus Christ on Earth.[3]

Looking at the text, disembodied from its context, mere Christianity; thus defined, could be seen as the presentation of the image of an ideal Christianity. Apart from the short but crucially important subtext about the "hereticating majority of Bishops" the passage could be a clear description of the position of a member of the Roman Catholic Church. Even with the subtext retained, the passage could serve as a definition of a Roman Catholic in England in 1680 who refused to kowtow to the "hereticating majority of Bishops" in the Anglican church. Indeed, Baxter was in fact referring principally to Anglican bishops, with whom he was at loggerheads. Baxter was not, however, a Roman Catholic but a Puritan divine.

The fact that the first person to coin the phrase "mere Christian" was a Puritan Protestant who called himself catholic highlights the difficulties involved in discussing and defining "mere Christianity." It also serves as a warning that eclecticism and eccentricity, the perennial enemies of orthodoxy, are a recurring temptation to those attempting to find the common ground that unites all Christians.

In Baxter's case, the eclecticism and eccentricity emerge once we return to the context in which his words were actually written. He was born into an England ripped apart by religious division. When not squabbling with each other, the contending Christian sects and parties were picking over the remains of the faith abandoned. The England of the seventeenth century was the inheritor of the chaos caused by Henry VIII's rupture of his realm from the unity of Christendom. This rupture led to further rupture. The fratricidal Civil War, during which Anglican Conformists fought their Nonconformist fellow countrymen to the death, was the result of the rise of hardline Puritanism, on the one side, and the perennial disunity within the Anglican church, on the other. Baxter took the side of the Puritan "Sect or Party" and acted as army chaplain to Cromwell's forces, being present at the sieges of Bridgewater, Bristol, Exeter, and Worcester. At the Restoration of the Monarchy he was appointed a royal Chaplain, but in 1662, when the Act of Uniformity sought to unite all Anglicans within a uniform framework of "merely Christian" worship, he dissented and left the Church of England. Thus we see that the original "mere Christian" was hardly a paragon of virtue as far as Christian unity was concerned.

Without wishing to descend to an *atgumentum ad hominem,* the apparent dichotomy between Baxter's laudatory words and his practical actions is extremely relevant. One who speaks of Christian unity while contributing to disunity is somewhat akin to one who speaks of chastity while practising adultery. Taken in context, as opposed to out of it, we see that Richard Baxter merely decided that his own eclectic and eccentric vision of what constituted "mere Christianity" was the true one. Having selected those aspects of Christianity that he personally liked the best, and having discarded those of which he disapproved, he moved throughout his life further from the center of Christian tradition. Baxter's "mere Christianity" was really the "do-it-yourself" Christianity that feels free to pick and choose from the deposit of faith. The result, three hundred years later, is that the Christian "Sects or Parties," only several in number during Baxter's day, are now several thousand in number; a plethora of "Parties or Sects," all claiming to represent "mere Christianity."

The paradox at the heart of Lewis's "mere Christianity" is that he is trying to solve the anarchy of contending "truths" caused by Christian eclecticism without abandoning the eclecticism itself. He was horrified by the effects of division but could not, or would not, identify the cause.

The question that confronts any conscientious student of Lewis is the extent to which his definition of "mere Christianity" conforms to objective criteria and the extent to which it succumbs to the subjectivism of personal prejudice. When is the "merely Christian" clearly Christian? A study of Lewis's *Mere Christianity* will help provide the answers.

Mere Christianity was a "revised and amplified edition . . . of the three books *Broadcast Talks, Christian Behaviour* and *Beyond Personality,*" and represents Lewis's effort "to explain and defend the belief that has been common to nearly all Christians at all times."[4] This was certainly a bold and commendable endeavor and follows in the noble tradition of G. K. Chesterton, who, in his *Orthodoxy,* published in 1908, sought to do exactly the same thing. At the commencement of his book, Chesterton defined what he meant by "orthodoxy" in terms that were similar to those that would later be used by Lewis to define "mere Christianity":

> These essays are concerned only to discuss the actual fact that the central Christian theology (sufficiently summarised in the Apostles' Creed) is the best root of energy and sound ethics. They are not intended to discuss the very fascinating but quite different question of what is the present seat of authority for the proclamation of that creed. When the word "orthodoxy" is used here it means the Apostles' Creed, as understood by everybody calling himself Christian until a very short time ago and the general historic conduct of those who held such a creed.[5]

Chesterton was, like Lewis, an Anglican at the time he outlined his "orthodoxy/mere Christianity" but, unlike Lewis, answered "the very fascinating . . . question of what is the present seat of authority for the proclamation of that creed" by his eventual reception into the Roman Catholic Church. Indeed, the most striking difference between Chesterton and Lewis is the extent to which one pursued the "very fascinating question" and the other avoided it.

Alluding to his own apparent reticence to discuss such matters, Lewis wrote in the preface to *Mere Christianity* that he hoped "people would not draw fanciful inferences from my silence on certain disputed matters":

> . . . such silence need not mean that I myself am sitting on the fence. Sometimes I am. There are questions at issue between Christians to which I do not think we have been told the answer. . . . But there are other questions as to which I am definitely on one side of the fence, and yet say nothing. For I was not writing to expound something I could call "my religion," but to expound "mere" Christianity, which is what it is and was what it was long before I was born and whether I like it or not.[6]

One is of course bound to draw inferences from anyone who chooses the Fifth Amendment, the right to remain silent implying the right of others to infer a meaning to the choice. It is, however, not what Lewis has *failed* to say in this one short paragraph that is of interest but what he *has* said or, more correctly, the *way* he has chosen to say it. According to Lewis, the "questions at issue" are not those to which we should try to find answers, they are questions to which *we* have not been told the answers. In other words, presumably, we can ignore the questions and the answers, and thus avoid the difficulty, because those things upon which we are not agreed have not in fact been "revealed," presumably by God, and are therefore irrelevant. Since Lewis insists on his right to remain silent as to which of these "questions at issue" he is referring, it is difficult to know exactly what he is talking about. However, since the questions at issue are hardly a secret, we can deduce that questions of authority, or the role and meaning of the Church, or the place of the Blessed Virgin, or the role of the sacraments, or that of the saints, or the liturgy are among the "questions" to which Lewis does "not think we have been told the answer." To avoid tackling such issues is not to *explain* "mere Christianity," it is to explain it away. In taking such an approach, Lewis is certainly in danger of confecting "mere Christianity" in his own image. At the very least, the confection is a fudge. He is fudging the central issues to try to please most of the people most of the time. He is succumbing to a politician's approach to Christianity. The kissing of the Baby but the refusal to recognize His Mother! In this light, it is more than a little ironic that Lewis should state that his aim is "the defence of what Baxter calls 'mere' Christianity."[7] Clearly what Baxter calls "mere Christianity" is not what many Christians would call it.

Immediately after this general explanation for his reticence to discuss disputed doctrines, Lewis defends his silence on the position of the Blessed Virgin by declaring that she is the one subject that can "be relied upon to wreck a book about 'mere' Christianity."[8] Thus, in a puzzling act of pragmatism, the subject of the Mother of Christ is dismissed as a wrecker of "mere Christianity."

There may be more to Lewis's "pragmatism" with regard to the Blessed Virgin than his dispassionate dismissal of her in the preface to *Mere Christianity* might suggest. Peter Milward, S.J., a former pupil of Lewis who conducted a long correspondence with him during the 1950s, made the following observation about his strange silence on the subject:

> I have no great quarrel with what Lewis says in *Mere Christianity*. My quarrel is rather with what he does not say, not so much in *Mere Christianity* as in his writings on mediaeval and Renaissance literature. For it is in these writings that one might expect him to say more about so central a figure in mediaeval and Renaissance art and literature as the Virgin Mary. Yet what do we find in them? In *The Allegory of Love* he merely speaks, inaccurately, once or twice about "the worship of the Virgin Mary." He quite fails to note that in Catholic and mediaeval terminology "worship" (*latria*) belongs to God alone, and it is clearly distinguished from the devotion or veneration (*hyperdulia*) paid to the Virgin Mary. He moreover contrasts this "worship of the Virgin Mary" with the cult of the Lady, or *Frauendienst*, which he cannot see as influenced in any way by the more widespread cult of Our Lady, though he is prepared to grant an influence in the other direction. Second, in his *Selected Literary Essays* there is only one entry in the index for "Saint Mary"; and this turns out to be in a quotation from *King Horn*, which serves to illustrate not any doctrine or devotion but the alliterative meter. Third, in his *English Literature in the Sixteenth Century* the Virgin Mary is passed over in complete silence, as it were to make way for the Virgin Queen, who took over so many of the Virgin Mary's prerogatives not least in Spenser's *Faery Queene*.
>
> So again I can't help wondering at the insensitivity of this scholar who, in his Inaugural Lecture *De*

Descriptione Ternporurn, claims to speak as a native of mediaeval England and to know "his way about his father's house" (p. 13), yet has no appreciation of her whom the people of the Middle Ages, including Dante and Chaucer, hailed as their queen and mother. Not that he has anything to say against her or the mediaeval devotion to her. He merely passes her over in silence. And in this silence I can't help feeling not so much reverence, or mere indifference, as suppression of a deep Protestant prejudice. For him as a Protestant the Virgin Mary has no place in "mere Christianity," despite the mention of her in the Apostles' Creed. Nor does he admit her to what he calls, in his *Preface to Paradise Lost,* "the great central tradition" (p. 92). . . .

But then, considering how impressive is the development of the doctrine and cult of Our Lady in Christian history, in both the Greek and the Latin Church, not only in the Middle Ages but well into the Renaissance and Baroque periods, any exposition of "mere Christianity" without mention of her is bound to be Protestant, or even Puritan, and so cut off from "the great central tradition" of the Church.[9]

Father Milward's critique of Lewis's inability or unwillingness to understand the prominence of the Blessed Virgin in the literature and culture of the Middle Ages and the Renaissance serves to undermine Lewis's status as a critic of the period. A critic must surely learn to empathize, even if unable to sympathize, with his subject and a failure to do so must prove fatal to any objective criteria upon which judgment is based. One who is not only unable to love the things that his subjects loved, but is unable to understand the love that they had, to such an extent that he cannot even bring himself to mention it, is not a very reliable judge. And what is true of the literary critic is true of the critic of religion. Failure to sympathize with, empathize with, or even mention, the Mother of Christ or, for that matter, the host of lesser saints who have been venerated down the centuries, is not to place oneself at the center of what "nearly all Christians at all times" have believed, it is to place oneself in the ranks of an iconoclastic minority who have only risen to prominence in relatively recent times on the outer fringes of mainstream Christian opinion. A "mere Christianity," thus formulated and propagated, is outside "the great central tradition" and cannot claim to be representative of it.

The principal difference between Lewis's "mere Christianity" and Chesterton's "orthodoxy" is a difference of principle. Chesterton placed at the center of his quest for the essence of Christianity, the Apostles' Creed; Lewis placed at the center of his quest, the Book of Common Prayer. To quote once again from the preface to *Mere Christianity:* "All this is said simply in order to make clear what kind of book I was trying to write; not in the least to conceal or evade responsibility for my own beliefs. About those, as I said before, there is no secret. To quote Uncle Toby: 'They are written in the Common-Prayer Book.'"[10] Chesterton began with the Apostles' Creed and discovered the Church of the Apostles; Lewis began with the Book of Common Prayer and was caught between the Church of the Apostles and the Compromise of Cranmer.

Ultimately, however, in spite of the limitations that "mere Christianity" had placed upon him, Lewis groped progressively towards "*more* Christianity," accepting as integral to the Christian faith, doctrines and dogmas that would have made Cranmer cringe. Lewis might have failed to escape completely from the Puritania of his prejudices, but he would evolve into a very Catholic sort of Protestant or, perhaps, a very Protestant sort of Catholic. At any rate, as we shall see, "mere Christianity" would make way for "more Christianity."

9

MORE CHRISTIANITY

Next to the Blessed Sacrament itself, your neighbour is
the holiest object presented to your senses.

—The Weight of Glory[1]

AFTER ANALYZING the anomalies of "mere Christianity" it is appropriate that we now concentrate on
Lewis's genuine search for "more Christianity." In the preface to *Mere Christianity*, Lewis had stressed that his intention
was to emphasize the highest common factors which united
Christians, and not, therefore, the lowest common denomi-
nators of the lowest common denominations. Presumably
the logic of Lewis's position, at least implicitly, is that those
denominations which do not affirm the highest common factors are not qualified to call themselves "mere Christians."
Thus, elsewhere in *Mere Christianity*, Lewis dismissed what he
termed "Christianity-and-water, the view which simply says
there is a good God in Heaven and everything is all right—
leaving out all the difficult and terrible doctrines about sin
and hell and the devil, and the redemption."[2] This form of
Christianity was "too simple" and was equated with atheism
as being an inadequate explanation of reality. Atheism and
watered-down Christianity were both dismissed by Lewis
as "boys' philosophies."[3] Those who denigrate dogma and

dilute doctrine are turning the wine of Christian truth into the water of unbelief. In so doing, the boys' philosophy of Christianity-and-water actually becomes, eventually, the boys' philosophy of atheism. Dilution and delusion are twin sisters of deception.

If diluted Christianity was unacceptable, what did Lewis consider the undiluted form? What were the highest common factors that were essential to anyone wishing to be "merely Christian"? "There are three things that spread the Christ life to us," Lewis asserts: "baptism, belief, and that mysterious action which different Christians call by different names—Holy Communion, the Mass, the Lord's Supper."[4] We know from Lewis's dismissal of Christianity-and-water that he doesn't mean "belief" to represent some vague nebulous "opinion;" he means it to be a definitive assertion of, and adherence to, a set of Christian principles that have been believed by those calling themselves Christians down the ages. Belief is not "opinion," it is *Creed, Credo, I Believe.* In short, and in essence, Lewis is declaring that the bare essentials of "mere Christianity" are the Creed (belief) and at least some of the sacraments (baptism and the Eucharist) as agents of grace. Immediately, therefore, Lewis is excluding the Protestant doctrine of *sola fide* from the "merely Christian."

The sacramental view of Christianity is reiterated by Lewis elsewhere in *Mere Christianity.* Having declared that "the whole mass of Christians are the physical organism through which Christ acts," Lewis concludes that this "explains why this new life is spread not only by purely mental acts like belief, but by bodily acts like baptism and Holy Communion, . . . God never meant man to be a purely spiritual creature. That is why He uses material things like bread and wine to put the new life into us. We may think this rather crude and unspiritual. God does not: He invented eating. He likes matter. He invented it."[5]

Lewis shows an even deeper affinity with Catholic doctrine in his chapter on the cardinal virtues, a mainstay of Catholic moral theology for centuries. Rather oddly, however, he sees fit to point out that the word "cardinal" has nothing to do with "Cardinals" in "the Roman Church."[6] This is, of course, technically true; but why, one wonders, did Lewis find it necessary to insert this particular parenthesis? It could be argued, and no doubt Lewis would have done so if asked, that it was simply to avoid any confusion on the point. The impression that could be gained, however, and whether Lewis intended it or not, is that the cardinal virtues themselves have nothing to do with the "Roman Church," which from Saint Augustine to Saint Thomas Aquinas has so carefully explicated them throughout her history. One might have forgiven Lewis for failing to mention such a cardinal reality, but it is hard to accept the insult added to injury implicit in his distancing the virtues from the Cardinals who have always taught them as part of the deposit of the Catholic faith.

Sinking deeper into debt to Catholic teaching, Lewis concludes the chapter on "Sexual Morality" in *Mere Christianity* by emphasizing that unchastity is not the "supreme vice." On the contrary, although the "sins of the flesh are bad," Lewis insists that "they are the least bad of all sins." In his insistence that the worst sins were "purely spiritual," Lewis was following the teaching of the Church, which relies in part on sacred tradition and not merely on *sola scriptura*. In particular, his theology resonates with that of Saint Thomas Aquinas, and also, of course, reflects the hierarchy of sins employed by Dante in the *Divine Comedy*. One is reminded also of the excellent little book *The Other Six Deadly Sins,* by Dorothy L.

Sayers, whom Lewis knew and respected. Since Sayers's book was the published transcript of a talk she had given in October 1941, it is possible that Lewis had been inspired by this earlier work to say something similar himself. Nonetheless, as Sayers was more of a Thomist than Lewis, and an even greater admirer of Dante, her own inspiration was at least as deeply rooted in the *Summa Theologiae* via the *Divine Comedy* as was Lewis's. And, of course, in stating in *Mere Christianity* that a churchgoing "self-righteous prig" might be "nearer to hell than a prostitute," Lewis was merely following the deeply Catholic and anti-Puritan path that he had taken in *The Great Divorce.* One wonders, in fact, whether Lewis recalled his words about "self-righteous prigs" a few years later, following his being banned from the "Protestant Hour Network" on American radio for his "startling frankness" on sexual love. "Professor Lewis," he was told, "I'm afraid you brought sex into your talk about Eros," to which he replied by asking how he could possibly talk about Eros "and *leave it out?*"[7]

Towards the end of *Mere Christianity* Lewis defends the discipline of theology in robust terms. "There is no good complaining that these statements are difficult. Christianity claims to be telling us about another world, about something behind the world we can touch and hear and see. You may think the claim false; but if it were true, what it tells us would be bound to be difficult—at least as difficult as modern Physics, and for the same reason."[8] This passage is reminiscent of Chesterton's memorable words in *Orthodoxy.*

> The complication of our modern world proves the truth of the creed more perfectly than any of the plain problems of the ages of faith. . . . This is why the faith has that elaboration of doctrines and details which so

much distresses those who admire Christianity without
believing in it. When once one believes in a creed, one
is proud of its complexity, as scientists are proud of the
complexity of science. It shows how rich it is in discov-
eries. If it is right at all, it is a compliment to say that
it's elaborately right. A stick might fit a hole or a stone
a hollow by accident. But a key and a lock are both
complex. And if a key fits a lock, you know it is the
right key.[9]

Lewis was aware of "the truth of the creed," as Chesterton
put it, and insisted that "mere Christianity" was not "an alternative to the creeds of the existing communions"[10] but merely
a means of understanding what the existing communions held
in common. The duty of all seekers after Christian truth was to
pass beyond "mere Christianity" to "more Christianity." The
problem, however, was that Lewis felt it difficult to broach
the subject of the Church, or church, or churches, for fear of
opening the Pandora's box of denominational differences and
difficulties. Eric Fenn, the assistant head of religious broadcasting at the BBC, expressed his concern that Lewis's failure
to make any reference to "the church" was compromising the
fullness of his message during the radio broadcasts that would
later be published as *Mere Christianity*. In December 1943,
Fenn, a Presbyterian, suggested that Lewis should "say a bit
more about the Christian community":

> With the exception of one or two references, you
> don't seem to mention that at all, and the scripts give,
> therefore, an impression of a purely individualistic
> approach. . . . You are thinking all the time about one
> man in relation to God, and not at all about the con-
> nection this always establishes with other men. I do

think it would strengthen the series to say something
more about the Church.[11]

Lewis replied that it was "difficult to go on long" about the
Church "without raising the denominational question"[12] and,
though he promised to try to say something about it, the whole
issue of the Church is conspicuous, for the most part, by its
absence from *Mere Christianity*. Since many Christians—and
Catholic Christians in particular—subscribe to an ecclesiology which sees the Church as the Mystical Body of Christ in
the world, and since Lewis's own sacramental approach suggests that this was a view to which he subscribed, the absence
of any full discussion of the role of the Church must be seen
as a sin of omission.

"After Lewis started broadcasting for the BBC he became
trapped by his own success," states Walter Hooper, endeavoring to explain these curious and conspicuous omissions. "He
suddenly became everyman's Christian apologist. Thereafter
Mere Christianity became a ring fence and he preferred to
stay out of theological dogfights."[13] Yet, though this might
be so, it is curious that there were some strange additions
to the recipe of "mere Christianity" that were singularly
and decidedly Catholic. Take for instance the allusion to
purgatory in Lewis's mention of the "purification . . . after
death,"[14] or his reference to the "Blessed Sacrament" as "the
holiest object presented to your senses."[15] These curiously
Catholic additions were due, in part, to Lewis's attachment
to Anglo-Catholicism, an attachment that he felt in spite of
his antagonism towards T. S. Eliot and those aspects of High
Church Anglicanism which he perceived that Eliot and his ilk
represented.

Lewis's sympathies with this particular wing of the

Anglican church could be gauged by the fact that he was a longstanding subscriber to *The Guardian,* a weekly Anglo-Catholic newspaper not to be confused with the present liberal-secularist newspaper of the same name. Founded in 1846 by R. W. Church and others to defend the High Church Tractarian principles of Pusey, Keble, and Newman (prior to his conversion, in the previous year, to Roman Catholicism), *The Guardian* continued to be the defender of such principles until it ceased publication in 1951. Lewis's respect for, and attachment to, this particular newspaper is evident from the fact that two of his finer works, *The Screwtape Letters* and *The Great Divorce,* were first published within its pages.

A further strong and enduring Anglo-Catholic influence on Lewis was his longstanding friendship with Sister Penelope, of the Convent of the Community of Saint Mary the Virgin. The Community of which Sister Penelope was a member had been founded in 1848 in the afterglow of the Oxford Movement and was one of the first of the Anglican religious orders to be founded since the Reformation. In one of her early books, *The Wood for the Trees: An Outline of Christianity,* she had defended the Church of England as a "real *via media,* retaining all the essentials of Catholicity." Lewis described Sister Penelope as his "elder sister" in the faith, and, according to Walter Hooper, "she more than anyone helped him to appreciate the Catholic side of Anglicanism."[16] She sent him a photograph of the Turin Shroud and, thereafter, he kept it on the wall of his bedroom for the rest of his life, venerating the relic as any good Catholic might have done.[17]

When unrestrained by the straitjacket of "mere Christianity," Lewis often flowered into the fullness of Catholicism, or at least the blushing bloom of near Catholicism, as was clearly the case with *The Pilgrim's Regress* and *The Great Divorce.* His work of popular theology *The Problem of Pain* was described by the Dominican Benet O'Driscoll, in *Blackfriars,* as being "in line with Catholic doctrine" and as "having much in common with the accepted Catholic teaching" on the Fall.[18] A review of the same book in the *Church Times,* an Anglican newspaper, declared that Lewis was a "defender of the Faith" who had taken "the Catholic position."[19] A reviewer of Lewis's *Beyond Personality* compared him with Jacques Maritain, the great French Thomist,[20] and Lewis declared of himself that he was "a dogmatic Christian untinged with Modernist reservations."[21]

Lewis's "Catholic" dogmatism was to the fore in a letter to his old friend Arthur Greeves, written at the end of 1944, in which Lewis dismisses his friend's defense of Unitarianism and his skepticism about the divinity of Christ:

> I don't think I can agree that the Churches are empty because they teach that Jesus is God. If so, the ones that teach the opposite, i.e. the Unitarians, would be full wouldn't they? Are they? It seems to me that the ones which teach the fullest and most dogmatic theology are precisely the ones that retain their people and make converts, while the liberalizing and modernizing ones lose ground every day. Thus the R.C.'s are flourishing and growing, and in the C. of E. the "high" churches are fuller than the "low."[22]

Clyde S. Kilby, in *The Christian World of C. S. Lewis,* emphasized the doctrinal foundation of Lewis's Christianity, stressing not only his striving for "orthodoxy" but his unremitting opposition to "modernism":

Doctrinally, Lewis accepted the Nicene, Athanasian, and Apostles' creeds. He was never failing in his opposition to theological "modernism." Some of his most acerose satire is employed against it in both his fiction and expository works. It is as ridiculous, he declares, to believe that the earth is flat as to believe in the watered-down popular theology of modern England. In *The Screwtape Letters* a major employment of hell itself is in encouraging theologians to create a new "historical Jesus" in each generation.[23]

ha ha!

Perplexingly, however, Lewis continued to oscillate between expositions of "orthodoxy" and proclamations of residual Protestant prejudice. For example, he states on one occasion that his arguments are based on three assumptions, namely, "the divinity of Christ, the truth of the creeds, and the authority of the Christian tradition;"[24] yet, on another occasion, he wrote to oppose moves in the Anglican church to include the veneration of the saints within the religious practice of the Church of England. "Thousands of members of the Church of England doubt whether *dulia* [the veneration of the saints] is lawful," he wrote to the *Church Times* in 1952.[25] Where, in this oddly unorthodox "doubt," was Lewis's assumption of "the truth of the creeds," all of which include the necessity of belief in the "communion of saints," or where was his affirmation in "the authority of the Christian tradition" which has always venerated the souls in heaven? One is tempted, in fact, to suggest that Screwtape and Company are at least as busy in creating a "Great Divorce" between the communion of saints in heaven and the communion of would-be saints on earth as they are with persuading modernist theologians to create a new "historical Jesus."

In the same letter to the *Church Times* in which he had cast a doubt on whether *dulia* is lawful, he had warned of the "frightful risks" of schism within the Church of England should the veneration of the saints be encouraged. The best riposte to Lewis's peculiar stance towards the "lawfulness" of venerating the saints would be his own words of warning from the chapter on "Hope" in *Mere Christianity.* "It is since Christians have largely ceased to think of the other world that they have become so ineffective in this. Aim at Heaven and you will get earth "thrown in": aim at earth and you will get neither."[26]

If it was dangerous to venerate saints as saints, it was safe enough to venerate them as writers. Saint Francis de Sales was, in Lewis's estimation, the author of "the *sweetest* of religious writings" in prose.[27] It was also safe to admire a saint before he had become a saint (or, at least, before he had been recognized as such by the authority of the Church), as was the case with Lewis's warm and fruitful friendship with Saint Giovanni Calabria, who was canonized by Pope John Paul II on April 18, 1999. Writing to Lewis in September 1947, Don Giovanni Calabria raised the "problem" of "the dissenting brethren whose return to the unity of the Body of Christ, which is the Church, is most greatly desired."[28] This commenced a long correspondence between Lewis and Calabria, conducted in Latin as the one language that they held in common, which lasted until the latter's death in 1954. "If only that plaguey 'Renaissance' which the Humanists brought about had not *destroyed* Latin," Lewis wrote to Calabria, ". . . we should then still be able to correspond with the whole of Europe."[29]

It was Calabria's hope that Lewis would "be able to perform something of greater moment in the Lord's vineyard, so that at last it may be seen that 'there is one fold and one

Shepherd.' "[30] If, however, it had been Don Calabria's desire that Lewis would himself be received into the Church and that, through his conversion, many others might be led into the "one fold," Lewis was not about to oblige him. He was not ready to be persuaded, or prayed, into the Church, even by a saint. "That the whole cause of schism lies in sin I do not hold to be certain," Lewis replied to another of Calabria's letters, adding that "we disagree about nothing more than the authority of the Pope: on which disagreement almost all the others depend."[31]

At around the time that Lewis began corresponding with Giovanni Calabria, he became embroiled in a heated debate with another Catholic, Professor Gertrude Elizabeth Anscombe, who is chiefly remembered within the sphere of Lewis studies as the one person reputed to have defeated him in open debate. Twenty years Lewis's junior, being born in 1919, Anscombe had become a convert to Catholicism as a teenager. She was a research fellow at Somerville College, only twenty-eight years old, when she gave a paper at the Socratic Club entitled "A Reply to Mr. C. S. Lewis's Argument That 'Naturalism' Is Self-Refuting." As a result of Professor Anscombe's line of reasoning, Lewis amended chapter three of his book *Miracles,* which had been the object of her criticism.

Apart from Lewis's friendly discussions with saintly Catholic priests such as Don Giovanni Calabria, or his arguments on the fundamentals of philosophy with robust Catholic philosophers such as Professor Anscombe, there remains the elusive nature of Lewis's own position within the theological spectrum. Exactly how close to the Catholic position was he? Did his occasional outbursts against the veneration of the saints or the primacy of the Pope signify an overriding Protestant bias, or did his quest for "orthodoxy" and his antagonism towards modernism, relativism, and other forms of Christianity-and-water suggest a strong tendency in the direction of Catholic Christianity?

Perhaps the best way of answering these questions is to return to the sacraments, and to consider Lewis's attitude towards them. We have already seen that Lewis considered the sacraments of baptism and Holy Communion essential elements of "mere Christianity." Since, however, the Catholic Church teaches that there are seven sacraments, Lewis's attitude to the other five will provide valuable evidence as to his position.

In spite of Lewis's controversial marriage to Joy Gresham, there is no doubt that he understood the Christian sacrament of marriage as binding before God "until death do us part." There is, therefore, no significant difference between his position and that of the Catholic Church as regards this particular sacrament.[32] The same could be said of his attitude to the sacrament of confirmation. More intriguing, and surprising, is Lewis's attitude towards confession. "I am going to make my first confession next week," Lewis informed Sister Penelope on October 24, 1940 and, thereafter, he went to the Anglican equivalent of confession regularly.[33] Writing of "Confession and Absolution" to another correspondent in January 1941, he asked her to "remember it's not the psychoanalyst over again; the confessor is the representative of Our Lord and declares His forgiveness—his advice or 'understanding' . . . is of secondary importance."[34] Twelve years later, Lewis differentiated between the Anglican and the Catholic view of confession:

> I think our official view of Confession can be seen in
> the form for the Visitation of the Sick, where it says,

"Then shall the sick person be moved (i.e., advised, prompted) to make a . . . Confession . . . if he feel his conscience troubled with any weighty matters." That is, where Rome makes Confession compulsory for all, we make it permissible for any; not "generally necessary" but profitable. . . . The quite enormous advantage of coming really to believe in forgiveness is well worth the horrors (I agree that they are horrors) of a first Confession. Also, there is the gain in self-knowledge. . . . I certainly feel that I have profited enormously by the practice.[35]

In spite of his differentiating between the way that Anglicans perceived confession and the way that the sacrament of penance is practiced within the Roman Catholic Church, the fact remains that Lewis was placing himself in a highly eccentric position within his own church. In going to confession he was not only beyond the pale as far as the Nonconformist churches were concerned; he was also partaking of a practice that was certainly frowned upon by most members of the Church of England. In theory Lewis was still seen by Christians of all persuasions as a "mere Christian," causing Tolkien to refer to him disparagingly as "Everyman's Theologian"[36]; in practice, however, and in private, he was indulging in what would be deemed as indubitably and "damnably" papist. It is also interesting to note that, in a letter to an American correspondent written a few months after the letter extolling the benefits of confession, he was referring to Holy Communion quite brazenly as "Mass," complete with the upper-case "M"![37] The language and practice of Lewis's faith had certainly come a long way from the streets of Puritania or Protestant Belfast!

Having succumbed to some form of apparent

crypto-Catholicism in the practice of confession, and some conception of Holy Communion as being Holy Mass, Lewis was also approaching a Catholic understanding of the nature of the priesthood. In July 1948 Lewis wrote to Dorothy Sayers on the subject of female ordination:

> News has just reached me of a movement . . . to demand that women should be allowed Priests' Orders. I am guessing that, like me, you disapprove of something which would cut us off so sharply from all the rest of Christendom, and which would be the very triumph of what they call "practical" and "enlightened" principles over the far deeper need that the Priest at the Altar must represent the Bridegroom to whom we are all, in a sense, feminine. Well, if you do, really I think you will have to give tongue.[38]

Sayers's reply was a concoction of contradictions, simultaneously sympathetic and antipathetic to Lewis's position, which seemed to illustrate, or prophesy, the explosive potential of an issue which was later to cause such turmoil in the Anglican church:

> Obviously, nothing could be more silly and inexpedient than to erect a new and totally unnecessary barrier between us and the rest of Catholic Christendom. (It would be rather a link than otherwise with some of the Free Churches, as tending to emphasise a ministry of the Gospel rather than a ministry of Sacraments and as involving a break with Apostolic tradition.)
>
> I fear you would find me an uneasy ally. I can never find any logical or strictly theological reason for it. In so far as the priest represents Christ, it is obviously

more dramatically appropriate that a man should be, so to speak, cast for the part. But if I were cornered and asked point-blank whether Christ Himself is the representative of male humanity or all humanity, I should be obliged to answer "of all humanity;" and to cite the authority of St. Augustine for saying that woman is also made in the image of God.[39]

On other occasions when discussing the issue of female ordination, Sayers was less petulant. She told her friend Barbara Reynolds that "considering Our Lord had the wisdom to be born as a man at the time when he was on earth, I think probably the whole thing is left better as it is."[40] In the course of editing Sayers's letters, Reynolds found further examples of her opposition to the ordination of women: "I found other letters in which she has said definitely that . . . when the churches are now showing signs of wanting to come together, this is something that will so alienate the Roman Catholic Church . . . that this is not something that I would want to promote."[41] This view was also expressed in her letter to Lewis, although it was coupled with an outright refusal to speak out on the issue: "It would be a pity to fly in the face of all the Apostolic Churches, especially just now when we are at last seeing some prospect of understanding with the Eastern Orthodox, and so on. . . . The most I can do is to keep silence in any place where the daughters of the Philistines might overhear me."[42]

For Lewis the silence was deafening, forcing him reluctantly to address the issue himself. Shortly after receiving the rebuff from Sayers, he wrote an article entitled "Priestesses in the Church?"[43] Lewis's tone was unusually apologetic, due possibly to the fear of being accused of misogyny which had been at the root of his desire that a woman should have written the article. Possibly with Sayers's reply in mind, he stressed that "no one among those who dislike the proposal is maintaining that women are less capable than men of piety, zeal, learning and whatever else seems necessary for the pastoral office." If women could preach as well as men, Lewis asked, why could they not do "all the rest of a priest's work"? The answer that Lewis gave to to such a question was rooted in a Catholic conception of the nature of priesthood: "We begin to feel that what really divides us from our opponents is a difference between the meaning which they and we give to the word 'priest.'" In line with the teaching of the Catholic Church, Lewis believed that the priesthood was not merely another "job" but was a mystical calling, sacramental in nature, which had been pre-ordained by God Himself as a masculine function as motherhood had been pre-ordained as a feminine function. Motherhood was eternally feminine; priesthood was eternally masculine:

> The innovators are really implying that sex is something superficial, irrelevant to the spiritual life. . . . One of the ends for which sex was created was to symbolize to us the hidden things of God. One of the functions of human marriage is to express the nature of the union between Christ and the Church. We have no authority to take the living and seminal figures which God has painted on the canvas of our nature and shift them about as if they were mere geometrical figures.
>
> This is what common sense will call "mystical." Exactly. The Church claims to be the bearer of revelation. If that claim is false then we want not to make priestesses but to abolish priests.[44]

As Lewis approached the end of his life there is little doubt that he was continuing the ascent towards the "High Church" principles of Anglo-Catholicism. There is also little doubt that the ascent was caused by his assent to those truly Catholic principles that represented not mere but more Christianity.

10

THE MERE AND THE MIRE

There is a good deal of Ulster still left in C. S. L. if hidden from himself

—*J. R. R. Tolkien*[1]

IN HIS final books, Lewis returned to the powerful influence of Dante, the quintessentially Catholic writer who had been a source of inspiration throughout the length of his literary career. *A Grief Observed,* inspired primarily and most potently by the death of his wife in July 1960, was also inspired by Dante's vision of hell and beyond. "The structure of it," Lewis explained to Walter Hooper, "is based on Dante's *Divine Comedy.* You go down and down and down. Then, as in Dante, when you hit bottom and pass Lucifer's waist you go *up* to defence of God's goodness."[2] In his final book, *Letters to Malcolm,* Lewis proclaimed that "Dante's Heaven is so right, and Milton's, with its military discipline, so silly."[3] He also employed Dante as an antidote to "the 'low' church *milieu* that I grew up in." Having recalled that his grandfather used to state that he "looked forward to having some very interesting conversations with St. Paul when he got to heaven," Lewis remarked on the preposterousness of the scenario thus imagined: "Two clerical gentlemen talking at ease in a club!" It never seems to have crossed his grandfather's mind that "an encounter with St. Paul might be rather an overwhelming experience even for an Evangelical clergyman of good family. But when Dante saw the great apostles in heaven they affected him like *mountains*."[4]

The most obvious effect of the lingering influence of Dante in the pages of *Letters to Malcolm* emerges in Lewis's reiteration of his belief in purgatory. "Of course I pray for the dead," he states categorically, describing his prayers for deceased friends as "spontaneous." He hardly knew how the rest of his prayers would survive "if those for the dead were forbidden." "At our age the majority of those we love best are dead. What sort of intercourse with God could I have if what I love best were unmentionable to Him?"[5] At this juncture, considering Lewis's injunction against the veneration of the saints, it is tempting to ask why God would make those that *He* loves best unmentionable to Him!

As usual, Lewis cannot announce his belief in a "papist" doctrine without attacking the "papists." He might be rejecting Protestantism and accepting one "papist" doctrine after another but he would not tolerate being called "Roman." Thus, after stating brazenly that "I believe in Purgatory," he defends the Reformers for throwing doubt on "the Romish doctrine concerning Purgatory." "If you turn from Dante's *Purgatorio* to the Sixteenth Century you will be appalled by the degradation," he states. Whereas Dante had the correct view of Purgatory, later "Romish" writers such as Saint Thomas More and Saint John Fisher emphasized the "retributive punishment" of purgatory, not its "purification." Regardless of whether Lewis's criticism of More and Fisher is justified, his logic is woefully awry. The "Reformers" did not quibble over whether Dante's view of purgatory was correct whereas the views of More and Fisher were wrong; they simply rejected the very existence of purgatory itself. Lewis is defending those who have thrown the baby out with the bathwater on the basis that those who had been charged previously with looking after the baby had failed to keep him as clean as they should.

The "right view" of purgatory "returns magnificently" in Newman's *Dream of Gerontius,* Lewis continues. Newman's *Dream* has the saved soul begging to be taken away and cleansed, re-establishing the purgative purity of purgatory. "Religion has reclaimed Purgatory," Lewis proclaims triumphantly. Which "religion," one wonders? Not the Protestants, nor the Anglicans. The Catholics, on the other hand, had never disowned it in the first place so had no need to reclaim that which had never been out of their possession. To which "religion," therefore, is Lewis referring? His own? Is Lewis making the ultimate mistake, according to his own criteria, of picking and choosing those doctrines he likes, much as a man in a supermarket selects products from the shelves? Is he concocting a do-it-yourself religion to suit his own preferences? If so, is he any different from the Modernists he criticizes? It is indeed ironic that Lewis should write elsewhere in *Letters to Malcolm* of the dangers of such picking and choosing to suit oneself: "Left to oneself, one could easily slide away from 'the faith once given' into a phantom called 'my religion.'"[6]

Certainly Newman did not believe that his "right view" had reclaimed purgatory for "religion." On the contrary, he believed that the "right view" of religion had claimed him. He accepted the "right view" of purgatory and the authority of the religion that proclaimed it as doctrine. Unlike Lewis, Newman saw the logic of his theological position. He responded by joining the Church of Dante, More, and Fisher. Newman joined the Faith of the Fathers; Lewis clung doggedly, but disbelievingly, to the faith of his grandfather. Newman genuflected before Authority and its Author; Lewis kowtowed before the traditions of his family and its prejudices, no longer believing what they believed, but unwilling or unable to make the break from them. Ultimately this is the tragicomic reality behind Lewis's merely Christian compromise.

In July 1963, three months after finishing his writing of *Letters to Malcolm,* Lewis suffered a heart attack and lapsed into a coma. Believing that he was dying, his Anglo-Catholic friends arranged for an Anglican clergyman to administer extreme unction, or the last rites, the sacrament of anointing with oil when a patient is *in extremis.* Since it can be safely presumed that Lewis's friends would have been aware that it would have been his desire to receive the Anglo-Catholic equivalent of the last rites, this can be taken as Lewis's acceptance of the seventh and final sacrament of the Catholic Church.

To everyone's surprise, Lewis woke from his coma and made a partial, if short-lived, recovery. "I was unexpectedly revived from a long coma," Lewis informed Sister Penelope, "and perhaps the almost continuous prayers of my friends did it—but it wd. have been a luxuriously easy passage, and one almost regrets having the door shut in one's face. . . . To be brought back and have all one's dying to do again was rather hard." Evidently, he was not expecting to wait long before having his "dying to do again" because his words to Sister Penelope conveyed a sense that he was signing off and bidding farewell to an old friend: "When you die, and if 'prison visiting' is allowed, come down and look me up in Purgatory."[7]

During his final illness Lewis was visited by Tolkien, which, considering their friendship, was not surprising. It was, however, a little surprising that Tolkien should bring his son,

Father John Tolkien, a Catholic priest, with him. Considering Tolkien's oft-expressed disappointment that Lewis had never converted to Catholicism, and his belief that Lewis's soul could be endangered should he fail to do so before his death, it is difficult to see his being accompanied by his son as anything other than an illustration of his hope that Lewis, at the last, would finally ask to be received into the Catholic Church. Lewis, however, showed no obvious inclination to convert and the two friends and the priest spent the time discussing the *Morte d'Arthur*.[8]

Lewis died on November 22, 1963. Two weeks later a letter from a Jesuit priest, Father Guy Brinkworth, published in the *Tablet*, suggested that Lewis, during the 1940s, had come close to conversion.

> In the letters I received from him, he time and time again asked specifically for prayers that God might give him "the light and grace to make the final gesture." He even went so far as to ask in a postscript to one of his letters for "prayers that the prejudices instilled in me by an Ulster nurse might be overcome."[9]

Unfortunately, by the time, seventeen years later, that Christopher Derrick, during the course of his research for *C. S. Lewis and the Church of Rome*, requested to see these letters, Father Brinkworth had lost them. One hesitates to suggest any dishonesty on the part of Father Brinkworth, so perhaps it is safest, in charity, to assume that Lewis was indeed considering conversion during the 1940s. Either way, Lewis never made the "final gesture" and, up to a point at least, the prejudices instilled by the Ulster nurse prevailed. This being so, perhaps it would be appropriate to look a little closer at the Belfast connection. To what extent was Lewis's sense and sensibility compromised by pride and prejudice?

Writing in *The Month* in May 1964, six months after Lewis's death and shortly after the posthumous publication of *Letters to Malcolm,* George Scott-Moncrieff, poet, novelist, and Scottish nationalist, wrote that Lewis, in his last book, was "concerned . . . with . . . taking the protest out of Protestantism." The problem, of course, was not so much the extent to which Lewis had succeeded in taking the protest out of Protestantism, as the extent to which he had failed to take the Protestantism out of himself. Scott-Moncrieff was, however, better placed than most to pass judgment on the struggle in Lewis between sense and sensibility, on the one hand, and pride and prejudice on the other. As a convert to Catholicism from a staunchly Protestant background, his own experiences paralleled those of Lewis to a remarkable degree. Born in 1910, he was the second son of the Reverend C. W. Scott-Moncrieff, a minister of the Church of Scotland. His grandparents were Presbyterians and his ancestors Covenanters, although his uncle Charles Scott-Moncrieff, the translator of Proust, Pirandello, and Stendhal, had broken with family tradition by converting to Catholicism when his nephew was still a child. Scott-Moncrieff, like Lewis, had imbibed the "no popery" rhetoric with his mother's milk. He shared the "supernatural dread" of Catholicism to which George Mackay Brown, another literary convert to Catholicism, referred in his short story "The Tarn and the Rosary."[10] Mackay Brown remembered as a child that "there was something sinister in the very word Catholic; all the words that clustered about it—rosary, pope, confession, relics, purgatory, monks, penance—had the same sinister connotations."[11] Scott-Moncrieff recalled, as a young man of twenty-five, witnessing an anti-Catholic riot in Edinburgh:

I remember bitterly the horror of seeing human beings, largely adolescents and women of disappointing mien, possessed beyond the reach of reason, screaming and rushing, ready for murder, upon the car in which Archbishop Andrew Joseph Macdonald drove up to the City Chambers. . . . This was "protest" and as such it was of the genesis of Protestantism. Whatsoever Protestantism had retained of Christianity . . . it seemed to me then to exist in distinction only as a negation, a protest against something that it did not appear even to wish to understand. . . .

I was not the only Protestant witness of those ugly scenes in the summer of 1935 who within a few years found himself no longer protestant, having progressively discovered how much of the stock picture of my country's history was mere myth.[12]

If this degree of hatred and bigotry could exist in the Orkneys of Mackay Brown's childhood or the Edinburgh of Scott-Moncrieff's reminiscence, how much more was it a factor in the formative psychology of those with their roots in Protestant Belfast? The asking of such a question is absolutely necessary to any understanding as to why Lewis failed, where Mackay Brown and Scott-Moncrieff succeeded, in overcoming the prejudices of childhood. Unfortunately, the asking of such a question is not the same as answering it. There are, however, clues to be gleaned from the lives of Lewis and his brother, Warnie, that throw some light on the shadow of Puritania and its lingering place in their respective psyches.

According to Christopher Derrick,[13] Warnie Lewis, at "some point in the early 1950s" was on the brink of making the "final gesture" himself. Suffering from alcoholism he found

himself, not for the first time, recovering under the care of the
Irish nuns at Our Lady of Lourdes Hospital in Drogheda,
County Louth, in the Republic of Ireland. "On this particular occasion . . . he felt moved to implement a long-standing
attrait towards Catholicism and actually embarked upon the
process of 'instruction,' preparatory to being received into the
Roman Catholic Church." As soon as his brother heard that
he was on the brink of succumbing to the seductions of the
"Scarlet Woman," he rushed to Ireland to rescue him from
her grasp. In his efforts to argue Warnie out of his intention,
Lewis became involved "in a long debate with the local priest,
a debate in which (according to Warren) Jack was thoroughly
worsted." In spite of apparently not being argued out of his
desire for conversion, Warnie allowed himself to be "coerced
into an immediate return to England."

> The point is that here, fairly late in his life, we see
> Lewis treating Catholicism as a fate from which his
> poor brother needed to be rescued. In that crisis, he
> seemed to have acted more like a Hamilton grandchild
> from Belfast than like a friend of Tolkien and lover of
> Dante.[14]

The source for this story, cited by Derrick, is that it was
"information received, through George Sayer, from Warren
Lewis." In other words, the source is the proverbial "horse's
mouth," albeit twice removed. It is at least possible that
George Sayer's memory was faulty. Compare, for instance, the
account given by Derrick with the entry in Warnie's diary for
June 30, 1947, which was not published until 1982, a year
after Derrick's book and therefore, presumably, unknown to
him:

On Friday 20th I realized I was a very sick man, and for once in a way showed some sense; [got hold of the local doctor, who got me into the Convent Hospital of Our Lady of Lourdes in Drogheda. . . . Rack] arrived, anxious and travel stained, on Monday morning, and the sight of him did me more good than any medicine. . . . From this moment I began to mend rapidly, and though I am still weak and shaky, I am obviously cured thanks to God and the Sisters of the Medical Missionaries of Mary. Once convalescent, I began to take a great interest in my surroundings. To the Protestant—or at any rate to me—there has always been something sinister, a little repulsive, almost ogreish, about the practice of the R.C. religion. So far as I had any idea of a convent, it was of something grey and secret, with sad faced women gliding about noiselessly; rarely speaking and never smiling, spying and spied upon. There could be nothing more preposterously unlike the truth: the first thing that strikes you is the radiant happiness of these holy and very loveable women, from Mother Mary Martin their superior down to the youngest novice: whatever else it is, it is a life of joy, and a place of laughter. As I got to know them better and gave them my preconceived ideas of conventual life, they exploded into delicious mirth. . . . I shall not soon or easily forget this little fortress of happy, valiant Christianity. The only bore was Father Quin, the chaplain, who would come to my room and try to convert me in a set piece oration: moreover, he was a Co. Tyrone man, and I could not explain to him that had he the tongue of men and angels, it would be ludicrously impossible for me to be converted by anyone talking with an Ulster accent!

> Finding J having tea with me one afternoon, he tackled him but here of course he caught a Tartar; his main point, if I understood him, seems to me to be absurd the honour of "our Lady" as the mother of *God*.[15]

Although Derrick states that Lewis's "rescuing" of his brother from the temptation to conversion was during a subsequent stay of convalescence at the convent, there are sufficient parallels in Warnie's diary entry for 1947 to raise the possibility, at least, of a faulty memory on Sayer's part. We see Warnie's prejudices being confronted by the holy example of the nuns but we see no temptation to convert; we see an argument between Lewis and the parish priest, though no suggestion that Lewis was "worsted."

There is also a further possible incongruity in Derrick's account. If one is to accept his version as true, what does one make of Warnie Lewis's later diatribes against the Catholic Church and his banging of the Orange drum of Ulster? On the Twelfth of July 1969, for example, wallowing in the pomp and circumstance of Ulster Protestant pride and prejudice, Warnie wrote of his sense of affinity with the bigotry of his native Belfast:

> Today is the greatest day on the calendar for us Ulster folk, the anniversary of the Battle of the Boyne in 1690 when William III and his Ulstermen beat James II and his Southerners—and it is in fact quite something to celebrate, for had we lost we would have been offered the alternative of becoming Roman Catholics or being hanged. By rights I ought to have an orange lily in my buttonhole this morning, but they do not seem to grow in these parts.[16]

A few months earlier he had written to another correspondent that, although he was "all in favour of the closest
collaboration between the various churches," he wanted no
"watering down of belief." Since "union without such a watering down" was impossible, he took a sectarian view, namely,
that "communion administered by anyone other than an
Ordained priest of my own church would not be a sacrament
at all."[17] Thus, on the assumption that the story about his earlier desire for conversion is true, Warnie had metamorphosed
from one who wanted to become a Catholic into one who
believed that the sacraments of the Catholic Church were not
even valid!

Having taken the sectarian position, if his words are to
be taken literally, that the Anglican church is the only true
church, Warnie seemed singularly uncomfortable as a member of it. "I am out of sympathy with all forms of Low Church,
if for no other reason, then because of their fanatical hatred
of the Cross; and as for the Anglo-Catholics they strike me as
plus royaliste que roi, more Roman than the Romans."[18]

Most shocking of all were Warnie's words about the situation in Ulster in August 1969, shortly after the recurrence of
the "Troubles" that would escalate so tragically in the years
that followed.

> Yes, my poor Ulster is passing through a bad patch,
> but I've seen many such before. The tragedy is that
> Protestant and Catholic are . . . *born* hating each other.
> I'm 3rd generation Ulster on my father's side and on my
> mother's, 5th; I've lived out of Ulster for fifty years: and
> the other night when I saw on the telly the Protestant
> boys marching and heard the band playing "The Boyne
> Water" I felt as if I could throw a bomb with the best of

them. Of course I said an instant prayer of forgiveness, but if I can react like that, imagine what the uneducated living cheek and jowl with their detested neighbours must be like! A sad, sad business.[19]

It would, of course, be perverse to ascribe Warnies's views to those of his brother but, considering that we are led to believe that, at one point at least, Warnie was far closer to Rome than was Lewis, his words might be more indicative of the gut feeling of both men than we might otherwise suspect. Certainly the strange schismatic schizophrenia that is present to such an alarming degree in Warnie's letters was present, albeit more mildly, in much of Lewis's confused ecclesiology also.

In a recently discovered letter by George Sayer to Dame Felicitas Corrigan,[44] Sayer seems to confirm Tolkien's belief that Lewis never managed to shake off his Ulster Protestant prejudices:

> He [Lewis] never recovered from his N. I. Prot [i.e., Northern Ireland Protestant] attitude to Our Lady. His grandfather Hamilton, the local Belfast vicar, was violently anti-R.C. [i.e., Roman Catholic]. But Tolkien in a letter to me (still unpublished) wrote: "I attribute whatever there is of beauty and goodness in my work to the influence of the Holy Mother of God."[45]

The sad truth is that Lewis, as regards Protestant Ulster, never managed to emulate the example of George Scott-Moncrieff, as regards Scotland. Whereas Scott-Moncrieff had "progressively discovered how much of the stock picture of my country's history was mere myth," Lewis's enslavement to "mere Christianity" was a product of his enslavement to the "mere myth" of Orange Ulster. Since the "papist" option was unthinkable for a Protestant Ulsterman, "mere Christianity" was Lewis's effort to escape the mire of modernism without submitting to the "Church of Rome." Unfortunately, however, and ironically, the merely Christian compromise would place him in an increasingly compromising position. As the mire of modernism advanced relentlessly within the Anglican church, C. S. Lewis, the most "Catholic" Protestant that Protestant Belfast had ever produced, would find himself increasingly isolated as a "protestant" Catholic within the Anglican communion. Everyman's theologian would find himself in no-man's-land. The mere would find itself in the mire.

MIRE CHRISTIANITY

The Modernists seem to me a far greater danger to
Christianity than the atheists.

—Letter to Miss Breckenridge (1960)[1]

A theology which denies the historicity of nearly everything in the Gospels to which Christian life and affec-
tions and thought have been fastened for nearly two
millennia . . . if offered to the uneducated man can
produce only one or other of two effects. It will make
him a Roman Catholic or an atheist.

—Fern Seed and Elephants (1959)[2]

IN HIS article "Priestesses in the Church?," Lewis warned
of the practical dangers of female ordination. Apart from
his objections in principle to such a move, he warned his
fellow Anglicans that the ordination of women would have
far-reaching consequences: "to cut ourselves off" from the
Christian past and to widen the divisions between ourselves
and other Churches by establishing an order of priestesses in
our midst, would be an almost wanton degree of imprudence.
And the Church of England herself would be torn in shreds
by the operation."[3] Walter Hooper has described these words
as "extraordinarily prophetic,"[4] and there is little doubt that

the issue has proved an explosively divisive force within the Church of England in the forty years since Lewis's death. The issue was itself, however, merely symptomatic of a more prevalent problem within the Anglican communion—the debilitating theological disease of modernism.

Lewis had written in 1960 that the modernists were "a far greater danger to Christianity than the atheists," a belief that was reflected in his sardonic depiction of modernists such as Mr. Broad in *The Pilgrim's Regress* and the ghost of the doggedly undogmatic Bishop in *The Great Divorce.* These characters were also "extraordinarily prophetic," in the sense that they would become incarnate in a new proliferation of modernist theologians and bishops within the Church of England.

In 1963, as Lewis entered his final illness, the publication of *Honest to God* by the doubting Bishop of Woolwich, J. A. T. Robinson, must have raised the specter of Modernism Ascendant to the ailing Lewis. If Christianity were to mean anything in the future to more than "a tiny religious remnant," the Bishop had argued, it would have to learn a new language in which "the most fundamental categories of our theology, of the supernatural, and of religion itself—must go into the melting pot." He suggested that Christianity needed a "Copernican Revolution" in which "the God of traditional theology" must be given up "in any form."[5]

As Lewis learned of the remarkable success of *Honest to God,* a publishing phenomenon—the book would sell almost a million copies within three years—he might have felt that he was actually being haunted by one of his own literary creations. Was the ubiquitous Bishop of Woolwich the shade of Mr. Broad or the ghost of the unbelieving Bishop from *The Great Divorce* who, on "holiday from Hell," had come to plague him in his final days?

The differences between Lewis and the Bishop of Woolwich were discussed saliently and succinctly by Adrian Hastings in his *History of English Christianity.* "In this [*Honest to God*], as in several of his other books, John Robinson was with little doubt the most effective writer of popular religious literature since C. S. Lewis, if in many ways Lewis's opposite. Both were highly persuasive. Lewis was . . . suspicious of modernity, unwilling to allow the smallest particle of traditional doctrine to be thrown overboard unexamined. Robinson was . . . apparently willing to de-mythologize almost anything of which modernity might conceivably be suspicious."[6]

Dismissing Robinson with humorous contempt as "The Bishop of Woolworth,"[7] Lewis nonetheless saw the danger that he represented, while at the same time refusing to be drawn into the controversy surrounding the book. "I had rather keep off Bishop Robinson's book," Lewis wrote on April 22, 1963. "I should find it hard to write of such a man with charity, nor do I want to increase the publicity."[8] One wonders, however, whether Lewis began to perceive in Robinson's best-selling *Honest to God* his own nemesis. His own powers were waning; Bishop Robinson's were waxing. Perhaps he saw in the "Bishop of Woolworth" the hideous shape of things to come.

As far back as 1945, Lewis had warned of the dangers of modernism, the mire Christianity that was "mere Christianity's" deadliest enemy. "A 'liberal' Christianity which considers itself free to alter the faith whenever the Faith looks perplexing or repellant *must* be completely stagnant."[9] The mere was, therefore, threatened by, and was in danger of sinking into, the mire. These words of Lewis, indubitably true in themselves, were a reiteration of Chesterton's anti-modernist rejoinder that we did not need a Church that would move *with* the world but a Church that would *move* the world. The words were more problematic, however, when seen within the context of Lewis's own singularly "mere Christian" position. Although, for instance, he occasionally placed allegorical representations of modern "modernists" in hell, he was always unwilling to criticize those "modernists" during the Reformation who felt "free to alter the faith" because the faith looked perplexing and repellent. This perplexing question came to the fore shortly before Lewis's death when a literary agent and a publisher proposed that a book about heresies should be commissioned. Lewis was consulted, and he gave his blessing to the project; yet, curiously, he sought to limit the book's scope. "Would a limitation, say down to 1400, be a good plan, so that it can remain a historical fact book and not become controversial?"[10] Commenting on these words, Christopher Derrick wrote that Lewis "clearly wanted the Reformation period to be excluded . . . as though 'heresy' was a matter of historical fact before that period, but during and after that period, a regrettably controversial matter about which it would be best to keep silent."[11] In essence, Lewis was stating that only "dead" heresies should be written about because, being dead, they were safe; living heresies, those arising out of the differences of the Reformation, should be avoided because, being alive, they were dangerous. Thus the danger goes unchallenged and is, presumably, left to thrive. Take, for instance, Lewis's refusal to be drawn into the debate over the modernism of *Honest to God.* Refusing to comment on Bishop Robinson's book, Lewis had written: "A great deal of my utility has depended on my having kept out of all dog-fights between professing schools of 'Christian' thought. I'd sooner preserve that abstinence to the end."[12] In these circumstances, the tacit acceptance of the limits of mere Christianity becomes an obstacle to the effective war against error. The mere actually becomes the mire.

As far as the present position of Lewis's "mere Christianity" is concerned, forty years after his death, it can be seen that its place within the Anglican church has become extremely tenuous. Posterity has shown that the war for the heart of Anglicanism between the "mere Christianity" of Lewis and the "mire Christianity" of modernism has resulted in the triumph of the latter.

Mercifully perhaps, Lewis died thirty years before his fears about the ordination of women became reality. The "almost wanton degree of imprudence" of "establishing an order of priestesses in our midst" has materialized and, as Lewis predicted, the Church of England has been "torn in shreds by the operation." Since the Anglican church has decided to cut itself off from the Christian past by making the priesthood merely another "job" and not a pre-ordained and masculine function instituted by Christ, where does it leave Anglicanism in the context of Lewis's definition of "mere Christianity"? Having moved so far in the modernist direction since Lewis's death, has Anglicanism become something less than "merely Christian"? If so, where would Lewis stand in relation to the Anglican church were he alive today? Perhaps this is ultimately unanswerable but, even so, it remains a perfectly pertinent question.

The question is certainly one that aroused the mischievous speculation of Lewis's friend Christopher Derrick. In 1996, Derrick mused over Lewis's likely reaction to the victory of the modernists in the Church of England.

> There was a rumour that he had Poped or that he was a
> Jesuit in disguise . . . literary men becoming Catholics

had been a phenomenon, and Lewis's conversion did seem likely to some but . . . I don't think he would have liked to have seen his own infallibility challenged by that of another Pope.

. . . it's difficult to imagine what he would make of today's Church of England. The Church of England is such a pathetic ghost nowadays. . . . You can't agree with it or disagree with it. There's nothing there.[13]

Derrick's imagery of the Church of England as a "pathetic ghost" is particularly potent. One imagines Lewis returning to *The Great Divorce,* after his real death, and meeting the ghost of the unbelieving Bishop for a second time. This time, however, he finds that the skeptic-souled ghost does not represent merely an heretical imaginary Bishop, nor even the real ghost of the "Bishop of Woolworth;" he discovers, to his horror, that it represents the Anglican church itself. What, for instance, would Lewis have made of the recent book by the Anglican Bishop of Oxford that criticizes the "outdated and chauvinist" assumption that God is a man? It was necessary, wrote the Right Reverend Richard Harries, in order to encourage greater understanding of the needs of women, to "alter our language and mental image of God." Christ could be seen "as mother" and the Holy Spirit "as feminine." Ann Widdicombe, a senior British politician who left the Church of England to become a Roman Catholic, responded to the Bishop's feminism in a manner which one imagines Lewis would have approved: "I think the bishop should remember that Jesus himself referred to God the Father. I have no time for arguments like this which simply empty the pews."[14] Fortunately, we know exactly how Lewis would have responded to the current Bishop of Oxford because, in August 1948, he had written:

Suppose the reformer stops saying that a good woman may be like God and begins by saying that God is like a good woman. Suppose he says that we might just as well pray to "Our Mother which art in Heaven" as to "Our Father." Suppose he suggests that the Incarnation might just as well have taken a female as a male form, and the Second Person of the Trinity be as well called the Daughter as the Son. Suppose, finally, that the mystical marriage were reversed, that the Church were the Bridegroom and Christ the Bride. All this, as it seems to me, is involved in the claim that a woman can represent God as a priest does. Now it is surely the case that if all these supposals were ever carried into effect we should be embarked on a different religion.[15]

Taking Lewis at his word, it would seem that Anglicanism is not merely sinking into the realm of mire Christianity, it is sinking beneath Christianity altogether into a new sub-Christian religion—a new religion in which priests are replaced by priestesses, and God, by a goddess.

It might of course be argued that the Bishop of Oxford is merely a rather eccentric oddity within the Church of England and that his views need not be taken too seriously. Presumably, one could not be quite so dismissive of the Archbishop of Canterbury, the most senior member of the Anglican hierarchy and, in theory at least, the one who speaks with most authority. At the beginning of August 2002, Rowan Williams, the new Archbishop, officially became a Druid, signifying at least a tacit compliance with the neopaganism that the modern Druids represent.

Even more scandalous was the result of a survey of two thousand Anglican clergymen carried out only a week before their most senior member became a Druid. The survey revealed that a third of Church of England clergymen do not believe in the Resurrection of Christ and that only half believed in the Virgin Birth. The survey also revealed that priestesses were more likely to be unbelievers than their male counterparts, with only a third of those questioned professing a belief in the Virgin Birth. Although a spokesman for a group called Cost of Conscience described the results of the survey as "a scandal," a representative of the Modern Churchperson's Union remarked that it simply illustrated that the church needed to "reassess" its doctrines "in the face of increasingly educated congregations."[16] Again, one hears echoes of the unbelieving Bishop from *The Great Divorce*, who might be termed the Ghost of Modernism Past, in the presence of the "Modern Churchperson's Union" representing the Spirit of Modernism Present. One can imagine Mr. Broad from *The Pilgrim's Regress* as the official "spokesperson" of the Modern Churchperson's Union (the very name of which warrants the allegorical attention of Lewis or, better still, the satirical ridicule of Waugh). Whereas the Churchpersons' spokesperson had spoken superciliously of "reassessing" doctrine based on the prejudiced presumption that "modern educated" congregations knew better than their primitive, backward, barbaric and, most damnable of all, "uneducated" forebears, Mr. Broad had spoken of the "very real danger" of making doctrines "too definite," and the burden of being "shackled to the formulae of dead men": "I don't say that they were not adequate once: but they have ceased to be adequate for us with our wider knowledge."[17] One also notices the ghost of the Unbelieving Bishop nodding sagely and quoting from his paper on the immaturity of Christ. "What a different Christianity we might have had if only the Founder had reached his full stature!" he muses.[18] "Or if He had been a She," interjects the Modern Churchperson. "Or a homosexual. . . ." Deep sighs all round. What Christianity might have been if only God had been more educated. . . .

Perhaps it is hardly surprising that Lewis's "mere Christianity" is now out of fashion in the Church of England. This brings us back to the "pertinent question." Exactly where would C. S. Lewis stand were he alive today? Russell Kirk, an American political philosopher, was asked at a conference in Seattle in 1990 whether he believed "T. S. Eliot and C. S. Lewis would have stayed in the Church of England had they been alive today." Kirk replied that he thought it "extremely unlikely for both of them but particularly so for Eliot."[19] Kirk's judgment is shared by Walter Hooper, Lewis's friend and most loyal defender. Asked in 1994 "whether Lewis would have become Catholic if he had lived longer," Hooper replied:

> I think so. . . . One of the last papers that he wrote was to Anglican seminarians in Cambridge. And in that well-known paper—called *Fern-seed and Elephants* he points out that, if they continue to talk that sort of liberalism that they were then talking—and increasingly more now—he said that their readers and hearers would leave the Anglican church and become either atheists or Roman Catholics, I think he would probably have had to include himself in that group. What do you do, when, in fact, the Anglican church becomes apostate—as it has truly become right now? Long before the Vatican gave us the document *Inter insigniores* in 1976, which is the statement on the ordination of women to the priesthood, Lewis had written about

the issue. . . . [H]is arguments about the priest standing in the place of Christ . . . are almost exactly those you find in the Vatican document. But I would stress the fact that his main point was that if you continued to talk about, say, God the Father, as a "she," and if you do have the ordained woman, it would be hard to resist that trend, and then you will have to change religions. . . . And so, it may be that if you find your religion has just changed, what else can you do except go where the faith actually still is Christian?[20]

Walter Hooper was an Anglican clergyman until his conversion to Catholicism in 1988, largely over the issue of priestesses. It could, therefore, be argued that, as a loyal devotee of Lewis and his legacy, he is himself the embodiment of Lewis's position projected into the future, forty years beyond his mentor's death.

We can't know for certain what Lewis would have done had he lived to see the triumph of modernism in the Church of England and the defeat of "mere Christianity." There is no doubt, however, that he would have felt strangely out of place in today's Anglican church. There is also no doubt that today's Anglican church sees him as a somewhat embarrassing part of their unenlightened and reactionary past. The sobering truth is that even if Lewis had not chosen to leave the Church of England, the Church of England has chosen to leave him. If this is so, who is still reading the books of C. S. Lewis? If not the Anglicans, who is responsible for his continuing popularity? Walter Hooper, as literary executor to the C. S. Lewis estate, is more qualified than anyone else to answer such a question:

I can say with absolute confidence that more and more Catholics are buying his books now because most of the translations that I've seen in recent years . . . have come from Catholic countries. In many instances it is Catholic publishers who are translating Lewis, as in Italy. The same is true in Spain where the translations are the work of Opus Dei—so we know that Catholics are reading them in vast numbers throughout the world. We know of course that there are a great many Protestants who read Lewis but I think there is a shift since he died insofar as he is read a great deal by the evangelical Protestants and less and less by the liberals. I don't think you would find that as many average Anglicans read him not liberal Anglicans, they wouldn't read him. I was surprised to see what used to be a very Anglo-Catholic magazine from America now saying "why did we ever read Lewis, he's far too doctrinal, he's far too Roman Catholic for us now." But there are still many Protestants out there, in this country and in the United States and many other countries, who admire Lewis for the same reason the Catholics do. They are supernaturalists and they need him as their ally in this battle. Lewis said in *Mere Christianity* that Christianity is a fighting religion and it looks as though only the evangelical Protestants and the Catholics are willing to get their hands dirty and fight. But the battle must have many soldiers in it because the number of Lewis's books which are read today is far in excess of anything that happened in his own lifetime.[21]

Lewis, it seems, has been abandoned by his own church but embraced by Catholics and evangelical Protestants. It is, therefore, a little ironic that his "mere Christianity," intended as a *via media* or center ground of traditional Christianity, is embraced by two such diverse theological traditions. Since Lewis insisted on the sacraments and the Creed as being necessary parts of "mere Christianity," it is clear that Protestants have to reach beyond their own beliefs if they are to embrace fully the beliefs of Lewis. In order to become "mere Christians," in Lewis's sense, they need to become *more* Christian. Catholics, on the other hand, are faced with the absence in Lewis's "mere Christianity" of certain doctrines that are central to the faith as taught by the Church. In other words, for a faithful Catholic, Lewis's "mere Christianity" is deficient; it is *less* Christian than the Church.

So much for the position of Protestants and Catholics in relation to "mere Christianity;" what about the position of Lewis himself in relation to it? "I hope no reader will suppose that 'mere' Christianity is here put forward as an alternative to the creeds of the existing communions," he wrote at the conclusion to the preface to *Mere Christianity.* It is not a home, still less Home, but merely a means to find the way Home. To use Lewis's specific analogy, it could be likened to "a hall out of which doors open into several rooms." The duty of everyone who arrives in the hall is to find which is the true room: "And above all you must be asking which door is the true one; not which pleases you best by its paint and paneling." [22]

Life, therefore, is the Quest for the True Door which leads one into the True Home.

Lewis clearly believed that he had found his True Home in Anglicanism. Yet, posthumously, he has been made homeless. He doesn't belong in the room he believed was the true one. He is not welcome there. Where then does he belong? Where is his Home? The Ultimate Home is, of course, with God in paradise; until or unless we reach that Home we remain in exile. Perhaps, however, considering that Lewis seems to have chosen the wrong door, it is not too fanciful to suggest that he will have to find his way to paradise via purgatory. Such a suggestion is hardly judgmental, considering that Lewis, a few weeks before he died, had written whimsically and wistfully to Sister Penelope that she should "look me up in Purgatory." Lewis was clearly expecting to go there.

Perhaps Lewis might come to realize, as part of his purgation, that the Anglican church was never the true room that he believed it to be. Perhaps, beyond the lands of shadow, it will be exposed as merely a Screwtaped illusion. Having desecrated the "Bare ruined choirs where late the sweet birds sang,"[23] the Church of England might appear to Lewis's newly opened eyes as "a separated porch."[24] slowly sinking into the swamps of quagmire "Christianity."

The final words are neither mine nor Lewis's, but Maurice Baring's. Entitled "Vita Nuova" and written after Baring's reception into the Catholic Church in 1909, they serve as both an epitaph for Lewis and as an epilogue to my book on his troubled relationship with the Church. Most important of all they serve as an epiphany of the new life that awaits the faithful soul "after this our exile" . . .

> One day I heard a whisper: "Wherefore wait?
> Why linger in a separated porch?
> Why nurse the flicker of a severed torch?
> The fire is there, ablaze beyond the gate.
> Why tremble, foolish soul? Why hesitate?
>
> However faint the knock it will be heard."
> I knocked, and swiftly came the answering word,
> Which bade me enter to my own estate.
> I found myself in a familiar place;

And there my broken soul began to mend;
I knew the smile of every long-lost face—

They whom I had forgot remembered me;
I knelt, I knew—it was too bright to see—
The welcome of a King who was my friend.

APPENDIX

C. S. LEWIS AND
CATHOLIC CONVERTS

THE GREAT American literary convert, Walker Percy, commenting on the numerous converts who had come to Catholicism through the writings of C. S. Lewis, remarked that "writers one might expect, from Aquinas to Merton," are mentioned frequently as influences, "but guess who turns up most often? C. S. Lewis!—who, if he didn't make it all the way, certainly handed over a goodly crew."[1] Here is an overview of some of the "goodly crew" to whom Percy alludes, those who have been influenced on their paths to Rome by C. S. Lewis. As the present author owes his own conversion, in part, to the works and wisdom of Lewis, it is gratifying to know that he is but one of many whom Lewis led Romewards.

Beginning with prominent British converts, the most famous is Group Captain **Leonard Cheshire**, who attained position number 31 in a BBC poll in 2002 to find the 100 Greatest Britons of all time. He was also listed in 1993 as one of "the 20 outstanding Christians of the twentieth century," alongside John Paul II, Dorothy Day, Thomas Merton, Simone Weil, Oscar Romero, Edith Stein, Martin Luther King, Billy Graham, Dietrich Bonhoeffer, Padre Pio, Albert Schweitzer, Desmond Tutu, John XXIII, Teilhard de Chardin,

Jackie Pullinger, Charles de Foucauld, Malcolm Muggeridge, Mother Teresa, and, last but not least, C. S. Lewis.[2]

Group Captain Cheshire is best known as the fearless commander of the famous "Dam Busters" squadron during World War Two, later the subject of an award-winning movie starring Richard Todd and Michael Redgrave. He received the Victoria Cross, the highest military honor awarded by the British monarch to members of the armed forces of the British Commonwealth, for exceptional bravery in the face of the enemy. He was also the official British observer of the dropping of the atom bomb on Nagasaki in 1945. This event, coupled with the general experience of warfare over the preceding six years, led him to a deep skepticism about the future of modern civilization. It was in this frame of mind and heart that Cheshire found himself receptive to the works of Christian apologists, including those of Lewis, whose broadcast talks for the BBC were being published at this time. Grappling with the problem of evil and sin, he had been particularly impressed by *The Screwtape Letters* which he described as "a rather good introduction to the Faith" and as "very compelling": "[R]eading through *The Screwtape Letters*, I could see myself in it and many of the sort of things that I went through."[3]

Cheshire was received into the Catholic Church on Christmas Eve, 1948. For the rest of his life, until his death in 1992, he would be a tireless worker for charity, especially on behalf of the disabled, and with his wife, Sue Ryder, also a convert, whom he married in 1959, he would establish some of the most successful and best known charities in the United Kingdom.

An earlier convert to Catholicism under Lewis's benign influence was Allan Griffiths, later **Dom Bede Griffiths,**

O.S.B. Lewis and Griffiths actually contributed to each other's conversion, so much so that Lewis considered Griffiths his "chief companion" on the road to Christianity.[4]

Lewis recalled in one of his letters that Griffiths had been "all mucked up with naturalism, D. H. Lawrence, and so on," when he had first arrived as an undergraduate at Magdalen College in 1925.[5] Lewis was Griffiths' tutor, becoming a significant influence on his student, though not, at first, in the direction of Christianity. "Lewis was at that time no more of a Christian than I was," Griffiths wrote, "but he had been through the same phase of romanticism as I was then passing through, and had reached a more rational philosophy of life."[6]

By the beginning of 1930, Lewis was referring to Griffiths as "my friend and former pupil" and was writing him long letters "on philosophical subjects."[7] It was a philosophical discussion between Griffiths, Lewis, and their mutual friend, Owen Barfield, which would prove instrumental in edging Lewis closer to Christianity (see page 66 of the present volume). It was clear by this stage of their respective journeys that the former pupil had now emerged from the shadow of his teacher and was prepared to make his own way towards conversion. The main influence on Griffiths' final approach to Rome was John Henry Newman. Griffiths would go on to follow a religious vocation with the Benedictines, eventually settling in India and authoring many books. Shortly before his death in 1993, an Australian film crew completed *A Human Search*, a film about his life.

Another of Lewis's former students to take the path to Rome was **George Sayer**. In the preface to his very fine biography of Lewis, Sayer recalled his first meeting with his new tutor. The two men discussed poetry and discovered a shared love for Chesterton's *Ballad of the White Horse*, which Lewis declaimed with gusto. As with Griffiths, Sayer would become a valued and trusted friend. He was one of relatively few students whom Lewis invited to his home. Years later, after Sayer had become an English Master at Malvern College, Lewis would visit him often, taking long walks with him in the Malvern Hills.

Sayer had been an atheist upon his arrival at Oxford in 1933 and it is not unreasonable to presume that Lewis, who had embraced Christianity less than two years earlier, had influenced his student in the direction of Christian belief. As with Griffith, however, Sayer began to feel the attraction of Catholicism and was received into the Church in 1935, whilst he was still Lewis's student. According to Walter Hooper, it was "almost certainly" Sayer to whom Lewis was referring in a letter to Griffiths in January 1936:

> "Neo-Scholasticism" has become such a fashion among ignorant undergrads that I am sick of the sound of it. A man who was an atheist two terms ago and admitted into your Church last term, and who had never read a word of philosophy, comes to me urging me to read the *Summa* and offering me a copy![8]

Another Oxford graduate who converted under Lewis's influence was **Meriol Trevor**, author of almost forty novels, as well as biographies of John XXIII, James II, and St. Philip Neri. Her two-volume biography of John Henry Newman was particularly highly acclaimed, winning the James Tait Black Memorial Prize for Biography in 1962.

Born in 1919 in London, Trevor had repudiated Christianity by the time she arrived in Oxford, from which she graduated in Greats in 1942. It was largely through the reading of C. S. Lewis that she became a Christian. After the war, she lived for a year in the Abruzzo region of central Italy, experiencing an indigenous Catholic culture for the first time. This positive experience led her towards the Church, which she entered in 1950. Following her death in January 2000, a writer in the UK's *Guardian* newspaper, paying tribute to her work, claimed that her children's stories were "often more successful in conveying the tenets of Christian faith through a fantasy format than C. S. Lewis's fiction,"[9] a flattering appraisal with which few presumably would concur.

Although Meriol Trevor's award-winning two volume biography of Newman is highly respected, her achievement as a Newman scholar has been eclipsed by that of **Fr. Ian Ker**, author of more than twenty books on Newman, including the generally acknowledged definitive biography published by Oxford University Press in 1990, on the centenary of Newman's death.

The lives of these two Newman scholars parallel each other in several significant respects. Like Trevor, though twenty or so years later, Ker went to Oxford University after having repudiated the Christianity with which he'd been raised. He ceased attending church upon his arrival at Oxford but, whilst an undergraduate, fell under the influence of Lewis, especially Lewis's books, *Surprised by Joy* and *Mere Christianity*. Like Trevor, he had a conversion experience in Italy, which brought him back to the practice of his Anglican faith. His final conversion to Catholicism would be influenced by his ongoing reading of the works of Lewis:

> It seemed to me that either you take the line that Christ
> is indeed God, or a bad man, as Lewis argues . . . in
> *Mere Christianity*. And it seemed to me the same was
> true of the papacy. I couldn't see how Anglo-Catholics

could avoid the papacy. . . . Either the Pope is the Vicar of Christ or he is the Anti-Christ .... You couldn't take a kind of halfway position. That seemed to me to be totally unreal because the Pope made certain claims and his Church makes claims for him and these had to be taken seriously.[10]

Having followed his vocation to the priesthood, Fr. Ker would go on to teach theology in universities in both Britain and the United States. He was for a time Catholic chaplain to the University of Oxford and is now a member of the Theology Faculty at Oxford University and is a Senior Research Fellow at Blackfriars in Oxford.

Like Father Ker, **John Redford** was raised as an Anglican, lapsed from the practice of his faith as a teenager, and came back to Anglicanism after reading the works of Lewis. After becoming a deacon in the Church of England he converted to Catholicism and was subsequently ordained to the priesthood. He is currently a lecturer in Scripture and Revelation Theology and is director of the graduate programs in theology and apologetics at Maryvale Institute in Birmingham. As was the case with Father Ker, the "mad, bad, or God" argument employed by Lewis in *Mere Christianity* was pivotal in Father Redford's conversion. This key aspect of Lewis's thought was central to the argument in Father Redford's book, *Bad, Mad or God?: Proving the Divinity of Christ from St. John's Gospel* (2004) and was also integral to his short book, *The Truth About Jesus*, published in 2006 to rebut the nonsense and hype surrounding *The Da Vinci Code*. In the latter book, Father Redford summarizes the persuasiveness of Lewis's argument:

What persuaded [C. S. Lewis] about the truth of Christian faith was the following argument, which he called "Bad, Mad or God?". Jesus claimed to be God, Lewis said. . . . If he did so claim, you could not understand that he was just a good man. If he made such a stupendous claim, he had either to be bad, a deceiver; or he had to be mad, like those unfortunate patients in a psychiatric hospital who have delusions of grandeur.

But, argues Lewis, the Gospels show us a man who is neither bad nor mad. On the contrary, all agree that Jesus of Nazareth was wise and sane. Furthermore, Lewis said, if God wishes to give us a revelation to believe, a God become man, that person would have to do mighty deeds to prove his credentials; like walk on the water and feed five thousand people with five loaves and two fishes; as well as being morally good. This is precisely what we find in the Gospel accounts.

After a lifetime's study of the four Gospels, I buy into that argument.[11]

One of the most unlikely converts to be helped on his path to Rome by Lewis was the German economist, **E. F. Schumacher**, who became known throughout the world in the early seventies as the author of the international bestseller, *Small Is Beautiful*. Schumacher was influenced by Catholic saints, such as Thomas Aquinas, Augustine, Teresa of Avila, and John of the Cross, and by an array of Catholic writers, including Dante, G. K. Chesterton, Jacques Maritain, Etienne Gilson, and F. C. Copleston. His *weltanschauung* was transformed by the social encyclicals of a succession of modern popes, particularly Leo XIII, Pius XI, John XXIII and Paul VI. There were, however, two very significant non-Catholics who nudged Schumacher in the direction of conversion. The first was Dorothy L. Sayers, whose writings on Dante's

Divine Comedy helped to re-shape Schumacher's understanding of the nature of man; the second was C. S. Lewis, whose books were a prized part of his personal library and whom his daughter recalled as someone her father admired.

Three prominent British journalists who were brought closer to Catholicism through the reading of Lewis, and who subsequently converted, were **William Oddie**, former editor of the *Catholic Herald*, **David Quinn**, former editor of the *Irish Catholic*, and **Michael Coren**, a well-known TV and radio talk show host and regular newspaper columnist in Canada, to which he moved from his native England in 1987. Amongst Coren's published books are biographies of Lewis, Tolkien, and Chesterton.

"My conversion to the Church came in stages, culminating in 1985," Coren wrote. "As a six-year-old I sat in awe and delight as a teacher read *The Lion, the Witch and the Wardrobe* to my school class. I rushed home and asked my mother to buy me the book. She did, I read it, and I am convinced that the seeds of my faith were planted there and then. It took another twenty years for me to find the courage to walk through Narnia and swim across the Tiber, but the journey was always inevitable."[12] Coren is convinced that Lewis was himself pretty close to the Tiber in his last years, without ever taking the plunge into its life-promising waters: "My great friend Walter Hooper, Lewis's secretary at the end of his life, always insists that Jack was effectively a Catholic in his later years, even though not formally a member of the Church. I think this is inescapable when you genuinely understand his theology and its development. One of the many wonders of his writing is that because he is not thought to be Catholic by most evangelicals, they still read him; after that, they move closer and closer to the Church, and then make the final decision."[13]

Having crossed the Atlantic with Michael Coren, it is time to move south of the border from Canada to look at some of the best known American Catholics who have swam the Tiber having been prompted to do so through the works of Lewis.

Al Kresta, who, like Coren, is a seasoned radio talk show host, recalls Lewis's role in his own conversion:

> I first encountered Lewis in 1973 while at Michigan State University and under the "New Age" influence of Edna, an aging harpist and Beulah, the massive grandmother of a multitude. Both channeled messages from the Ascended Masters, radiant, powerful beings who governed the spiritual evolution of the human race from higher realms of consciousness. We *chelas*, i.e., disciples, worked to purify our desires, live ascetically, and achieve release from our karmic debt. After many reincarnations, we would ascend into the company of these Masters. I lived the discipline and read hundreds of their channeled dictations; yet I found myself no closer to godhood. Worse, their dictations were cliched, insipid, and repetitious. Our Masters may have raised their bodies from this earth but they would never ascend beyond a D+ in any creative writing class.
>
> I happened upon Lewis in his essay headlined, "Man or Rabbit?" Irritably, I said, "What a stupid question." Then his first line asked: "Can't you lead a good life without believing in Christianity?" Now that *was* a good question. I longed to reconcile the non-Christian, Ascended Masters' instructions with Christianity. But all religions could not be "one," as the Masters taught, if some spiritual leaders were legitimately dubbed "false

prophets" as this Lewis taught. Later, his "trilemma" argued that Jesus was God in human flesh, not merely one of many ascended masters. A Savior was necessary, he wrote, contra the Masters, who urged all to discover their own divinity. The Masters belittled reason. Lewis, however, exercised intellectual courage and met all objections. Further, Lewis's words embraced reality with a simplicity, clarity and colourfulness that was wise, not merely pious. Having once thought that spiritual truths were purely subjective and beyond rational discussion, I rejoiced in Lewis's reasoned presentation. Christianity was true to the way things are, good not merely pragmatic, beautiful not merely utilitarian, and true not merely consoling.

In March of 1974, largely through Lewis, my allegiance finally shifted from the New Age Jesus to the Jesus of the New Testament. Later that year, as I was unwittingly engaging in *lectio divina*, poring over Lewis's *Mere Christianity* and Pope John XXIII's *Journal of a Soul*, I "heard" an interior directive accompanied by an overwhelming peace: "Disseminate the Faith." For forty years, this command has guided my life, work, marriage and family, not perfectly but truly. That Lewis and the Pope were in on it from the beginning both amuses and strengthens me.

"Mere Christianity" still invites us to heal the broken Christian community through a sacramental and liturgical vision of life. Lewis respected the beauty of holiness expressed in the Anglican Book of Common Prayer. Without it, I would likely have remained identified with the more pragmatic, low church evangelicalism that surrounded me as a young man. In the providence of God, however, Lewis's "*Mere Christianity*" flowered into Fr. Dwight Longenecker's "*More Christianity.*" Without the "mere," I could never have recovered the "more." Lewis formed me as a Christian. His overall vision, however, I found most faithfully and concretely embodied in the Catholic Church.[14]

Fr. Dwight Longenecker, to whose book *More Christianity* Al Kresta refers, is another convert who was prompted and prodded in the direction of Rome by his youthful encounter with Lewis. Longenecker was an undergraduate at Bob Jones University, that hub and hotbed of anti-papist Protestant Fundamentalism, when he first came across the works of Lewis. Falling under Lewis's spell he began to attend an Episcopalian church near to the Bob Jones campus. After graduation, besotted with anglophilia and a desire to experience the Oxford of the Inklings, Longenecker moved to England to study for the Anglican priesthood. After a short period as the vicar of a parish on the Isle of Wight, he and his wife felt increasingly drawn to the Catholic Church into which they were eventually received in 1995. He returned to the United States ten years later and is now a popular writer and author of many books.

Francis Beckwith cites Lewis as a significant influence on his journey from Evangelical Protestantism to Catholicism in his book, *Return to Rome: Confessions of an Evangelical Catholic*, published in 2009, two years after his reception into the Church. Beckwith is best known as an indefatigable Christian apologist and controversialist and is the author or editor of more than a dozen books. He is currently an associate professor of Church-State studies at Baylor University in Texas.

Mark Brumley, president and CEO of Ignatius Press, is another convert from Protestantism who credits Lewis as being a major contributor to his spiritual and intellectual progress:

> C. S. Lewis made me a Catholic. Well, of course, that puts it too simply. God made me a Catholic; Lewis was a human instrument in the process. And he was aided and abetted by G. K. Chesterton, Frank Sheed, Louis Bouyer, and others. Still, Lewis started it all for me.
>
> I remember when I first encountered Lewis. *Mere Christianity* sat innocently on the bookrack at a neighbourhood bookstore. I confused Lewis with Lewis Carroll of *Alice in Wonderland* fame. What could a weaver of children's tales teach me about Christ?
>
> An odd question, given that Jesus himself said that we must become as little children to enter the kingdom of God. Ironic, for Lewis was, unbeknownst to me, renowned for the extraordinary children's books *The Chronicles of Narnia.*
>
> Lewis quickly became my best friend, theologically speaking. He challenged me to understand Christ and his truth. And he moved me beyond the narrow world of my Fundamentalist Christianity to "historic Christianity," which I eventually came to regard as found fully only in the Catholic Church.[15]

Brumley states that Lewis's "mere Christianity" prompts people to seek "full Christianity," "which leads one to ask, *What is the Church?*, a question Lewis seemingly never fully confronted, but which many of his non-Catholic readers do. And when they do, they often come up with the Catholic answer—as I did."[16]

In discussing Lewis's role in his own conversion, Brumley refers to another well-known convert, **Sheldon Vanauken**, whose extraordinary book, *A Severe Mercy*, recounts his and his wife's friendship with C. S. Lewis and their conversion to Christianity. *A Severe Mercy* was published in 1977, four years before Vanauken's reception into the Catholic Church. This is Mark Brumley on Vanauken and Lewis:

> Sheldon Vanauken, friend of Lewis and former Anglican, once spoke of his mentor as "Moses"—one who led the way into the promised land of the Catholic Church yet never entered himself. What Lewis himself could not see in the Catholic Church, others standing upon his broad Christian shoulders, have seen. Hence the steady stream of converts Lewis has helped into the Catholic fold.[17]

H. Lyman Stebbins, founder of Catholics United for the Faith, was converted to Catholicism as a direct result of his correspondence with Lewis during the closing months of World War Two. Raised as an Episcopalian in a vague and lukewarm way, Stebbins had been given a gift of *The Screwtape Letters* for Christmas in 1942. "All at once," his wife wrote many years later, "a light went on in him and over the dull landscape of his life. . . . That book, which obviously made a deep impression on him, opened the enormous C. S. Lewis door. He started reading all his books and was enthralled."[18] It was, therefore, as a devotee or disciple of Lewis that Stebbins was emboldened to write to his mentor in April 1945. Describing himself to Lewis as "one of the many people, I am certain, who have been led by your books to a reconsideration of Christ, of Christianity, and of the Church," he asked Lewis to help him refute the claims of the Catholic Church that it was the true Church and the seat of Christian authority.

Lewis's reply is enlightening insofar as he expresses his reasons for opposing Catholicism with a rare candour that is seldom seen in his private correspondence and never in his books. He dismissed Catholic theology on the Blessed Virgin, Catholic "papalism" with regard to the authority of Peter, and the doctrine of Transubstantiation. "In a word, the whole set-up of modern Romanism seems to me to be as much a provincial or local variation from the central, ancient tradition as any particular Protestant sect is."[19] Stebbins replied, defending the Catholic position on the Blessed Virgin and the Blessed Sacrament, and arguing that "papalism" was tooted in the authority that Christ Himself had given to the Church:

> The true sequence seems to me to be as follows: I am satisfied that the New Testament is reliable historically; from reading that history I become convinced that Jesus Christ was God; I become convinced that He founded an infallible Church which should endure until the end of time; in the course of time this Church pronounces the inerrancy of Scripture; therefore, whatever can be proved from Scripture is truth. I cannot see any other way by which one can arrive at the conclusion, and it all requires an infallible authority.[20]

Many years later, in 1987, Stebbins summarized the importance of this correspondence in convincing him that he had no logical or theological reason for not becoming a Catholic:

> I wrote to C. S. Lewis and got a fascinating and interesting reply. That letter of Lewis practically put me into the Church, because that man for whose intellect I had boundless admiration very carefully wrote a stupid

letter, the stupidest thing he ever wrote. He summoned all that he could dream up to say as an argument against my becoming a Roman Catholic and there was no substance in any of it. My immediate response was that if this is the best this marvelous man can think of as an argument against it, then I'm all for it. So then when I was in London, I went to the Jesuit church at Farm Street on May 28, 1946, blessed day. I was received into the Catholic Church.[21]

The historian **Warren Carroll**, founder of Christendom College and author of the multi-volume *History of Christendom*, first read Lewis's Space Trilogy as a boy. "In these remarkable books, Lewis sketches the Christian universe without saying it is Christian," Carroll explained. "So when I read them at the age of ten and eleven, I did not know that they were Christian, but I never forgot them."[22] Rediscovering Lewis years later, he read *Mere Christianity*, *Miracles*, and *The Problem of Pain*, becoming convinced of the Divinity of Christ: "Lewis does not let you evade the fundamental question: Who was this Man? He shows you why you must answer that He is God Himself."[23] As with the other Lewis-inspired converts, there were other factors at work, apart from the reading of Lewis. In Warren Carroll's case he is convinced that the prayers of his wife, a cradle Catholic, led him to a final acceptance and embrace of the claims of the Church.

Ronda Chervin, well-known Catholic philosopher and author of over fifty books, was brought to Rome from a Jewish background:

> When I first read C. S. Lewis I was an atheist, aged 21, a philosophy graduate student, from a Jewish cultural background. *Mere Christianity* was the book I read.

Lewis's famous part about how we can't see Jesus just as a great thinker or great holy man but either as divine, crazy, or a liar was absolutely decisive for my conversion to Christianity. Obviously, I could not become a Catholic if I didn't believe in the Divinity of Christ. My mentors were Dietrich and Alice Von Hildebrand who subsequently introduced me to all of Lewis's books. In fact now at 76 years old, when all my possessions fit into six boxes, as I go around to different teaching situations, the books of C. S. Lewis are among the only ones I "have to have" with me. I teach *The Problem of Pain*, *The Four Loves*, and often recommend the Space Trilogy and *Till We Have Faces*. *Surprised by Joy* is also a favorite because of our common atheist background. Another favorite is *The Great Divorce*. *A Grief Observed* was a great help to me facing the suicide of my son. My children and grandchildren love Narnia.[24]

Ross Douthat, a *New York Times* columnist and contributor to the *Wall Street Journal*, the *Weekly Standard*, *GQ*, and *National Review*, converted at the young age of seventeen. He summarized C. S. Lewis's role in the process with unequivocal succinctness: "You start reading C. S. Lewis, then you're reading G. K. Chesterton, then you're a Catholic. I knew a lot of people who did that in their 20s—I just did it earlier, and with a different incentive structure."[25]

Thomas Howard was raised as an Evangelical, became an Episcopalian in his mid-twenties and converted to Catholicism in 1988, at the age of fifty. He is one of the finest prose stylists writing in the United States today and is the author of many fine books, including *C. S. Lewis: Man of Letters* and *The Novels of Charles Williams*. His conversion story, *Lead Kindly Light: My Journey to Rome*, was published by Ignatius Press. Although he owes his conversion, under grace, to great Catholic intellectuals, such as Newman, Knox, Chesterton, Guardini, Ratzinger, Karl Adam, Louis Bouyer, and St. Augustine, he was accompanied on his journey by Lewis, whose abiding presence guided him towards Rome:

> The question as to C. S. Lewis's possible influence on one's itinerary towards the Catholic Church has an irony in it, since, as everyone knows, Lewis not only had no interest whatever in exerting any such influence, but he avoided ecclesiastical discussions like the Black Plague. He once cut off his brother Warnie, who had innocently adverted to the topic, with a curt reply and added, "And that's the last time we'll speak of that."
>
> Nevertheless, there is a compound irony here, since the net effect of Lewis's writing, or shall we say his vision—has perhaps drawn more than one Protestant believer in the direction of the Ancient Church. Lewis would scarcely welcome any such testimony; but, upon reflection, he might have admitted that his work could have had such an effect.
>
> His influence on my progress into the Church was subliminal. I don't think that I ever thought, "Oh, Lewis is evoking the Catholic vision here" as I read his apologetics, his general essays, and his imaginative works. Perhaps one way of trying to locate the thing would be to say that Lewis speaks, not so much as a conscious Reformation Christian, in spite of his repeated references to his being an Ulsterman, but rather as a catholic Christian. (N.B., that lower-case c there.) He was at home in the Anglican liturgy, which

reflects the liturgy of the Church. He used such terms as the Blessed Virgin, the Blessed Sacrament, and so forth. And he apparently made use of the confessional. My Protestant imagination noted such details as these, but I can't remember any conscious ecclesial stirring in my mind as I encountered them.

It was the shape and the radiant immensity of Lewis's vision that must have worked, unbeknownst to me, to draw me towards what I now know as Catholicism. Protestantism does not characteristically run easily in the direction of "fantasy," for one thing. Tolkien's work is Catholic, by his own explicit testimony. Whether Narnia and the "space trilogy" could have arisen from strictly Reformational categories, I would hesitate to insist. I think the *sola scriptura* rubric at work in Reformed religion may exercise a certain restraint on authors' attempts to write fantasy, but that opens onto a question far too weighty to address in this short piece.

In any event, the blissful reaches of playful joy, titanic glory, and sheer magnificence that Lewis evokes did, I think, ultimately make inevitable my being received into the Ancient Church.[26]

Ian Hunter, Professor Emeritus in the Faculty of Law at Western University in London, Ontario, and author of *Malcolm Muggeridge: A Life*, listed Lewis as one of four people who had a profound influence on his conversion:

> The story of my conversion is the story of four men: Pope John Paul II, my father (albeit, an unwitting guide), C. S. Lewis, and Malcolm Muggeridge. It is the story of the Church's decision to publish a

comprehensive Catechism of the Christian faith, and of a priest willing to go beyond the requirements of his office to fetch one lost sheep out of the wilderness. It is the story of faithful Catholics who prayed. And above all, first, last, and always, it is the same old story that it always is—a story of God's grace and forgiveness and love. *Deo gratias*.[27]

"All my Christian life I have been reading and learning from C. S. Lewis's books," Hunter continues, "particularly to pick three—*Mere Christianity, Surprised by Joy*, and *The Great Divorce*." More controversially, Hunter is convinced that Lewis would also be a Catholic, were he alive today, and that anyone who reads Lewis is being moved closer to conversion:

> If C. S. Lewis were alive today, he would almost certainly be a Roman Catholic. That is the short answer— and, I believe, the most convincing answer—to the Lewis paradox. When I discovered that I believed that, then my last feeble justification for remaining an Anglican—"If it was good enough for C. S. Lewis, then it's good enough for me"—was gone. I believe now that anyone who reads and understands Lewis is on the path to Rome.[28]

Bobby Jindal, the Governor of Louisiana and chairman of the Republican Governors Association, converted to Catholicism from Hinduism as an undergraduate at Brown University. In an interview with *Christianity Today* in 2011 he revealed that he had "spent many years reading books by authors like C. S. Lewis" prior to his conversion.

Peter Kreeft, professor of philosophy at Boston College, is perhaps the most prolific and lucid Catholic apologist in

the English speaking world. Like Bobby Jindal, he converted
to Catholicism as an undergraduate: "Though my doubts
were all resolved and the choice was made in 1959, my senior
year at Calvin, actual membership came a year later, at Yale."[29]
As with so many others, Lewis led him towards Rome:

> I discovered CSL as an undergraduate at Calvin College,
> in the Fifties. My philosophy professor assigned *The
> Problem of Pain*, and I distinctly remember my reaction
> to it. I did not fully understand it upon first reading,
> but I knew this was wholly my fault, not his. Somehow,
> even through my confusion his utter clarity shone forth.
> I had never read an author who thought and wrote that
> clearly. (I still haven't.) I've re-read it at least ten more
> times, and every single time it has become clearer than
> before. (I think the light of Heaven must be like that.)
>
> A second assignment was to make a detailed out-
> line of *The Abolition of Man*. . . . My confidence that
> the clarity was there, if only I could find it, led me to
> hack through the jungles of my own confusion and into
> the light. I had never read anyone who could be both
> so clear *and* so profound *at the same time*. (I had not
> yet discovered Thomas Aquinas, one of the very few
> authors who is even better than Lewis at that.)[30]

Having caught the Lewis habit, Kreeft then proceeded, on
his roommate's recommendation, to read *Mere Christianity*:

> I had no problem understanding this book, as I did the
> other two, but I was such a fool as to think that any
> book that was that clear must, deep down, be shallow.
> (Of course that's a self-contradiction, but smart-ass col-
> lege students believe in themselves, not in logic.) Later,

I came to understand that it was a masterpiece. It has probably accounted for more conversions than any other book in the century. . . . It was not a specifically Catholic book, though there is nothing in it at odds with the Catholic doctrine or spirit. Paradoxically, its very "mereness" gave me a good reason to become a Catholic, for Catholicism, I came to see, did the most justice to each of the "mere" essentials. (That was the concluding argument of my *Handbook of Catholic Apologetics*.)[31]

Lorraine Murray, writer, novelist, former professor of philosophy and author of *Confessions of an Ex-Feminist*, recalls Lewis's impact upon her as quite literally life-changing:

In college I turned my back on Catholicism, my childhood faith, and became a radical, gender-bending feminist and a passionate atheist. After getting a doctorate in philosophy with a concentration in feminist ethics, I went on to teach philosophy and English at colleges in Atlanta. Although I was well aware that philosophers are expected to examine both sides of every issue—and present ideas neutrally in the classroom—I slyly advocated for my own radical agenda, which included a woman's "right" to abortion, the "compassionate" need for euthanasia, and full acceptance of the homosexual lifestyle.

When we explored Christianity in my philosophy classes, I unwittingly became my own version of St. Paul before his conversion, taking delight in dismantling every shred of evidence for belief in God and faith in His Son. Still, despite my efforts to derail Christianity, there were Christian students in my classes who knew better, and who quietly managed to withstand my atheistic onslaughts. One of them, a girl named Jill, shyly gave me a book as a present one day. It was a hardbound version of *Mere Christianity*, and she wrote inside that she thought I "might like the arguments." I thanked her politely, and then thrust the book upon a shelf, chuckling at the notion that someone as enlightened as myself might like anything to do with Christianity. What a surprise it was when, many years later, this very book seemed to "light up" on my shelf, begging me to take it down and read it. And that's exactly what I did.

How astonished I was to find a brilliant and logical explanation of the faith I had so passionately and arrogantly discarded! Reading Lewis, I found something that I must have been quietly hungering for all along, which was a reasoned approach to my childhood beliefs, which had centred almost entirely on emotion. As I turned the pages of this book, I could no longer ignore the Truth, nor turn my back on the Way and the Life. Little by little, and inch by inch, I found my way back to Jesus Christ and returned to the Catholic Church.

Years later, I discovered that, in *Surprised by Joy*, Lewis had written that "Providence quite overrules our previous tastes when it decides to bring two minds together." He also suggested that the feeling of being drawn to an author can be as involuntary and improbable as falling in love. It was certainly improbable that an atheist and radical feminist would read Lewis with such zeal. It was certainly improbable that she would fall in love with Lewis because of his brilliant mind and his passionate defence of Christianity.

When I later read *The Screwtape Letters*, it helped

me considerably in understanding how the devil works in the ordinary circumstances of our lives. I saw how thoroughly the prince of darkness had weaseled his way into my heart in those dark days when I persecuted Christ in the classroom, before I was so fortuitously knocked off my high academic horse in my own version of a St. Paul conversion.[32]

Jef Murray, an internationally acclaimed fantasy artist, best known for his illustrations of the works of Lewis and Tolkien, owes a considerable debt to both of the writers whose works are the subjects of his Muse:

> For me, I can say that CSL was a somewhat earlier but perhaps less powerful influence on my own conversion than was JRRT. I first recollect being read chapters from *The Lion, the Witch, and the Wardrobe* at nearly the same time that I was read *The Hobbit* by my mother; that is, in the form of bedtime stories when I was in second grade. And I've ever since conflated the two tales in that enchanted and mysterious realm of childhood glamour that is remembrance.
>
> Later, when I was in high school, I read *The Screwtape Letters*, and was simultaneously fascinated and repelled by the figures both of Screwtape and of his hapless nephew, Wormwood. Lewis convinced me that evil was real, and even that it took the form of Personality, even if I let that knowledge lie buried during my college years.
>
> After a very long hiatus from the naive Christianity that I had held as a child and teenager, *Mere Christianity*, read for the first time as an adult, made an enormous impression upon me; but by this time, the Hound of

Heaven was already nipping at my heels, and Lewis's brilliant logic simply reinforced what my heart was already telling me.

I came to the Catholic faith, appropriately enough, when I was 33 years old, but I only fully embraced all of the faith a decade later, when first I encountered JRRT's *Letters* and realized, viscerally, that "my God, it's all true!!!" It was only then that I could rediscover, as an artist and illustrator, the profundity of CSL's Narnia tales. Those same bedtime stories that first entranced me I found to be far deeper and far more beautiful than they had seemed even then, when haloed by childhood innocence and wonder.[33]

One of the most astonishing and dramatic conversions of the twentieth century, or of any century, is that of **Bernard Nathanson**, one of the pioneers of the movement to legalize abortion in the United States. By his own admission, Nathanson personally performed more than 60,000 abortions before realizing that his actions were intrinsically and barbarically evil. In 1979 his book *Aborting America* exposed the ugliness and dishonesty of the abortion industry. In 1984 he directed and narrated *The Silent Scream*, a film that opened the eyes of many to the true horrors of *in utero* infanticide.

Nathanson, who had always described himself as a Jewish atheist, was received into the Catholic Church at St. Patrick's Cathedral in New York in December 1996. Echoing the words of G. K. Chesterton who had famously said that he had become a Catholic in order to have his sins forgiven, Nathanson responded to those who asked why he had become a Catholic that "no religion matches the special role for forgiveness that is afforded by the Catholic Church."[34]

Surprisingly enough, Nathanson cited Lewis as a significant influence on his path to conversion. In his autobiography, *The Hand of God: A Journey from Death to Life*, he discussed the intellectual dimension to his spiritual progress: "In my case, I was led to a searching review of the literature of conversion, including Karl Stern's *Pillar of Fire*. I also read Malcolm Muggeridge, Walker Percy, Graham Greene, C. S. Lewis, Cardinal Newman and others. It was entirely in character for me that I would conduct a diligent review of literature before embarking on a mission as daunting and threatening as this searching for God."[35]

Kevin O'Brien, founder and artistic director of Theater of the Word Incorporated, is another well-known Catholic who has made the journey from atheism to Catholicism, via C. S. Lewis:

> I was an atheist from the age of nine—an evangelizing atheist, trying to convince anyone I could of the folly of religious belief. By the time I was in my late thirties, I had softened enough to admit the existence of something outside of my material existence that I could not explain. But I had simply settled into the philosophy of the day—a benign spiritualism that recognized what I called an "intentionality" in the universe, but that was far from believing in any sort of personal god.
>
> I picked up, almost at random, a book from the library that appealed to me—*God in the Dock*, an anthology of writings by C. S. Lewis, the title of which seemed to indicate the legal case that man could make against his creator, as Job had dreamed of doing. But much to my surprise I found that the evidence was all

on God's side, and that this chap Lewis was a believer—
and unlike the Christians I had known, was a first class
thinker and one of the best writers I had ever encountered. "Perhaps you don't have to sacrifice your intellect
to be a Christian," I began to tell myself.

The more I read Lewis, the more I liked him, and
the more I began to read writers that he read—G. K.
Chesterton in particular. Chesterton I found to be far
and away the best essayist I had ever dreamed of reading, and one of the most penetrating thinkers of any
era. And Chesterton's friend Belloc was more direct and
even more convincing.

And so by the grace of God, Lewis led me to
Chesterton, Chesterton led me to Belloc, and all three
of them led me to the Catholic Faith.

My wife and I were received into the Catholic
Church on July 30, 2000—which I later learned was
the 78th anniversary of Chesterton's reception. And, to
echo Maurice Baring, this was "the only action in my
life which I am quite certain I have never regretted."[37]

Carl Olson, author of *Will Catholics Be "Left Behind"? A
Catholic Critique of the Rapture and Today's Prophecy Preachers*
and co-author of *The Da Vinci Hoax: Exposing the Errors in
The Da Vinci Code*, is emphatic about Lewis's role in his own
conversion: "Lewis was very helpful to me, in particular in
helping me appreciate the intellectual and spiritual depth
of the Christian faith, which aided me in later pursuing the
fullness of that faith in the Catholic Church." Olson, who is
also a regular columnist for *Our Sunday Visitor* and editor of
Ignatius Insight, states that "*Mere Christianity, The Abolition
of Man*, and *The Great Divorce* were especially important for

me as a young man (late teens, early twenties) trying to make sense of my beliefs and 'world view.' "[38]

Olson's story is particularly interesting because his roots are in a radical form of Protestant Fundamentalism that is suspicious of Lewis and his works:

> I first heard the name, "C. S. Lewis," when I was five years old. But I didn't read any of his books for another thirteen years or so. My parents were leaders in a small Fundamentalist group. There was concern in the group about some of the teens reading *The Chronicles of Narnia* since the books included witches and apparently used a lion to represent the person of Jesus. It was recommended that *The Chronicles* be avoided for fear of the teenagers being misled.
>
> Lewis, however, proved to be a surefooted guide for me in my late teens and early twenties, and reading his work paved the way toward and into the Catholic Church in my late twenties. There are three reasons for this.
>
> First, when I read *Mere Christianity* I was a committed but somewhat confused Fundamentalist. On one hand, I wanted to do the right thing; on the other hand, I often found myself at the mercy of my emotions and the pull of dubious attractions. Although I had been schooled fairly well in Scripture, the foundations of my faith were weak in many ways, especially in terms of logical, intellectual reasons for believing in Scripture, in Jesus Christ, and the whole of Christianity. Lewis helped firm up those weak areas and showed me that I didn't have to sacrifice one bit of intellectual curiosity to be a serious Christian—quite the contrary! That fact,

a few years later, emboldened me to study and examine the history and teachings of the Catholic Church.

Secondly, Lewis impressed upon me the need to thoughtfully engage with other belief systems and perspectives—not with a relativistic mindset, but with a clear-eyed and, hopefully, rigorous interest. *The Abolition of Man* certainly stands out in this regard. He and Francis Schaeffer instilled in me an interest in the "why" and "how" of atheism and skepticism. Because of that, I would eventually discover other authors—such as Chesterton, Walker Percy, and John Paul II—who would take me even deeper into such matters. And those great men, of course, helped to open the door to the Catholic Church.

Finally, I discovered in the writings of Lewis (especially in *Surprised by Joy* and *The Four Loves*) a sense of joy, wonder, and gratitude that was often lacking in my Fundamentalist upbringing. He delighted in mystery, and I found that I, too, thought that the mystery of life and existence, rather than being frightening or a path into ruin, was a call to both deeper humility and wonder. This eventually led me, again, to Chesterton, who was so vital in my decision to become Catholic. Lewis, far from being misleading, was a key member of the communion of saints whose catholicism pointed the way to Catholicism.[39]

Richard Purtill, Professor Emeritus of Philosophy at Western Washington University, is a well-known writer of fantasy fiction, as well as being the author of many books of philosophy. In addition, he is author of *Lord of the Elves and Eldils: Fantasy and Philosophy in C. S. Lewis and J. R. R.*

Tolkien (1974), *C. S. Lewis's Case for the Christian Faith* (1981) and *J. R. R. Tolkien: Myth, Morality and Religion* (1984). He converted to Catholicism as a teenager "largely due to reading Lewis's *The Screwtape Letters* and a lot of works by G.K. Chesterton. So Chesterton and Lewis sort of guided me into the Catholic Church, even though Lewis wasn't a Catholic."[40] Purtill describes Chesterton as his "father in the faith" and Lewis as his "older brother in Christianity."[41]

There are remarkable parallels between the conversion of Richard Purtill and that of another well-known fantasy author, **Gene Wolfe**. Born within a few weeks of each other in 1931, they both converted as young men under the informative influence of both Chesterton and Lewis. Although Wolfe's conversion is often dismissed in secular circles as being nothing but the consequence of his marriage to a Catholic, his intellectual engagement with the Faith and philosophical and theological acceptance of its tenets are clear from his works of fiction and were made abundantly clear in an interview he gave in 1992:

> I became interested in it, read and studied, and talked to people about it and so forth, and eventually converted. . . . I didn't read a lot of theology. . . . I read Chesterton's book on St. Thomas Aquinas . . . and ended up reading everything of Chesterton's that I could find. I had gone through very much the same thing earlier with C. S. Lewis.[42]

Thomas Storck, author of *The Catholic Milieu* (1987), *Foundations of a Catholic Political Order* (1998) and *Christendom and the West* (2000), is one of the best known and most respected writers on Catholic social teaching. He credits Lewis with being a significant influence on his journey from atheism to Catholicism:

C. S. Lewis played a complicated though mostly indirect role in my trajectory from atheist to theist to (Anglican) Christian which began in the summer before my junior year in high school and was completed the following summer when I received baptism in the Episcopal Church.

In the first place, it was reading an article about Lewis that made me decide to investigate whether the Christian revelation might be true after all. I was impressed that an obvious intellectual and scholar could be a Christian. He, however, had nothing to do with my realization, a month or so later, that God did exist, for it was another author who presented me with some rudimentary arguments for the existence of God. Lewis was a direct influence on my transition from theist to Christian, however, for it was his analogy (in *Surprised by Joy*, chap. XIV) of a playwright writing a part for himself into his own drama, of how "Shakespeare could . . . make himself appear as Author within the play, and write a dialogue between Hamlet and himself," that helped me accept the Incarnation, how God could be both Creator of this world yet live among us in it for a time. Although this analogy hardly constitutes proof of the claims of the Christian revelation, at the time it was sufficient for me.

But I think the most crucial part which Lewis played in my fledgling Christian faith was in his arming me against the skepticism that I would meet as an undergraduate. I entered Kenyon College in the fall of 1969, an institution officially affiliated with the Episcopal Church, but whose prevailing intellectual atmosphere simply assumed that the Christian revelation was not merely false but irrelevant, and thus not even worth refuting. Here Lewis was of signal help, especially his *Screwtape Letters*, with their exposure of the hollowness of the many intellectual and moral methods of undermining religious faith. Historically, I think, many more people have abandoned their Christian faith because they found themselves in a milieu which tacitly assumed that supernatural religion is silly and irrelevant, than were convinced by any brilliant exposition of atheism or devastating refutation of the Christian claims. After reading *Screwtape* it was hard for me to be much impressed by such an atmosphere, and as a result I experienced very few intellectual obstacles to my Christian faith as an undergraduate.

Lewis, of course, played no part in the final step in my conversion, when, a few years after I graduated, I entered the Catholic Church. As a matter of fact, his ecclesiology is probably the weakest part of his presentation of the Christian religion, and even in high school I had been influenced much more on this point by authors such as Ronald Knox and Newman. So while Lewis is hardly the all-purpose doctor of the church that some Protestants make him out to be, nevertheless as a solid witness to the reasonableness of religious belief in the midst of modern academic and intellectual skepticism, he was for me, as for many others, a teacher to whom I will always be indebted.[43]

No overview of celebrated Lewisian converts would be complete without reference to **Walter Hooper**, who served as Lewis's secretary in the final months of Lewis's life and who has devoted himself tirelessly to promoting Lewis's legacy for half a century since his mentor's death. He is the author, with Roger Lancelyn Green, of one of the finest biographies of Lewis and is also the author of the *Companion and Guide* to Lewis's work, an indispensable resource for scholars. He is editor of the three volumes of Lewis's letters, a magnificent scholarly achievement in its own right.

As someone who might realistically be considered a lifelong disciple and devotee of Lewis, it is intriguing and surely noteworthy that Hooper was received into the Catholic Church in 1988, twenty-five years after Lewis's death. Considering that few people, if any, are more steeped in the ideas of Lewis, Hooper's conversion could be seen as a projection of Lewis's own likely destiny if he had lived long enough to see the triumph of modernism in the Anglican Church. Hooper felt that he could no longer remain as an Anglican following the decision to ordain women to the priesthood, a momentous decision on the part of the Anglican hierarchy that exploded any claim that Anglicanism was part of the universal Church. Hooper's decision was the ratification of the conclusion which Lewis had himself reached in his essay, "Priestesses in the Church," published in 1948, and in the talk, "Fern-seed and Elephants," given shortly before his death, as Hooper himself explains:

> [W]ould C. S. Lewis have become a Catholic had he lived? I think so. . . . One of the last papers that he wrote to give to an audience in England was to a group of seminarians—Anglican seminarians—in Cambridge. And in that paper—it is a very well-known paper— called *Fern-seed and Elephants*—he points out that if they continue to talk that sort of liberalism that they were then talking—and increasingly more now—that

their readers or hearers were more and more likely to fall into two groups: they would leave the Anglican church and become either Atheists or Roman Catholics. I think he would probably have had to include himself in that group. What do you do, when, in fact, the Anglican Church becomes apostate—as it has truly become right now? Even long before the Vatican gave us the document *Inter Insigniores* in 1976, which is the statement on the ordination of women to the priesthood, Lewis had written about the issue as far back as 1948, in an essay called *Priestesses in the Church,* in which his arguments about the priest standing in the place of Christ predate those of the Holy See. His reasons are almost exactly those you find in the Vatican document.[43]

Today, fifty years after his death, the controversy continues to rage over whether or not Lewis would have converted had he lived to see the demise of Anglicanism. Regardless of Lewis's own position, there is no doubt whatever that he has ushered many people into the Catholic Church. This living witness to his power as a teacher of Christian orthodoxy is an important part of this remarkable man's astonishing legacy.

NOTES

INTRODUCTION TO THE FIRST EDITION:

1. C. S. Lewis, *Mere Christianity* (repr. New York: Simon and Schuster, 1996), p. 6.
2. Ibid., p. 8.
3. Peter Kreeft, "The Achievement of C. S. Lewis: A Millennial Assessment," address given at Boston College, 1998.
4. C. S. Lewis, *Surprised by Joy* (New York: Harcourt Brace Jovanovich, 1955), pp. 228–29.
5. Walker Percy, introduction to *The New Catholics: Contempormy Converts Tell Their Stories*, ed. D. O'Neill (New York: Crossroad, 1987), p. xv.
6. Lewis, *Mere Christianity*, p. 139.
7. C. S. Lewis, *Letters to Malcolm: Chiefly on Prayer* (New York: Harcourt Brace and World, 1963), pp. 108–9.
8. Lewis, *Mere Christianity*, p. 64.
9. Ibid., pp. 64–65.
10. John A. Harcion, S.J., *Modern Catholic Dictionary* (New York: Doubleday, 1980).
11. Thomas Howard, "Why Did C. S. Lewis Never Become a Roman Catholic?" *Lay Witness* (November 1998), p. 8.
12. Ibid., p. 9.
13. C. S. Lewis, *The Allegory of Love* (Oxford University Press, 1936), p. 323.

PREFACE:

1. G. K. Chesterton, *Autobiography* (1936), Collected Works, vol. 16 (San Francisco: Ignatius Press, 5988), p. 187.

CHAPTER 1:

1. C. S. Lewis, *The Pilgrim's Regress*, 3d ed. (London: Geoffrey Bles, 1943), p. 20.
2. Ibid., p. 5.
3. Perhaps it would be appropriate to mention that I have experienced the prejudiced politics of Ulster at first hand. Prior to my conversion I was, for a time, embroiled in the politics of Loyalist extremism. At the age of seventeen I was present at a major Loyalist riot on the Waterside in Derry and later became involved with Loyalist paramilitaries, forging friendships with leading members of the Ulster Volunteer Force (UVF) and the Ulster Defence Association (UDA). See, Pearce, *Race with the Devil: My Journey from Racial Hatred to Rational Love* (Charlotte, NC: Saint Benedict Press, 2013).
4. Unpublished "Lewis Papers," cited in Roger Lancelyn Green and Walter Hooper, *C. S. Lewis: A Biography*, rev. ed. (London: HarperCollins, 2002), p. xx.
5. Green and Hooper, *C. S. Lewis: A Biography*, p. 119.
6. C. S. Lewis, *Surprised by Joy* (London: HarperCollins, Fount ed., 1998), p. 4.
7. Ibid.
8. Ibid.
9. Ibid., p. 7.
10. Unpublished "Lewis Papers," cited in Green and Hooper, *C. S. Lewis: A Biography*, p. 119.
11. Walter Hooper, ed., *They Stand Together: The Letters of C. S. Lewis to Arthur Greeves (1914–1963)* (New York: Macmillan, 1979), pp. 432–33.
12. G. K. Chesterton, *George Bernard Shaw* (1909), Collected Works, vol. II (San Francisco: Ignatius Press, 1989), pp. 385–86.
13. Ibid., p. 386.
14. Ibid., pp. 374–75.
15. Michael Holroyd, *Bernard Shaw*, vol. 1, *The Search for Love* (Loudon: Chatto, 1988), p. 5.
16. W. H. Lewis, "C. S. Lewis: A Biography" (unpublished manuscript); Wade Collection, Wheaton College, Wheaton, Illinois.
17. W. H. Lewis in conversation with George Sayer, in Chris-

topher Derrick, *C. S. Lewis and the Church of Rome* (San Francisco: Ignatius Press, 1981), pp. 26–27.

18. Walter Hooper, ed., *C. S. Lewis: Collected Letters* (London: HarperCollins, 2000), 17.
19. Ibid., p. 8.
20. Lewis, *Surprised by Joy*, pp. 24–25.
21. Ibid., p, 49.

CHAPTER 2

1. C. S. Lewis, *Surprised by Joy* (London: HarperCollins, Fount ed., 1998), p. 148.
2. Ibid., p. 124.
3. Walter Hooper, ed., *C. S. Lewis: Collected Letters* (London: HarperCollins, 2000), 1:230–31.
4. Ibid., 1:234.
5. Ibid., 1:235.
6. Ibid., 1:379.
7. G. K. Chesterton, *Collected Poetry*, part i, Collected Works, vol. 10 (San Francisco: Ignatius Press, 1994), pp. 523–24.
8. Hooper, *C. S. Lewis: Collected Letters*, 1:397.
9. Ibid., 1:443.
10. Ibid.
11. Ibid., 1:281.
12. Ibid., 1:311.
13. Ibid., 1:277.
14. Orange is the color of allegiance of Protestant Ulster. The Orange Order, an anti-Catholic secret society whose membership is open to Protestants only and which is still a hugely influential organization in Ulster, was named after William, Prince of Orange, whose victory at the Battle of the Boyne in 1690 effectively secured the success of the "Glorious" Revolution and the ending of the Catholic Monarchy.
15. Hooper, *C. S. Lewis: Collected Letters*, 1:330. Patsy Macan is a character in "The Crock of Gold," a story by the Irish poet James Stephens, published in 1912.
16. Ibid., 1:303–6. Plunkett, along with Padraic Pearse and others, was executed for his part in the Easter Rising in Dublin in 19:6, only a year before Lewis and Butler met.

17. Ibid., 1:307.
18. Ibid., 1:307, 315.
19. Ibid., 1:212.
20. Ibid., 1:285.
21. Lewis, *Surprised by Joy*, pp. 147–48.
22. Ibid., p. 148
23. Hooper, *C. S. Lewis: Collected Letters*, 1:169–70.
24. From Lewis's preface to *George MacDonald: An Anthology* (London: Geoffrey Bles, 1946), quoted in Roger Lancelyn Green and Walter Hooper, *C. S. Lewis: A Biography*, rev. ed. (London: HarperCollins, 2002), p. 27.
25. Ibid.
26. C. S. Lewis, *The Great Divorce* (New York: Macmillan, 1952), p. 61.
27. Hooper, *C. S. Lewis: Collected Letters*, 1:275.
28. Ibid., 1:303.
29. Ibid., 1:65–66.
30. C. S. Lewis, *Prayer: Letters to Malcolm*, centenary ed. (London: HarperCollins, Fount ed., 1998), p. 104.
31. Hooper, *C. S. Lewis: Collected Letters*, 1:359.
32. Ibid., 1:353.
33. Ibid., 1:475–76,
34. Ibid., 1:520.
35. G. K. Chesterton, *The Everlasting Man* (1925), Collected Works, vol. 2 (San Francisco: Ignatius Press, 1986), p. 147.
36. Ibid., pp. 156–57.
37. Lewis, *Surprised by Joy*, p. 166.
38. Ibid., p. 173.

CHAPTER 3

1. C. S. Lewis, *Surprised by Joy* (repr. London: HarperCollins, 1998), p. 168.
2. C. S. Lewis, *All My Roads before Me: The Diary of C. S. Lewis, 1922-1927* (New York: Harcourt Brace, 1991), pp. 431–32.
3. Ibid., p. 432.
4. Walter Hooper, ed., *C. S. Lewis: Collected Letters* (London: HarperCollins, z000), 1:901.
5. Ibid., 1:904.

6. Ibid., 1:915.
7. Ibid., 5:857.
8. Lewis, *Surprised by Joy*, p. 168.
9. Lewis, *All My Roads before Me*, pp. 392–93.
10. Humphrey Carpenter, *The Inklings* (London: George Allen and Unwin, 1978), p. 28.
11. Ibid., p. 30.
12. Ibid., p. 32.
13. Letter from Tolkien to Clyde Kilby, 18 December 1965; Wade Collection, Wheaton College, Wheaton, Illinois.
14. Walter Hooper, interview with the author, Oxford, 20 August 1996.
15. Humphrey Carpenter. *J. R. R. Tolkien: A Biography* (London: George Allen and Unwin, 1977), p. 151.
16. Further details of Tolkien's exposition of the nature of myth and its relationship with Christianity can be found in much of his own writing, particularly in the essay "On Fairy Stories," in his short allegory "Leaf by Niggle," in his poem "Mythopoeia," in his published letters; and in the creation myth in *The Silmarillion*.
17. Carpenter, *The Inklings*, p. 44,
18. Lewis, *Surprised by Joy*, pp. 178–79.
19. Carpenter, *The Inklings*, p. 45.
20. Waiter Hooper, ed., *They Stand Together: The Letters of C. S. Lewis to Arthur Greeves (1914–1963)* (New York: Macmillan, 1979), pp. 427–28.
21. Carpenter, *The Inklings*, p. 52.

CHAPTER 4

1. C. S. Lewis, *The Pilgrim's Regress*, 3d ed. (London: Geoffrey Nes, 1943), p. 168.
2. Walter Hooper, ed., *C. S. Lewis: Collected Letters* (London: HarperCollins, 2000), 1:915.
3. Ibid., 1:926.
4. Ibid., 1:933.
5. Ibid., 1:974.
6. C. S. Lewis, unpublished manuscript in the Bodleian Library, Oxford; quoted in Walter Hooper, ed., *C. S. Lewis: A Com-*

panion & Guide (London: HarperCollins, 1996), p. 181.

7. Ibid., pp. 181–82.
8. Bystander (8 October 1930), quoted in Joseph Pearce, *Literary Converts* (San Francisco: Ignatius Press, 1999), p. 167.
9. Roger Lancelyn Green and Walter Hooper, *C. S. Lewis: A Biography*, rev. ed. (London: HarperCollins, 2002), pp. 126–27.
10. Lewis, *The Pilgrim's Regress*, p. 20.
11. Ibid., p. 26.
12. Ibid., p. 35.
13. Ibid., pp. 57–58.
14. Ibid., pp. 63–64.
15. Ibid., p. 68.
16. Ibid., p. 76.
17. Ibid., pp. 77–78.
18. Ibid., pp. 80–81.
19. Quoted in Green and Hooper, *C. S. Lewis: A Biography*, p. 132.
20. Quoted in William Griffin, *C. S. Lewis: The Authentic Voice* (Tring, Herts, England: Lion Publishing, 1988), p. 167.
21. Lewis, *The Pilgrim's Regress*, p. 169.
22. Ibid., p. 170.
23. Ibid., p. 171.
24. Humphrey Carpenter, ed., *The Letters of J. R. R. Tolkien* (London: George Allen and Unwin, 1981), pp. 53–54.
25. This compendium of quotations from various reviews has been gleaned from citations in Griffin, *C. S. Lewis: The Authentic Voice*, pp. 127–28; and Hooper, *C. S. Lewis: A Companion & Guide*, p. 185.

CHAPTER 5

1. Humphrey Carpenter, ed., *The Letters of J. R. R. Tolkien* (London: George Allen and Unwin, 1981), pp. 95–96.
2. Roger Lancelyn Green and Walter Hooper, *C. S. Lewis: A Biography*, rev. ed. (London: HarperCollins, 2002), p. 132.
3. Arthur Hazard Dakin, *Paul Elmer More* (Princeton University Press, 1960), p. 327.
4. Christopher Derrick, *C. S. Lewis and the Church of Rome* (San Francisco: Ignatius Press, 1981), pp. 148–49.

5. C. S. Lewis, *The Allegory of Love* (Oxford: Clarendon Press, 1936), p. 322.
6. C. S. Lewis, *The Pilgrim's Regress*, 3d ed. (London: Geoffrey Bles, 1943), p. 14.
7. Derrick, *C. S. Lewis and the Church of Rome*, p. 152.
8. Ibid.
9. Ibid., p. 153.
10. William Griffin, *C. S. Lewis: The Authentic Voice* (Tring, Heats, England: Lion Publishing, 1988), p. 127.
11. Ibid.
12. Humphrey Carpenter, *The Inklings* (London: George Allen and Unwin, 1978), p. 50.
13. W. H. Lewis, "C. S. Lewis, A Biography" (unpublished manuscript, pp. 267–68); Wade Collection, Wheaton College, Wheaton, Illinois.
14. From a sketch Lewis wrote for the dust jacket of the first American edition of *Perelandra* (New York: Macmillan, 1944); quoted in Walter Hooper, *C. S. Lewis: A Companion & Guide* (London: FlarperCollins, 1996), p. 16.
15. C. S. Lewis, *The Four Loves* (London: Collins, Fontana ed., 1963), p. 62.
16. W. H. Lewis, "C. S. Lewis, A Biography," pp. 268–69.
17. Cited in Green and Hooper, *C. S. Lewis: A Biography*, p. 166.
18. Lewis, *Surprised by Joy*, p. 180.
19. Bede Griffiths, *The Golden String* (New York: Kenedy, 1954), p. 120; quoted in Joseph Pearce, *Literary Converts* (San Francisco: Ignatius Press, 1999), p. 220.
20. Hooper, *C. S. Lewis: A Companion & Guide*, p. 671.
21. Owen Barfield, interview with the author; quoted originally in Joseph Pearce, *Literary Converts*, p. 220.
22. Clyde S. Kilby and Marjorie Lamp Mead, eds., *Brothers and Friends: The Diaries of Major Warren Hamilton Lewis* (San Francisco: Harper and Row, 1982), p. 193.
23. Ibid., p. 200.
24. Carpenter, *The Letters of J. R. R. Tolkien*, p. 95.
25. Ibid., pp. 95–96.
26. For more details of Campbell's experiences during the Spanish Civil War, see Joseph Pearce, *Bloomsbury and Beyond: The Friends and Enemies of Roy Campbell* (London: HarperCollins, 2001).

27. Carpenter, *The Letters of J. R. R. Tolkien*, pp. 95–96.
28. Ibid.
29. Ibid.
30. Carpenter, *The Inklings*, p. 192.
31. George Orwell, *Homage to Catalonia*, in *Collected Works* (London: Seeker and Warburg/Octopus, 1980), p. 260.
32. Roy Campbell, *Light on a Dark Horse* (London: Hollis and Carter, 1951), pp. 320–21.
33. Ibid., p. 317.
34. Lewis, *The Pilgrim's Regress*, p. 13.
35. Kilby and Mead, *Brothers and Friends*, p. 209.
36. Many other contemporary critics, apart from Lewis, had failed to appreciate the philosophical and spiritual nuances in Eliot's *The Waste Land* and *The Hollow Men*. Chesterton, for instance, had been vocal in his disapproval of Eliot's earlier verse but had come to recognize, particularly after publication of *Murder in the Cathedral*, that he and Eliot were kindred spirits who shared the essentials of a common faith and a common desire to communicate its beauty through the medium of literature.
37. W. H. Lewis, "C. S. Lewis, A Biography," p. 265,
38. Kilby and Mead, *Brothers and Friends*, p. 197.

CHAPTER 6

1. W. H. Lewis, ed., *Letters of C. S. Lewis* (New York: Harcourt, Brace and World, 1966), p. 167.
2. W. H. Lewis, "C. S. Lewis, A Biography" (unpublished manuscript, p. 302); Wade Collection, Wheaton College, Wheaton, Illinois.
3. Humphrey Carpenter, ed., *The Letters of J. R. R. Tolkien* (London: George Allen and Unwin, 1981), pp. 63–64.
4. Walker Hooper, ed., *C. S. Lewis: Collected Letters* (London: HarperCollins, 2000) 1:908–9
5. G. K. Chesterton, *Culture and the Coming Peril* (London: University of London, 1927), pp. 16–17.
6. W. H. Lewis, *Letters of C. S. Lewis*, pp. 166–67.
7. Ibid., p. 167.
8. Hooper's preface to C. S. Lewis, *Of This and Other Worlds* (repr. London: HarperCollins, Fount ed., 1984), p. 17.

9. Ibid.
10. Ibid.
11. Ibid., p. 18.
12. C. S. Lewis, *Surprised by Joy* (repr. London: HarperCoLlins, Fount ed., 1998), p. 26.
13. Humphrey Carpenter, *J. R. R. Tolkien: A Biography* (London: George Allen and Unwin, 1977), pp. 173.
14. Christopher Beiting, "Science and Temptation of C. S. Lewis's Space Trilogy," *Saint Austin Review* 2, no. 6 (June 2002).
15. C. S. Lewis, *The Cosmic Trilogy: Out of the Silent Planet, Perelandra, That Hideous Strength* (London: Bodley Head, 1990), p. 105.
16. Ibid., p. 196.
17. Ibid., p. 198.
18. Ibid., p. 201.
19. Ibid., p. 109.
20. Roger Lancelyn Green and Walter Hooper, *C. S. Lewis: A Biography*, rev. ed. (London: Harpereollins, 2002), p. 198.
21. Carpenter, *The Letters off. J. R. R. Tolkien*, p. 172.
22. Walter Hooper, ed., *C. S. Lewis: A Companion & Guide* (London: HarperCollins, 1996), p. 222.
23. Dante, *Purgatorio*, canto xxviii, 11.34–42 (Henry Wadsworth Longfellow's translation).
24. Lewis, *Perelandra*, in *The Cosmic Trilogy*, p. 171.
25. Dorothy L. Sayers, commentary to canto xxviii of Dante's *Purgatorio*; Dante, *The Divine Comedy: Purgatory*, trans. Dorothy L. Sayers (London: Penguin Classics, 1955), pp. 293–94.
26. Hooper, *C. S. Lewis: A Companion & Guide*, p. 222.
27. Green and Hooper, *C. S. Lewis: A Biography*, pp. 200–201.
28. Edith Sitwell, *Taken Care Of: An Autobiography* (London: Readers Union, 1965), p. 154.
29. Lewis, *That Hideous Strength*, in *The Cosmic Trilogy*, p. 338.
30. Green and Hooper, *C. S. Lewis: A Biography*, p. 212.
31. Lewis, *That Hideous Strength*, in *The Cosmic Trilogy*, p. 544.
32. Green and Hooper, *C. S. Lewis: A Biography*, p. 210.
33. Lewis, *That Hideous Strength*, in *The Cosmic Trilogy*, p. 569.
34. Christopher Derrick, *C. S. Lewis and the Church of Rome* (San Francisco: Ignatius Press, 1981), pp. 23–24.
35. Ibid., pp. 25–26.

CHAPTER 7

1. C. S. Lewis, *The Great Divorce* (New York: Macmillan, 1952), p. 63.
2. Roger Lancelyn Green and Walter Hooper, *C. S. Lewis: A Biography,* rev. ed. (London: HarperCollins, 2002), p. 282.
3. Humphrey Carpenter, ed., *The Letters of J. R. R. Toikien* (London: George Allen and Unwin, 1981), p. 71.
4. Reginald Heber, ed., *Jeremy Taylor: Whole Works* (London: 1822), 5:45, quoted in Walter Hooper, *C. S. Lewis: A Companion & Guide* (London: HarperCollins, 1996), p. 279.
5. This translation, first published in Hooper's *C. S. Lewis: A Companion & Guide*, is by Father Jerome Bertram of the Oxford Oratory.
6. Prudentius Aurelius Clemens, from his "Hymn for the Lighting of the Lamp" in *Liber Cathemerinon*, quoted in Hooper, *C. S. Lewis: A Companion & Guide*, p. 280.
7. Clyde S. Kilby and Marjorie Lamp Mead, eds., *Brothers and Friends: The Diaries of Major Warren Hamilton Lewis* (San Francisco: Harper and Row, 1982), pp. 102–3.
8. To be precise, *The Great Divorce* was first published in fifteen instalments in *The Guardian* between 10 November 1944 and 14 April 1945, and it was published in book form by Geoffrey Bles in January 1946.
9. Lewis, *The Great Divorce*, p. 62.
10. *The Voyage of Saint Brendan*, trans. John J. O'Meara (Dublin: Dolmen Press, 1978), p. 57.
11. I am indebted to Father Bertram for his exposition of this whole issue, the full text of which is published in Hooper, *C. S. Lewis: A Companion & Guide*, pp. 280–81. Father Bertram's sources also are given in Hooper's *Companion*
12. Cited in W. A. Jurgens, ed., *The Faith of the Early Fathers* (Collegeville, Minn.: Liturgical Press, 1979), 3:152.
13. Lewis, *The Great Divorce*, p. 63.
14. Ibid., p. 69.
15. Ibid., p. 65.
16. Green and Hooper, *C. S. Lewis: A Biography*, p. 164.
17. Lewis, *The Great Divorce*, pp. 28–29.
18. Ibid., pp. 31–40.

19. Ibid., pp. 56–58.
20. This is still more evident in the way in which, a few pages later, Lewis handles the miserable state of the prurient or lustful Ghost, whose damnable destiny is a symbolic representation of the Magdalen Unrepentant.
21. In this whole passage Lewis presents, in poetic imagery, a foreshadowing of the mystical profundity of Pope John Paul II's "Theology of the Body."
22. Lewis, *The Great Divorce*, p. 63.
23. Ibid., p. 129.
24. Ibid, p. 129.

CHAPTER 8

1. C. S. Lewis, introduction to *The Incarnation of the Word*, trans. Sister Penelope (New York: Macmillan, 1946); cited in Walter Hooper, *C. S. Lewis: A Companion & Guide* (London: HarperCollins, 1996), p. 579.
2. Ibid, pp. 295–96.
3. Richard Baxter, "What History Is Credible, and What Not," *Church-history of the Government of Bishops and Their Councils* (1680), p. xv; quoted in Roger Lancelyn Green and Walter Hooper, *C. S. Lewis: A Biography*, rev. ed. (London: Harper-Collins, 2002), p. 247.
4. C. S. Lewis, *Mere Christianity* (London: Coffins, Fontana ed., 1955), p. 6; Lewis's words are, of course, an echo of the Vincentian Canon (A.D. 434), one of the earlier tests for Catholicity: "that which has been believed in all places at all times by all people."
5. G. K. Chesterton, Orthodoxy (San Francisco: Ignatius Press, 1995), p. 17.
6. Lewis, *Mere Christianity*, pp. 6–7.
7. Ibid., p. 6.
8. Ibid., p. 7.
9. Peter Milward, S.J., *A Challenge to C. S. Lewis* (London: Associated University Presses, 1995), pp. 61–63.
10. Lewis, *Mere Christianity*, p. 8.

CHAPTER 9

1. C. S. Lewis, "The Weight of Glory," published in *Screwtape Proposes a Toast and Other Pieces* (London: HarperCollins, Fount ed., 1977), pp. 109–10
2. C. S. Lewis, *Mere Christianity* (London: Collins, Fontana ed., 1955), p. 42.
3. Ibid.
4. Ibid., p. 59.
5. Ibid., p. 62.
6. Ibid., p. 70.
7. Roger Lancelyn Green and Walter Hooper, *C. S. Lewis: A Biography*, rev. ed. (London: HarperCollins, 2002), p. 388.
8. Lewis, *Mere Christianity*, p. 133.
9. G. K. Chesterton, *Orthodoxy* (London: Sheed and Ward, Unicorn ed., 1939), pp. 134–35.
10. Lewis, *Mere Christianity*, p. 12.
11. Walter Hooper, *C. S. Lewis: A Companion & Guide* (London: HarperCollins, 1996), p. 311.
12. Ibid.
13. Walter Hooper, interview with the author.
14. Lewis, *Mere Christianity*, p. 168.
15. Lewis, *Screwtape Proposes a Toast*, pp. 109–10.
16. Hooper, *C. S. Lewis: A Companion & Guide*, p. 719.
17. Ibid., pp. 719–20.
18. Benet O'Driscoll, in *Blackfriars* 21 (December 1940): 718–20; cited in Hooper, *C. S. Lewis: A Companion & Guide*, p. 302.
19. *Church Times* 123 (29 November 1940). Cited in Hooper, *C. S. Lewis: A Companion & Guide*, p. 302.
20. *Times Literary Supplement* (21 October 1944). Quoted in Green and Hooper, *C. S. Lewis: A Biography*, p. 265.
21. C. S. Lewis, *Christian Reflections* (London: HarperCollins, Fount ed., 1981), p, 65.
22. Walter Hooper, ed., *They Stand Together: The Letters of C. S. Lewis to Arthur Greeves (1914–1963)* (New York: Macmillan, 1979), p. 502.
23. Clyde S. Kilby, *The Christian World of C. S. Lewis* (Appleford, Abingdon, Berks, England: Marcham Manor Press, 1965), p. 157.
24. Lewis, *Christian Reflections*, p. 43.

25. William Griffin, *C. S. Lewis: The Authentic Voice* (Tring, Herts, England: Lion Publishing, 1988), p. 313.
26. Lewis, *Mere Christianity*, p. 116.
27. W. H. Lewis, ed., *Letters of C. S. Lewis* (New York: Harcourt, Brace and World, 1966), p. 235.
28. C. S. Lewis and Don Giovanni Calabria, *The Latin Letters of C. S. Lewis* (South Bend, Ind.: St. Augustine's Press, 1998), p. 31.
29. Ibid., p. 37.
30. Ibid., p. 31
31. Ibid., p. 41.
32. The highly romanticized presentation of Lewis's marriage in the two movie versions of *Shadowlands* should not overshadow the real anomalies or irregularities in Lewis's mode of proceeding with his wedding to Mrs. Gresham. Aware that one should not judge lest one be judged, I have no inclination or desire to discuss the rectitude or otherwise of Lewis's actions. There is, however, a real indication of the confusion within the Anglican church that a bishop could refuse to conduct the wedding on the grounds that Mrs. Gresham was a divorcee but that another Anglican clergyman could ignore his judgment end marry them regardless. It is interesting to note that, in Catholic Canon Law, it is likely that Joy Gresham's first marriage would have been nullified as having been contracted between two atheists who had no concept of the sacramental nature of their union (besides the fact that her first husband was already a divorcee at the time of their marriage). It is ironic, even if ultimately hypothetical, that Lewis could have, as a Catholic, married Joy without the mess that overshadows the way his marriage was contracted as an Anglican.
33. Hooper, *C. S. Lewis: A Companion & Guide*, p. 755.
34. W. H. Lewis, ed., *Letters*, p. 191.
35. Ibid., pp. 249–50.
36. Humphrey Carpenter, *J. R. R. Tolkien: A Biography* (London: George Allen and Unwin, 1977), p. 155.
37. C. S. Lewis, *Letters to an American Lady* (Grand Rapids, Mich.: William B. Eerdmans, 1967), p. 23.
38. Barbara Reynolds, *Dorothy L. Sayers: Her Life and Soul* (London: Sceptre, 1993), p. 406.

39. Ibid., pp. 406–7.
40. Barbara Reynolds, interview with the author, Cambridge, England, 19 September 1996; cited originally in Joseph Pearce, *Literary Converts* (San Francisco: Ignatius Press, 1999), p. 272.
41. Ibid.
42. Reynolds, *Dorothy L. Sayers*, p. 407.
43. C. S. Lewis, "Priestesses in the Church," in *God in the Dock* (London: HarperCollins, Fount ed., 1979), pp. 88–94.
44. Ibid.

CHAPTER 10

1. Humphrey Carpenter, ed., *The Letters of J. R. R. Tolkien* (London: George Allen and Unwin, 1981), pp. 95–96.
2. Walter Hooper, "C. S. Lewis and C. S. Lewises," in Michael H. MacDonald and Andrew A. Tadie, eds., *G. K. Chesterton and C. S. Lewis: The Riddle of Joy* (London: Collins, 1989), p. 45.
3. C. S. Lewis, *Prayer: Letters to Malcolm*, centenary ed. (London: HarperCollins, Fount ed., 1998), p. 110.
4. Ibid., p. 11.
5. Ibid., p. 103.
6. Ibid., p. 11.
7. W. H. Lewis, ed., *Letters of C. S. Lewis* (New York: Harcourt, Brace and World, 1966), p. 307.
8. Roger Lancelyn Green and Walter Hooper, *C. S. Lewis: A Biography*, rev. ed. (London: HarperCollins, 2002), p. 430.
9. *The Tablet* (7 December 1963).
10. George Mackay Brown, *Hawkfall and Other Stories* (London: Hogarth Press, 1974), p. 191.
11. George Macicay Brown, *For the Islands I Sing* (London: John Murray, 1997), p. 49.
12. George Scott-Moncrieff, *The Mirror and the Cross: Scotland and the Catholic Faith* (London: Burns and Oates, 1960), pp. 153–54.
13. Christopher Derrick, *C. S. Lewis and the Church of Rome* (San Francisco: Ignatius Press, 1981), pp. 39–40.
14. Ibid., p. 40.

15. Clyde S. Kilby and Marjorie Lamp Mead, eds., *Brothers and Friends: The Diaries of Major Warren Hamilton Lewis* (San Francisco: Harper and Row, 1982), pp. 201–2.

16. W. H. Lewis to Edward A. Allen, 12 July 1969; Wade Collection, Wheaton College, Wheaton, Illinois.

17. W. H. Lewis to Blanche Briggs, Easter Day 1969; Wade Collection, Wheaton College, Wheaton, Illinois.

18. W. H. Lewis to Blanche Briggs, 23 June 1969; Wade Collection, Wheaton College, Wheaton, Illinois.

19. W. H. Lewis to Blanche Briggs, 28 August 1969; Wade Collection, Wheaton College, Wheaton, Illinois.

CHAPTER 11

1. C. S. Lewis to Miss Breckenridge, 16 August 1960; quoted in W. H. Lewis, "C. S. Lewis: A Biography" (unpublished manuscript, p. 442); Wade Collection, Wheaton College, Wheaton, Illinois.

2. C. S. Lewis, "Tern Seed and Elephants," repr. in *Christian Reflections* (London: HarperCollins, Fount ed., 1981), p. 192. In a U.S. edition (William B. Eerdmans, 1967), this essay was entitled "Modern Theology and Biblical Criticism."

3. C. S. Lewis, *God in the Dock* (London: HarperCollms, Fount ed., 1979), p. 88.

4. James T. Como, ed., *C. S. Lewis at the Breakfast Table* (London: Collins, 1980), p. 147.

5. Quoted in Roger Lancelyn Green and Walter Hooper, *C. S. Lewis: A Biography*, rev. ed. (London: HarperCollins, 2002), p. 425.

6. Adrian Hastings, *A History of English Christianity 1920–1990*, 3d ed. (London: SCM Press, 1990), p. 537.

7. Green and Hooper, *C. S. Lewis: A Biography*, p. 423.

8. Ibid., p. 422.

9. Walter Hooper, *C. S. Lewis; A Companion & Guide* (London: HarperCollins, 1996), p. 607.

10. Christopher Derrick, *C. S. Lewis and the Church of Rome* (San Francisco: Ignatius Press, 1981), p. 53.

11. Ibid., pp. 53–54.

12. Green and Hooper, *C. S. Lewis: A Biography*, p. 422.

13. Christopher Derrick, interview with the author, September 1996; quoted in Joseph Pearce, *Literary Converts* (San Francisco: Ignatius Press, 1999), p. 274.

14. Ann Widdicombe, *Sunday Telegraph* (18 August 2002).

15. Lewis, *God in the Dock*, pp. 83–84.

16. *Daily Telegraph* (31 July 2002).

17. C. S. Lewis, *The Pilgrim's Regress*, 3d ed. (London: Geoffrey Bles, 1943), pp. 118–19.

18. C. S. Lewis, *The Great Divorce* (New York: Macmillan, 1952), p. 40.

19. Iain T. Benson, letter to the author, 22 August 1996; quoted in Pearce, *Literary Converts*, p. 408.

20. Crisis (July–August 1994).

21. "Tolkien and C. S. Lewis: An Interview with Walter Hooper," in *Tolkien: A Celebration*, ed. Joseph Pearce (San Francisco: Ignatius Press, 2001), pp. 196–97.

22. C. S. Lewis, *Mere Christianity* (London: HarperCollins, Fount ed., 1955), p. 12.

23. William Shakespeare, "Sonnet 73."

24. Maurice Baring, *Collected Poems* (London: William Heinemann, 1925), p. 66.

APPENDIX

1. Walker Percy, introduction to Dan O' Neill, ed., *The New Catholics: Contemporary Converts Tell Their Stories* (New York: Crossroad Publishing Company, 1987).

2. Sheilah Ward Ling, *Your Glory Reflected: 20 Outstanding Christians of the Twentieth Century* (Staten Island, NY: Alba House Books, 1993).

3. Leonard Cheshire, *Where is God in All This?* (Slough, Berkshire, UK: St. Paul Publications, 1991), p. 26.

4. Lewis, *Surprised by Joy*, p. 182.

5. Walter Hooper, ed., *C. S. Lewis: Collected Letters Volume 1* (London: HarperCollins, 2000), p. 881.

6. Dom Bede Griffiths, *The Golden String* (New York: P. J. Kenedy & Sons, 1954); quoted in Walter Hooper, ed., *C. S. Lewis: Collected Letters Volume 2* (London: Harper Collins, 2004), p. 1044.

7. Hooper, ed., *C. S. Lewis: Collected Letters Volume 1*, p. 858.
8. Walter Hooper, ed., *C. S. Lewis: Collected Letters Volume 3* (London: Harper Collins, 2007), pp. 1708–09.
9. Caitlin Matthews, *The Guardian* (31 January 2000).
10. Fr. Ian Ker, interview with Marcus Grodi for *The Journey Home* (EWTN Audio Library).
11. Quoted in John Beaumont, ed., *Roads to Rome* (South Bend, IN: St. Augustine's Press, 2010), p. 353.
12. Michael Coren, correspondence with the author (June 2013).
13. Ibid.
14. Al Kresta, correspondence with the author (June 2013).
15. Mark Brumley, correspondence with the author (June 2013).
16. Ibid.
17. Ibid.
18. Madeleine Stebbins, "The Boldness of a Stranger: Correspondence between C.S. Lewis and H. Lyman Stebbins", *Lay Witness* (November 1998).
19. Ibid.
20. Ibid.
21. Ibid.
22. Lorene Hanley Duquin, A Century of Catholic Converts (Huntington, Indiana: *Our Sunday Visitor* 2003), p. 170
23. Ibid.
24. Ronda Chervin, correspondence with the author (June 2013).
25. Mark Oppenheimer, "Ross Douthat's Fantasy World", *Mother Jones* (January–February 2010).
26. Thomas Howard, correspondence with the author (June 2013).
27. Ian Hunter, "My Path to Rome," in *That Time of Year: The Best of Ian Hunter*, Ottawa, ON: Justin Press, 2010, pp. 16–31
28. Ibid.
29. Peter Kreeft, "Hauled Aboard the Ark," www.peterkreeft.com.
30. Peter Kreeft, correspondence with the author (June 2013).
31. Ibid.
32. Lorraine Murray, correspondence with the author (June 2013).
33. Jef Murray, correspondence with the author (June 2013).
34. Quoted in "Dr. Bernard Nathanson, R.I.P." on www.catholicleague.org (22 February 2011).

35. Quoted in Fr. John McCloskey's review of the book in *L'Osservatore Romano* (English Edition) (20 November 1996).
36. Kevin O'Brien, correspondence with the author (June 2013).
37. Kevin O'Brien, correspondence with the author (June 2013).
38. Carl Olson, correspondence with the author (June 2013).
39. Ibid.
40. "An Interview with Dr. Richard Purtill," Ignatius Insight (June 2005: www.ignatiusinsight.com).
41. Richard L. Purtill, "Chesterton, the Wards, the Sheeds, and the Catholic Revival" in Michael H. Macdonald and Andrew A. Tadie, eds., *G. K. Chesterton and C. S. Lewis: The Riddle of Joy* (London: Collins Religious Publications, 1989), p. 22. This excellent article was also republished as an appendix in *Richard Purtill, Reason to Believe* (San Francisco: Ignatius Press, 2009).
42. Gene Wolfe, interview with James B. Jordan in 1992, republished in Peter Wright, ed., *Shadows of the New Sun: Wolfe on Writing/Writers on Wolfe* (Liverpool: Liverpool University Press, 2007), p. 102.
42. Thomas Storck, correspondence with the author (June 2013).
43. John Mallon, "A Conversation with Walter Hooper", *Crisis* (July–August 1994).
44. A Benedictine nun and writer who served as a spiritual adviser to the converts Siegfried Sassoon and Alec Guinness.
45. Unpublished letter, a copy of which was sent to me by Stratford Caldecott on 22 November 2006, coincidentally on the anniversary of Lewis's death.

INDEX

MORE GREAT TITLES FROM
SAINT BENEDICT † PRESS

◀ Race with the Devil

My Journey from Racial Hatred
to Rational Love

Joseph Pearce

Before he was the world's foremost Catholic biographer, Joseph Pearce was a leader of the National Front, a British-nationalist, white-supremacist group. Before he published books highlighting and celebrating the great Catholic cultural tradition, he disseminated literature extolling the virtues of the white race, and calling for the banishment of all non-white from Britain. *Race with the Devil* is one man's incredible journey to Christ, but it also much more. It is a testament to God's hand active among us and the infinite grace that Christ pours out on his people, showing that we can all turn—or return—to Christ and his Church. *264 pgs.*

978-1-61890-064-4 Hardcover

Bilbo's Journey ▶

Discovering the Hidden Meaning
of *The Hobbit*

Joseph Pearce

In Bilbo's Journey: Discovering the Hidden Meaning of the Hobbit, go beyond the dragons, dwarves, and elves and discover the surprisingly deep meaning in this beloved classic. Bilbo's quest to find and slay the dragon Smaug is a riveting tale of daring and heroism. But as renowned Tolkien Scholar Joseph Pearce brilliantly shows, it is so much more. *The Hobbit* is a story of grace and faith, good and evil, love and sacrifice. It is a story of Bilbo's journey, and an invitation to one of our own—a journey to learn the value and cost of sacrifice, the difference between luck and providence, and the power of grace. *120 pgs.*

978-1-61890-058-6 Paperbound

SaintBenedictPress.com • (800) 437-5876

CATHOLIC COURSES

Learn More

The Hidden Meaning of ▶
The Lord of the Rings
The Theological Vision in
Tolkien's Fiction

Joseph Pearce

Despite the absence of any direct mention of Christ or the Catholic Church, Tolkien described his work as "fundamentally religious and Catholic." Tolkien's profound faith shaped his creative philosophy, which emerges in *The Lord of the Rings* as an unmistakable Catholic presence. *Eight 30 minute lectures.*

978-1-61890-019-7 DVD / CD

◀ The Hobbit

Discovering the Grace and
Providence in Bilbo's Adventures

Joseph Pearce

In this course, Joseph Pearce shows that Tolkien's own words about The Lord of the Rings being a "fundamentally religious and Catholic work" also apply to *The Hobbit.* Some readers mistakenly believe that Tolien's novel *The Hobbit* is just a simple children's story. Tolkien might have written the book for his children's entertainment, but the best children's literature always has a deep level of meaning, and *The Hobbit* is no exception. *Eight 30 minute lectures.*

978-1-61890-077-7 DVD / CD

CatholicCourses.com • **(800) 437-5876**

SAINT BENEDICT + PRESS

Saint Benedict Press publishes books, Bibles, and multimedia that explore and defend the Catholic intellectual tradition. Our mission is to present the truths of the Catholic faith in an attractive and accessible manner.

Founded in 2006, our name pays homage to the guiding influence of the Rule of Saint Benedict and the Benedictine monks of Belmont Abbey, just a short distance from our headquarters in Charlotte, NC.

Saint Benedict Press publishes under several imprints. Our TAN Books imprint (TANBooks.com), publishes over 500 titles in theology, spirituality, devotions, Church doctrine, history, and the Lives of the Saints. Our Catholic Courses imprint (CatholicCourses.com) publishes audio and video lectures from the world's best professors in Theology, Philosophy, Scripture, Literature and more.

For a free catalog, visit us online at
SaintBenedictPress.com

Or call us toll-free at
(800) 437-5876